THE MARKET: ETHICS, KNOWLEDGE AND POLITICS

Following the failure of 'actually existing socialism' in Eastern Europe and Asia, a consensus has grown, on Left and Right, around the virtues of market economies. *The Market: Ethics, Knowledge and Politics* calls for a reappraisal of that consensus. It reviews the strongest arguments offered in defence of market economies and contends that they are often less compelling than the recent opinion would suggest.

The arguments discussed include: those for markets from liberal neutrality, from welfare, from autonomy and freedom and from the forms of recognition it is taken to foster; the Austrian arguments at the heart of the socialist calculation debate concerning the 'calculational' and 'epistemic' virtues of the market; and arguments from within the public choice tradition. The author defends non-market institutions against the growing incursions of market norms, including a detailed discussion of the changing conceptions of intellectual property rights in science, and develops a case for associational socialism.

This is a genuinely multidisciplinary book, spanning economics, philosophy, political science and sociology. It will be of special interest to Austrians, Marxists, political economists, institutionalists, public choice theorists and all those who harbour suspicions about the efficacy of markets.

John O'Neill is Reader in Philosophy at Lancaster University. He is the author of *Ecology, Policy and Politics*, and *Worlds without Content* – both published by Routledge.

ECONOMICS AS SOCIAL THEORY

Series edited by Tony Lawson

University of Cambridge

Social theory is experiencing something of a revival within economics. Critical analyses of the particular nature of the subject matter of social studies and of the types of method, categories and modes of explanation that can legitimately be endorsed for the scientific study of social objects, are re-emerging. Economists are again addressing such issues as the relationship between agency and structure, between the economy and the rest of society, and between enquirer and the object of enquiry. There is renewed interest in elaborating basic categories such as causation, competition, culture, discrimination, evolution, money, need, order, organisation, power, probability, process, rationality, technology, time, truth, uncertainty and value, etc.

The objective for this series is to facilitate this revival further. In contemporary economics the label 'theory' has been appropriated by a group that confines itself to largely a-social, a-historical, mathematical 'modelling'. *Economics as Social Theory* thus reclaims the 'theory' label, offering a platform for alternative, rigorous, but broader and more critical conceptions of theorising.

Other titles in this series include:

ECONOMICS AND LANGUAGE
Edited by Willie Henderson

RATIONALITY, INSTITUTIONS AND ECONOMIC METHODOLOGY
Edited by Uskali Mäki, Bo Gustafsson and Christian Knudson

NEW DIRECTIONS IN ECONOMIC METHODOLOGY
Edited by Roger Backhouse

WHO PAYS FOR THE KIDS?
Nancy Folbre

RULES AND CHOICE IN ECONOMICS
Viktor Vanberg

BEYOND RHETORIC AND REALISM IN ECONOMICS
Thomas A. Boyland and Paschal F. O'Gorman

FEMINISM, OBJECTIVITY AND ECONOMICS
Julie A. Nelson

ECONOMIC EVOLUTION
Jack J. Vromen

ECONOMICS AND REALITY
Tony Lawson

THE MARKET

Ethics, knowledge and politics

John O'Neill

London and New York

First published 1998
by Routledge
11 New Fetter Lane, London EC4P 4EE

Simultaneously published in the USA and Canada
by Routledge
29 West 35th Street, New York, NY 10001

Typeset in Times by
Ponting–Green Publishing Services
Chesham, Buckinghamshire

Printed and bound in Great Britain by
Clays Ltd., St. Ives PLC

British Library Cataloguing in Publication Data
A catalogue record for this book is available
from the British Library

Library of Congress Cataloging in Publication Data
A catalogue record for this book has been requested

ISBN 0–415–09827–0 (hbk)
ISBN 0–415–15422–7 (pbk)

FOR YVETTE

CONTENTS

ACKNOWLEDGEMENTS

The ideas and commitments that inform this book have a long history. My ideas bear the imprint of conversations I have had down the years with my father, Bill O'Neill, who for much of his working life was a building worker and shop steward. They also owe much to conversations I had many years ago with another building worker, Joe McGechie. An anarchist in the 1930s and later a socialist, Joe combined wide political reading with a broad cultural knowledge: it is to Joe that I am indebted for my first acquaintance with classical political economy. I was also fortunate in being raised on a council estate in a new town which for the first generation had a large population of immigrants from Clydeside, the Welsh mining valleys, Ireland and the North of England. The arguments in the pubs were amongst the most literate I have had about politics. The intellectual and political values of these self-educated traditions of the working class still count a great deal for me and my hope is that something of them still permeates this book.

However, the book is also a product of many years spent working in universities. The arguments have been influenced by the many good friends and colleagues who have over the years done their best to put me right. The errors in the following are there despite their best efforts. Several have read and commented on final drafts of chapters for this book: my thanks to Andrew Collier, Steve Fleetwood, Russell Keat, Paul Lancaster, Tony Lawson, Jimmy Lenman, Andrew Sayer, John Shepherd, Yvette Solomon, and Geoff Smith for their comments. There are many others to whom I am indebted for conversations and written comments on earlier versions of arguments developed here. They include Jonathan Aldred, John Benson, Ted Benton, Ric Best, Bob Brecher, John Broome, Shanti Chakravarty, Roger Crisp, Paul David, Rob Eastwood, Mary Farmer, Tim Hayward, Geoff Hodgson, Alan Holland, Michael Jacobs, Anton Leist, Uskali Mäki, Joan Martinez-Alier, Scott Meikle, Giuseppe Munda, Martin O'Connor, Mark Sagoff, Peter Schaber, Darrow Schecter, Anthony Skillen, Barry Smith, Clive Spash and Donald Winch. Drafts of a number of arguments were read to university seminars and conferences at Bangor, Cambridge, Cardiff, Edinburgh, Lampeter, Lancaster, London, Paris, Sussex, Tampere in Finland, Usti nad Labem in the Czech Republic, York and Zurich: my thanks to all those who made many helpful comments on those occasions. Earlier versions of parts of chapters 1, 2, 8, 9, 10, 11 and 12 have appeared in *Analyse &*

Kritik, Environmental Politics, History of Political Thought, Social Policy and Philosophy, The Monist, Political Studies, Politics, Philosophical Forum, Radical Philosophy; my thanks both for permission to reuse the material and the many helpful comments from editors and referees. Finally, I would like to express my gratitude to all my colleagues in the Philosophy Department at Lancaster for their support in writing this book and to all those students who over the years have had to endure earlier versions of the arguments stated here: their incisive comments are a reminder of the value of teaching.

1

IN PARTIAL PRAISE OF ADVERSARIES

1.1 The spirit of Hayek

The art of argument begins with the choice of opponents and whether it goes well or ill depends on the quality of those one has chosen to oppose. This book is a response to a number of major arguments for market economies. Those of a number of distinguished figures past and present will be discussed. Adam Smith, J. S. Mill, Jevons, Marshall, Menger and Mises all make appearances. But if one spectre haunts this book perhaps more than any other it is that of Hayek. While this book will criticise both Austrian and neo-classical defences of the market economy, it is the former, and in particular Hayek's version of it, that in the end I believe forms the more powerful foundation for a normative case for the market economy. Since it is Hayek's position that provides a powerful case for the market, it also forms a major but not the only object of criticism. Much of this book is a conversation with Hayek.

However, the spirit of Hayek also pervades the book in a quite different way. There is a sense in which the book is also written in the spirit of Hayek. In particular, for all my differences with Hayek, I accept an assumption of his earlier writings that there is a clear distinction between political defeat and defeat in an argument. Victory and defeat in a political battle is a question of power. Victory and defeat in political argument is a question of truth and validity. Hayek clearly recognises the difference between the two. To write a book like *The Road to Serfdom* in the conditions he did, just after the war when the case for a centralised planned economy was, in Europe at least, almost universally accepted, required the recognition of that distinction. What is distressing about so much of recent work that purports to be socialist is just how much it is founded on the denial that there is a distinction to be made. The ancient sophist position that the pragmatic criterion of effectiveness in persuasion is the only norm that governs argument is held widely either as an explicit position,[1] or as a practical attitude to political argument. Thus one finds many analyses of why the New Right was politically effective, but, with a few notable exceptions,[2] few about the strength of the arguments it offers in its favour. One finds many suggestions about how one might state the case for 'the Left' in a way that wins power, but few on what arguments might be offered for socialism that give good reasons for doing so. Indeed to engage in such arguments is often seen as a little vulgar in the polite society of post-modern discourse. Politics is reduced to a matter of mere taste.

At the same time there has been a tendency amongst political radicals to relinquish the economic argument to liberal defenders of the market. As far as the traditional arguments between socialist criticism of the market and its liberal defenders go, many on the socialist side of the argument have given up. If there are criticisms of market economies around they are largely to be found in the realm of political ecology in discussions of the ecological limits of commercial society. Elsewhere there is a new consensus on the economic virtues of market economies. Now there is a good reason for this. It is clearly the case that the economies of Eastern Europe and Asia that went under the title of 'really existing socialism' were failures, not just in gross accumulation of goods, but on more or less all other indicators of a good economic order: the well-being of citizens, ecological sustainability, political and social freedoms, democratic accountability, and the distribution of wealth and power. In no instance did they offer a particularly happy alternative to liberal market orders. Their record has encouraged the verdict in that previous critics of the possibility of rational non-market economic order were right.

The response of the left has been twofold. The first has been simply to accept that, in the modern world, any rational economic order has to have the market as its central economic mechanism. The main task is then taken to be to show that socialism is compatible with the market: the market socialist project is the main intellectual child of this thought,[3] although there are others, including the criticisms of 'market essentialism' I discuss later in this chapter. The second move, often combined with the first, has been to shift the radical political argument away from the economy altogether, towards either a political debate about citizenship or a cultural argument about identity, recognition and voice. While these issues are of importance, to treat them in isolation from the economy is for reasons I outline later implausible.

These moves appear to leave the critic of the market with a dilemma, for the alternative position of defending a centrally planned economy governed by some powerful state bureaucracy is quite rightly seen a non-starter. However, the alternatives never were only market and state. One of the great myopias of twentieth-century political economy has been the tendency to assume just four institutions in economic life: the state, the market, the household and the firm, with the firm being seen as a kind of miniature planned economy within the market. That was never the choice. There has always been an associational component to the economic order that this picture ignores. In market societies there exists a variety of economic and non-economic associations that are directly or indirectly central to economic life. Consider for example the increasingly threatened non-commercial scientific community: it exists as a non-market community whose members relate to each other in non-contractual ways; the incursion by both market and state is quite properly seen as a threat to its integrity; its products are central to

2

the economic life of the modern world. Neither is it the case that non-market associations were always seen as peripheral to the arguments of political economy. It is forgotten that the early defenders of commercial society like Smith were as much concerned with criticising the associational blocks to mobile labour represented by guilds as they were to the activities of the state. The history of socialist thought includes a long associational and anti-statist tradition prior to the political victory of the Bolshevism in the east and varieties of Fabianism in the west. This blindness to non-market associations and relations has also had an other dimension: the failure to address issues of market colonisation, of the invasion of market norms into non-market spheres, which until recently was lost to standard political debate.

This book is written from within the tradition of associational socialism. Its main aim is to maintain criticism of the market, criticism that is in danger of disappearing as political radicals turn either to rhetoric and culture, or to the embracement of the market. However, clearly it will not be possible here to review all the arguments for and against markets and I have not attempted to do so. My selection of arguments here has followed two principles. First, I have attempted to limit myself to those that are primarily about the market as such, and not the specifically capitalist form it might take. Hence, with some reluctance I have left aside material to do with class conflict and proletarian unfreedom. Second, I have tried to limit myself to what I believe to be the strongest grounds for defending markets. There are a variety of arguments against market economies, for example those that concern the distributional consequences of market choices or the ecological limits of markets, which I leave aside here. I do so not because I think they are unimportant. The opposite is the case: I think them the most pressing failures of market economies. I do so rather because I do not think this is where the strength of the case for market economies lies. I want to argue that even where the case for the market economy appears strongest, it is less convincing than might initially be thought. What these arguments are will be clear from the topics of the different chapters. Chapters 2 to 8 look at arguments for markets from liberal neutrality, from welfare, from autonomy and freedom and from recognition. Chapters 9 to 12 examine the arguments at the heart of the socialist calculation debate, with the 'calculational' and 'epistemic' virtues of the market. Chapter 13 looks at arguments from within the public choice tradition which give the most sophisticated version of the claim that the market runs with and not against the self-interested side of the human character. In each case I will attempt to show that the argument is weaker than is normally assumed. At the same time running through the argument will be a defence of the centrality of non-market associations to a good social and economic order.

The terms 'market', 'markets', 'commercial society' and 'market economies' will be used more or less interchangeably in the book. There are problems in doing so. There can be localised 'markets' in societies that are not 'market economies' in the sense I define it below. The term 'market' can be used at different levels of abstraction: when I tell my children I am writing a book about the market they assume that I am talking about a local market of the kind that pigs go to, not a set of institutional arrangements for the transfer of property rights. The term 'market' and 'market economy' can be used to describe a variety of different types of institutions at a variety of different levels of abstraction.[4] Some delineation of our topic is required. The central concern of this book is the defensibility of market economies. To give an initial definition, by a market economy I mean those social and institutional arrangements through which goods are regularly produced for, distributed by and subject to contractual forms of exchange in which money and property rights over goods are transferred between agents. A few comments on the definition.

First, the term 'institutional arrangements' here can be understood in a narrow or a wide sense. In the narrow sense they refer specifically to those institutional arrangements for the transfer of property rights over commodities. In a wider sense they can refer to all those institutional arrangements required for exchange to be possible, from the institutions that allow the actual transport and distributions of goods, the social institutions that make possible the conditions of social trust that are required for contractual arrangements to work, the legal arrangements required to define property rights and their legitimate transfer and so on.[5] As long as one is aware that market exchanges in the narrow sense are dependent upon background institutions, nothing much hinges upon the use of a narrower or wider reading. For the most part in this book I will refer to the institutional preconditions of markets, hence analytically at least separating these from markets understood in the narrower sense. I return to some of the implications of this point in the next section.

Second, markets are institutions for 'contractual forms of exchange': market economies are constituted by a particular form of exchange rather than the exchange of goods *per se*. Thus it is possible, for example, to have economic arrangements founded upon the exchange of gifts. While these tend to be discussed in terms of distant economies, such as the Kula exchanges of the Trobriand Islands, some parts of not only our personal lives, but also our public transactions are still founded upon gift relationships.[6] There is also a long tradition, from Aristotle onwards, that takes the best form of economic arrangement to be one founded upon something like public gift relationships through which private ownership is combined with common use.[7] Gift and contractual exchange have different social meanings: gift is constitutive of a particular social relationships – failure in reciprocity where it is due is indicative that the relationship is not in order. Failure of contract has a different social meaning in virtue of having an instrumental and impersonal significance. Hence, the different kinds of exchanges have different ethical implications: thus, for example, the gift to bodily parts or the use of the womb does not raise the same objections as the sale of bodily parts or the commercial rent of wombs in surrogacy contracts.

Third, markets involve the exchange of money and property rights over goods. I will assume that we are talking about market economies in which money is a universal medium of exchange and not simple commodity production. More important, what is transferred in market exchange is property rights over goods not goods *per se*: the point is significant in that it allows, contrary to some fairly common bad arguments, that the goods that can be exchanged need not be material entities, but can also include for example skills, information, knowledge, and capacities to work. Anything over which a set of property rights can be defined is potentially an item for exchange in markets. It follows that labour power can be a commodity.[8] However, labour power need not be a commodity in a market. The defining feature of specifically capitalist markets is that labour power is a commodity that is bought and sold. It is possible to have non-capitalist markets, for example, markets of small producers all of whom own their own labour power and exchange the fruits of their labour power: market socialism in its basic sense envisages a version of such an economy, in which all enterprises take the form of cooperatives.

A central difference between market economies and non-market economies is the ways in which decisions are made and enacted. In market economies, agents by necessity respond to the relative prices of goods, and their choices are constrained and regulated by the movements in the exchange values of different goods. The exchange value of objects becomes a common unit through which decisions are made. The shifts in exchange values are the unintended consequence of the collective outcomes of individual actions of agents. Hence, they are independent of any social or ethical ends that might be held either individually or in common. Market economies are in this special sense disembedded economies:[9] decisions are not constrained directly by social custom and ethical goals, but rather respond to a system that proceeds independently of these. The economies are amoral. In contrast, in non-market economies, economic decisions are constrained directly by social custom and needs, and operate directly in terms of the nature of the goods involved.

The observation that there is such a difference between market and non-market economies is one that goes back to Aristotle.[10] This very general difference is also the source of an ancient set of objections to market economies that also go back at least as far as Aristotle: precisely because in market economies, economic decisions are not constrained directly by ethical considerations the economies are ethically indefensible. Much of the argument in defence of market economies can be stated as a response to that general worry. One liberal justification of market economies is one that simply reverses the Aristotelian objection. It is precisely a virtue of market economies that decisions and outcomes are not determined by any ethical goal. It is not the job of public economic and political institutions to promote the 'good' under some particular conception of it. The perfectionist account of public institutions should be rejected. We live in pluralistic societies and in such societies the best institutional arrangement are those which are neutral between different conceptions of the good. The market offers an institutional arrangement that realises this liberal principle of neutrality.[11] I discuss this appeal to neutrality in chapter 2.

5

An alternative response might be to say that it is just a truth that the best human life is to be found in societies that are economically organised in ways that do not make the good life the end of decision making. Hence, just as there is a paradox of hedonism – that if you want a life of pleasure do not make pleasure your end – or a paradox of self-fulfilment – that if you want self-fulfilment do not think about your self – it may be simply a paradox that the good life develops in societies that do not make it the aim of economic and political life. That there is a paradox here is noted by some of the market's critics. Marx notes:

> Wealth appears as an end in itself only among the few commercial peoples ... who live in the pores of the ancient world ... [T]he old view, in which the human being appears as the aim of production ... seems to be very lofty when contrasted to the modern world, where production appears as the aim of mankind and wealth as the aim of production. In fact, however, what is wealth other than the universality of human needs, capacities, pleasures and productive capacities etc., created through universal exchange.[12]

While clearly not Marx's position, it is open to the defender of the market to show that markets best realise the human good as an unintended consequence of the pursuit of other ends. This strategy is at the centre of many of 'the invisible hand' defences of market economies. One central argument for the market economy is that it is the best institutional arrangement to deliver human welfare. The argument can take different forms depending upon the account of welfare offered. The different welfarist arguments for markets are discussed in chapters 3 and 4. Another central liberal argument for the market is that it is through markets that individual autonomy is best realised. This appeal to autonomy, if the concept of autonomy is understood in a thin sense, can be understood as a version of the neutrality argument. However, if autonomy is understood more substantially as a desirable state of character, as I shall argue it should be, then the argument is perfectionist in form. The complex of arguments that centre around the concept of autonomy are discussed in chapters 5 to 8.

Another response to the Aristotelian objection that is consistent with these welfarist and libertarian arguments is that the market facilitates rational decision making not possible in non-market economies precisely because it does introduce a universal unit of comparison in making choices. The claim forms the principal argument developed by Mises in the opening chapter of the socialist calculation debate. It gives way in the Austrian tradition through Hayek's work to a stronger set of arguments concerning epistemic properties of market economies, their capacity to discover and distribute to different actors that information required for the coordination of their plans. These arguments form the substance of chapters 9 to 11. Finally there is the claim that markets are institutions that work because they go with the grain of human nature. Humans are self-interested or at best beings of limited altruism. However, through markets the activities of self-interested agents can produce outcomes which, from the perspective of an impartial altruist, would be best. I discuss this argument in chapter 12.

Before proceeding to the substance of these arguments, however, a methodological preliminary is warranted; for there is an objection to the whole enterprise of the book which has some current influence: that it is 'essentialist'. Those interested in the substantive argument can leave aside the remainder of this chapter. However, since the objection has influence in current debates it needs to be dealt with.

1.2 Arguing about the market: some methodological preliminaries

The references to 'the market' and 'the market economy' in the last section and the typology of arguments presented point to another assumption that the arguments of this book share with Hayek, one which goes against the grain of some recent intellectual fashions. The assumption is that it makes sense to argue about the defensibility of the market or market economies. That assumption looks innocent enough. It is shared by a great body of both liberal and socialist theorists, by Smith, Hume, J. S. Mill, Mises and Hayek for example on the one side, and Marx, Morris, Tawney, Neurath and Titmus on the other. Socialists and liberals have engaged in a long-standing debate in political philosophy about the desirability of markets. These debates have focused on a series of questions about the market: the kind of moral character it fosters, its tendency to enhance or diminish human welfare, the distribution of goods it promotes, its relationship to political democracy and freedom, its compatibility with socialist goals, and so on. However, the very possibility of this debate has been questioned. The whole tradition of argument about the market has been rejected on the grounds that it assumes an 'essentialist' view of the market.[13] Both defenders of the market and its traditional socialist critics assume that it is possible to talk of 'the market'. They assume that different markets share some essential nature such that one can engage in a general discussion of the relation of the market to the moral character, welfare, justice, freedom, democracy and so on. However, recent argument goes, all such essentialist assumptions should be rejected; the standard arguments between defenders and critics of the market rest on a mistake.

This rejection of the idea of any essence to 'the market' has clear appeal in an intellectual world dominated by a variety of positions that employ that most empty of prefixes 'post'. Thus, the rejection of market essentialism is attractive to those 'post-Marxists' and 'post-liberals' who argue that the market is an achievement which the recent demise of 'actually existing socialism' shows that we no longer need to discuss. The debate over the relation between socialism and the market is one that we can put behind us since it depended on the assumption that the market has certain essential properties which render it incompatible with socialism. In the 'post-Marxist' and 'post-liberal' world, the debate moves on to new territory concerning the proper institutional framework in which markets can operate.[14] Amongst 'post-modernists' the term 'essentialist' is used as a term of abuse: we live in a world without essences, one in which Heraclitus is proclaimed a hero. Essentialism is rejected variously for being incompatible with the recognition of 'difference', for entailing a reduction of social categories to non-social natural categories; it is taken also to be philosophically naïve, having been effectively demolished by Wittgenstein. The post-modern moves against essentialism are most frequently employed in discussions of gender. However, the same moves can and have been made in debates in political economy and appear in particular in discussions of 'market essentialism'.

Now if this rejection of essentialism and the basis of traditional debate about the market was sustainable then much of this book could be set aside; for this book is a contribution to that debate. Fortunately the questions about the market that have been traditional to political philosophy can be defended against these recent anti-essentialist arguments. In the rest of this chapter I argue that *if* essentialism is presupposed by these questions, the debate is none the worse for it. If essentialist assumptions are made then neither liberal defenders of the market nor its socialist critics are in error in making them. The essentialist position is immune to the recent anti-essentialist wave of arguments offered by the various position that are 'post' this or that. However, to reject bad philosophical criticism of essentialism is not to render essentialist claims about the market immune from empirical criticism and I will outline what a defensible and empirically grounded criticism of essentialist assumptions about the market would need to look like. However, I will suggest that much in the traditional debate can still survive such empirical criticism.

If it wasn't for the anti-essentialist philosophical fashions of the moment, the criticism of the traditional debate for being essentialist would look a fairly odd one. Many in the debate would take it not as a criticism but a complement. While neo-classical economics has had its flirtations with instrumentalism,[15] many in both Austrian and Marxian traditions have been self-consciously essentialist in their methodological assumption and have taken this to be a virtue. The essentialism in the Austrian tradition can be traced back to its founder, Menger,[16] and runs through much of the Austrian tradition.[17] Amongst the exceptions are Mises[18] and possibly Hayek who has an ambivalent relation to essentialism. While Hayek's economic thought has been presented as essentialist by some of his recent anti-essentialist critics, for example Hindess,[19] others, notably Gray, have given a strong anti-essentialist reading to Hayek's own methodological claims about his work.[20] My own view is that, whatever Hayek's own philosophical conception of his work, his writing is best understood in realist[21] and essentialist terms.[22] In the Marxian tradition, Marx's own work shows clear essentialist assumptions that are made openly and without apology.[23] What the Austrian and Marxian traditions share here is a common heritage in Aristotelian thought from which a philosophically sophisticated essentialism is inherited. Moreover, that inheritance is also implicit in the work of theorists about the market influenced by Aristotelian economics, for example Polanyi. I discuss this work in more detail in the next chapter.

It is worth outlining some of the basic features of this Aristotelian essentialism. What is criticised in recent anti-essentialism is in fact a caricature which is defended by nobody. In outlining the central features of Aristotelian essentialism I leave aside here a number of more specific elaborations of the position found in Aristotle himself and later writers like Hegel and Marx, in particular the attempt to give a teleological specification to essences. I present here the minimal essentialist position.

The essential properties of an entity of a particular kind are those properties of the object that it must have if it is to be an object of that kind. Accidental properties of an entity of a particular kind are those properties it has, but could lack and still be an entity of that kind.[24] To take a familiar example from the modern natural sciences, consider what it is for a substance to be copper. There are properties an entity must have if it is to be a specimen of copper, e.g. ductility, malleability, fusibility, electrical conductivity, atomic number 29, and so on. There are other properties possessed by some or all samples of copper that they could lack and still be copper. Thus, for example, it may be this lump of copper is a door knob. It is a property it could lack and still be copper. It may be that all copper comes in lumps smaller than that of the Taj Mahal. However, that property, if it is true of all lumps of copper, is not one that they must have. It is possible, given the nature of copper, for them to come in sizes greater than that.

A few standard observations about essences thus defined:

1   Essence precedes investigation and requires investigation. The essential properties of objects are properties that we discover by investigation, not by simply looking at them or by looking in a dictionary. The electrical conductivity of copper and its specific atomic number are properties that we once did not know copper possessed and that we now know that it does. The essence of an object precedes its discovery. The appearance of an object does not reveal to us directly its essence.

2   Many essential properties of objects are dispositional properties that are actualised only in certain circumstances. Thus ductility, malleability, fusibility and electrical conductivity are all dispositional properties – capacities and powers that particular samples of copper have, which they exhibit in certain conditions. To discover those properties requires that those conditions be realised. A sample of copper may never exhibit the powers and capacities that it possesses. This is one reason why the discovery of the essences of natural objects involves experimental investigation: powers can be discovered by setting up those conditions in which they are exhibited.

3   Some essential properties of objects are dependent upon others and part of the purpose of scientific investigation is to discover those dependencies: it is the atomic structure of copper that explains its ductility, malleability, fusibility and electrical conductivity.[25] However, the dependent essential properties of objects are no less real than those that are explanatory prior to them. To explain is not to explain away.

Compare this minimal account of Aristotelian essentialism with the picture of essentialism portrayed by recent critics. Here is Hindess criticising the market essentialism attributed to both defenders of free markets such as Hayek, and socialist critics of the market such as Marx:

> These various positions arrive at their assessments of the market in rather different ways, but they nevertheless share an essentialization of the market and the problems that this generates for social analysis. To write of essentialism in this context is to say that the market is analyzed in terms of an essence or inner principle which produces necessary effects by the mere fact of its presence.[26]

The criticism offers a caricature of what it is to say that an entity has an essence, and results in an account of essentialism about the market that neither its liberal proponents nor its socialist critics hold. In using the language of essences one is not, as Hindess claims, describing inner principles that produce 'necessary effects' by the mere fact of their presence. Rather, one is concerned with the nature and explanation of the capacities and powers of objects to produce certain effects. The liberal and socialist theorists that Hindess criticises claim that the market has certain dispositional properties – for example, to take a disparate and contested list to facilitate the accumulation of capital without limit, to foster vices, say that of *pleonexia*, or virtues, such as those of the autonomous character, to determine a particular price for a commodity. The theorist aims also to explain these dispositional properties. It does not follow that these dispositions are always exhibited. Hindess's mischaracterisation of essentialism undermines his more substantial criticisms of market essentialism. The criticisms are aimed at positions that nobody holds.

At the centre of Hindess's substantive criticism of market essentialism is the claim that markets do not and could not exist in an institutional vacuum. Markets appear in a variety of institutional contexts. In elaborating this claim Hindess makes two points – that markets presuppose other institutions, and that markets operate in different institutional contexts. Both points can and should be accepted. Neither, however, entails the falsity of essentialism.

In criticising Hayek's essentialism, Hindess accuses him of inconsistency in also holding that market institutions presuppose non-market institutions.

> [I]n parts of *The Constitution of Liberty* (especially Ch. 4, 'Freedom, Reason and Tradition') he suggests that the effective workings of the market depend on the presence of the appropriate traditions and moral codes. But in spite of that recognition his anti-planning polemic achieves its superficial appearance of plausibility by essentializing 'the market'.[27]

Hayek's recognition that market transactions presupposes a set of prior non-market institutions sets him against pure contractarian versions of liberalism which hold that all relations could be modelled on contract. However, Hayek is guilty of no logical inconsistency in combining non-contractarianism about markets with essentialism. That a particular kind of object or institution can exist only given particular conditions is quite irrelevant as to whether the object or institution has essential properties. Hayek's claim that the market has institutional prerequisites is quite consistent, for example, with the claim that it is essentially a catallactic order that reduces coercion and thereby cultivates human freedom.

Hindess's second point is that markets operate in different institutional contexts:

> what is shared by all markets is little more than the fact that something is marketed in them. Otherwise they are highly differentiated. Markets always operate under specific institutional conditions, which can vary considerably from one case to another. What is meant by institutional conditions in this context are: the market actors (large corporations, government departments, small businesses, producer and retail co-operatives, private individuals, etc.) and the resources made available to them; legislative regulation and other forms of administrative and political controls; customary and other informal constraints on acceptable behaviour; linkages with and spillovers into other markets engaging different actors and controls.[28]

That markets operate under a number of distinct institutional conditions and have different effects given these conditions is uncontentious. However, it does not follow that essentialism about markets is false or that the *only* general statement one can make about markets is that 'something is marketed in them'.

Two initial general points are in order here. First, there is nothing in essentialism that disallows variation in the properties of different instances of some kind of entity: the distinction between accidental and essential properties serves in part to distinguish what is of the nature of a thing and what varies. Second, that the essential properties of markets might be exhibited only in certain institutional conditions does not entail that they are not always present or that reference to them might not feature in the explanations of the behaviour of markets.

An essentialist account of the market clearly allows that there exist a variety of accidental features of specific market relations in particular institutional contexts. These conditions will often entail that the powers of markets are not exhibited. There may exist constraints that 'inhibit' the exercise of those powers. Consider Polanyi's claim that it is only in modern conditions, in which the market is 'disembedded', that the potentialities of a market economy based on the principle of the unrestrained acquisition of wealth without limit are fully exhibited. In saying that the market is disembedded in modern capitalism Polanyi is not claiming that markets here exist without any institutional context. He recognises that it is the product of, and still relies upon, a particular political and legal framework.[29] When Polanyi refers to the disembedding of the market he is referring to the disappearance of legal and customary regulatory constraints on the working of markets. In these conditions certain potentialities of markets become visible. However, these potentialities existed within markets in their embedded state. The relation between markets and surrounding institutional contexts was one of tension.

The coexistence of non-market relations alongside market relations between agents might also entail that the market does not exhibit its essential properties. For example, it might be the case that, as Hegel claims, market relations are essentially impersonal, and this might be taken to be a virtue or vice of markets. However, the impersonality of market relations might often not be exhibited in virtue of other personal ties between particular actors. Ties of kinship, particular historical loyalties between members of a community, and so on, might mean that market transactions within a small village community do not exhibit the impersonality of those of the city. The defender of the claim that markets are essentially impersonal might still quite properly argue that the personal bonds are accidental features of those specific market transactions: as the surrounding accidental ties are eroded, markets tend to impersonality.

The recognition that essentialism about the market is compatible with acceptance of the existence of variation in markets in different institutional conditions also undermines a criticism of essentialism which is popular in post-modern literature. The term 'essentialist' has, in post-modernist circles, become a term of abuse. The major reason is a perception that essentialism is incompatible with difference. Post-modernists celebrate difference and diversity and any claim that an entity of certain class has an essential nature shared by all the class is taken to entail a denial of difference. In the post-modern thesaurus the term 'essence' appears in the same list as 'uniformity' and 'homogeneity'. Similarly, the assumption that essentialism is incompatible with difference underlies the rejection of essentialism about markets. It is assumed that to talk of there being an essential nature of markets involves a denial of the possibility of differences between distinct markets. That assumption is false for the reasons outlined. Essentialism is quite compatible with the recognition of variation. The claim that a number of entities share some common nature is quite consistent with the existence of differences between them.

To say this is not to deny that there is a danger associated with essentialism of taking properties of one particular variant of a species of being to be essential properties of all. Thus, for example, where feminists criticise essentialism, it is often the way that culturally specific attributes and relations are taken to be shared by all women that is the object of criticism. Likewise it is a mistake to assume specific accidental properties of a particular market order, say that in western Europe or the United States, to be essential properties of all markets. However, the defensibility of specific essentialist claims needs to be distinguished from the defensibility of essentialism. That some essentialist theorists make false claims does not entail the falsity of essentialism. It merely points to the proper fallibility of claims about essences.

Thus far I have outlined the essentialist position by way of parallels between the use of the language of essences to describe natural objects and its use in social theory. Such parallels between essentialist claims about human beings and social institutions, and essentialist claims about natural objects, can be misread in a way that invites another familiar criticism of essentialism in social theory. Thus another reason why some feminists are critical of essentialist accounts of the nature of women is a suspicion that it entails biological reductionism and a commitment to a purely biological explanation of gender differences and power relations. If this is the case then the anti-essentialist criticism would be well founded. However, essentialism need not involve any such failure to recognise the differences in the nature of the objects of the human sciences and those of the natural sciences. More specifically, the essentialist can accept that institutions like markets are not natural objects: in particular essentialism is consistent with the claim that social objects are constituted by relationships and acts which have social meanings whereas natural objects are not. Consider, for example, the account offered by Hegel, a strong essentialist in the Aristotelian tradition, of the essential differences between the contractual market sphere of civil society on the one hand and the family on the other. Hegel claims that 'marriage, so far as its essential basis is concerned is not a contractual relation'.[30] The relationship of marriage partners is such that one's identity is partially constituted by that relationship. In contrast contracts are essentially between persons considered as 'self-subsistent persons', whose identity is independent of the contractual relation. Whatever might be said for or against Hegel's position, his arguments are based on differences in the social meanings of different relationships and acts. Contractual relations and personal relations are essentially different in virtue of the meanings constitutive of them. In this respect at least, the essential natures of social objects are different from those of natural objects. However, the essentialist need have no difficulty in recognising that the objects of the human sciences do have such distinct properties.

Another source of inspiration for the rejection of essentialism is Wittgenstein's well-known criticism of the 'craving for generality':

> There is ... the tendency to look for something in common to all the entities which we commonly subsume under a general term. – We are inclined to think that there must be something in common to all games, say, and that this common property is the justification for applying the general term 'game' to the various games; whereas games form a *family* the members of which have family likenesses.[31]

I have no dispute at all with Wittgenstein's argument here. However, I do not believe that it undermines essentialism. It is quite true that there is no reason to assume that there *must* be something in common to all entities that fall under a general term which justifies the application of the term. However, no general conclusion follows from that about the truth of essentialism. The scientific endeavour to specify and explain the nature of copper or certain species of animal or plant is not ruled out by Wittgenstein's argument. The legitimate conclusion to draw from Wittgenstein's discussion is that one cannot assume in advance that there must be a set of essential properties shared by all entities that fall under some concept, not that there are no essential properties of objects. Turning to markets, it is quite possible that different markets, like games, may turn out to share only some family resemblances. It does not follow that the attempt to discover essential properties is a mistake. It does mean that one may be unsuccessful. In the end it is a matter of empirically informed investigation.

Two further points need to be added. First, Wittgenstein's conclusion is quite independent of the nominalist thesis that the only thing in common between all entities that fall under a general term X is that they are called X, such that, in principle, we could extend the reference of term to whatever we like. The entities that fall under a term do share family resemblances – 'a complicated network of similarities overlapping and crisscrossing: sometimes overall similarities, sometimes similarities in detail'.[32] Those similarities are real – there does exist a network of properties that thread together entities that fall under a term. If it is the case that markets are, like games, united only by a set of family likenesses, those likenesses are real.

Second, this existence of real family resemblances is sufficient for the intelligibility of many of the traditional questions asked about markets in political philosophy. For example questions like 'What effects do markets have on the moral character?' and 'What effects does engagement in games have on the moral character?' make perfect sense even in the absence of any single essential property shared by all markets or all games. Likewise it makes sense to investigate the reasons for blocking markets in certain goods – votes, bodily parts, blood and so on – just as it makes sense to ask of games whether it is appropriate to play them at a funeral. The existence of a family network of real resemblances will suffice for such traditional questions raised in political philosophy.

Wittgenstein's argument does highlight the openness of essentialist claims to empirical criticism. It is important to distinguish between general arguments aimed against essentialism and specific empirical arguments aimed against particular essentialist claims about some set of entities that fall under a general term. My criticism of anti-essentialism in this section has been of those arguments aimed quite generally against essentialism. The failure of general anti-essentialist arguments fail does not yet show that there must be some form of market essentialism that is true. There could be good empirical evidence specifically aimed only against essentialism about markets.

This last point can be developed in essentialist terms. It may be that in exploring the differences between markets, what looked like one species is in fact many. Dore opens a paper on 'What makes the Japanese different?' as follows:

> Sheep come in all shapes and sizes. So do goats. In fact some sheep look
> like goats, and vice versa. But as biological systems they are distinct;

they won't interbreed. Shoats and geep don't exist. Are capitalisms like that? Is it true that there are different types of capitalism, and that the differences between them are systematic.[33]

Superficially similar beings can turn out to be essentially different. It might be the case that, as Dore suggests, superficially similar economic orders turn out to have quite different natures. The differences are systematic. Those claims not only are consistent with essentialism about social orders, but also assume an essentialist programme. What is denied is the more specific essentialist claims about the market. If this denial were right, some of the essentialist claims made about *the* market would turn out to be false, and theorists like Marx, Polanyi and Hayek would have failed to distinguish essentially different social orders. Whether this is the case is in the end a question of empirically informed investigation.

To say all of this, however, is to simply accept that essentialist claims about the market are fallible – and this is just as it should be. It clearly does not show that essentialist claims about the market are false. Theoretical and empirical investigation of market economies still offers good prima facie reasons for an essentialist approach to markets. A commitment to specific essentialist claims about market economies is presupposed in the initial definition and characterisation offered earlier in this chapter and in the arguments developed in the following chapters. As such the arguments of this book are open to empirically grounded criticism. But any book about real social objects and processes like markets has to accept the possibility of empirical criticism. Such empirical criticism of market essentialism is not to be confused, however, with those founded on a general rejection of the language of essences discussed in this section. The anti-essentialist philosophical fashions of recent times ought to leave us unmoved.

2

POLITICS, ECONOMY, NEUTRALITY

In the last chapter I noted that many of the criticisms of market economies have an Aristotelian heritage: market economies are disembedded in the sense that decisions within them are determined by shifts in the exchange values of goods, not by shared ethical and political ends. The goods of human life and their proper distribution are not the goals of economic life. This Aristotelian objection is open to a liberal response: the criticism presupposes a mistaken perfectionist account of political and economic institutions. Thus recent liberalism has been characterised, in opposition to perfectionism, as the view that public decisions and institutions are to be neutral between conceptions of the good. Such neutrality is required it is argued in virtue of the pluralism characteristic of modern society. Perfectionist conceptions of politics of the kind defended by Aristotle are incompatible with this pluralism. Given the pluralism characteristic of modern society, perfectionism entails a political practice which is at best authoritarian, at worst totalitarian. It necessarily involves the imposition of a contested conception of the good life by coercive means. Hence, modern pluralistic societies require economic and political institutions, the market economy and liberal state, that are themselves neutral between different conceptions of the good. This chapter contests this claim. It outlines and defends an Aristotelian conception of a pluralist politics and of the associational picture of civil society for which it provides a basis, and it rejects the non-perfectionist defence of liberal political and economic institutions. The most plausible defences of markets are those that are themselves perfectionist.

2.1 Liberalism, pluralism and neutrality

A major theme in recent liberal thought has been that liberalism be characterised as the view that the political and social institutions should be neutral between different conceptions of the good. Liberalism thus defined is set in opposition to perfectionist views of politics,[1] exhibited most clearly in the classical political writing of Plato and Aristotle for whom the purpose of politics is the good life of its citizens. Thus for Aristotle, 'the end and purpose of the polis is the good life',[2] where the good life is characterised in terms of the virtues: hence the comment that the best political association is that which enables every man to act virtu-

16

ously and to live happily.[3] Liberal neutrality is standardly defined in terms of a rejection of this conception of politics.

The doctrine of liberal neutrality is open to a variety of specific forms. The term neutrality itself is open to several interpretations, a point well rehearsed in recent literature.[4] It can refer to neutrality of justification – that political and social actions and procedures should not be justified or undertaken on the grounds that they promote some conception of the good – or neutrality of effect – that they should not have the effect of promoting one conception of the good over another. Liberals standardly defend neutrality of justification and I will assume that this characterisation of neutrality in the remainder of this chapter.

While there is a widespread recognition of the different meanings of 'neutrality', less commonly noted are ambiguities about the site of neutrality. What is the site of neutrality? Is it specific laws and decisions that are to be neutral, or political institutions, or economic and social institutions, or all of these? The point is important in assessing the plausibility of both modern liberalism and its perfectionist opponents. Neutrality is often assumed to concern government decisions. Hence Dworkin characterises liberalism thus: 'political decisions must be, so far as possible, independent of any particular conception of the good life, of what gives value to life.'[5] Neutrality is often, however, extended beyond specific decisions to include political procedures and constitutional arrangements: a liberal polity is one that is procedurally neutral between different conceptions of the good life. Finally, neutrality can also be extended to include a society's basic economic arrangements. Hence a central component of recent liberal arguments in defence of the free market is that the market is a procedurally neutral device through which consenting adults can by way of free contractual arrangements pursue their own conceptions of the good life. For this reason interference by political bodies in the workings of the market is sometimes taken to be an instance of the state departing from neutrality.

That neutrality can occur at different sites is of importance in giving a proper characterisation of the perfectionist opponents of neutrality. Behind many defences of neutrality is a concern that the state should not impose a particular conception of the good life by decree or law. It is assumed that the critic of neutrality is concerned to reject neutrality at the level of particular political decisions. Some conservative critics of neutrality do defend that position, most notably Devlin.[6] However, to characterise perfectionist opponents of neutrality in these terms is misleading. The most plausible versions of perfectionist social and political theory have been concerned mainly with the nature of political and social institutions rather than specific laws: Aristotle's *Politics* is concerned with the forms of vice and virtue associated with different constitutional arrangements; Mill, a perfectionist liberal, likewise frames the issue in terms of institutions – 'the first question in respect to any *political institutions* is, how far they tend to foster in members of the community the various desirable qualities moral and intellectual';[7] Marx, in criticising the market, is concerned with the social and economic arrangements that allow the realisation of our characteristically human capacities. To reject political neutrality is not thereby to embrace a paternalistic state. Perfectionist political theory tends to be concerned with the promotion of the good life through particular social institutions, not through particular state decisions.

A common theme that runs through defences of neutrality is that neutrality is required by the pluralism characteristic of modern societies. However, two distinct responses are made to that pluralism each associated with a distinct account of the nature of the site of neutrality. One response is a dialogical response according to which pluralism requires a space for conversation between competing conceptions of the good, a space which is itself neutral between those conceptions. A second response is a non-dialogical response which rejects the possibility of rational conversation between different conceptions of the good and argues that pluralism requires arational mechanisms which will allow individuals with different conceptions to coordinate their activities without conversation. These two responses to pluralism entail different accounts of the social and political arrangements that form the site of neutrality. In the dialogical account, the forum is the model of political and civil society, whereas the non-dialogical account assumes a market model of public life.

The dialogical response to the existence of a plurality of different beliefs about the good is to insist on a public space for conversation that is itself neutral between those competing beliefs. Neutrality is required to resolve, or to come to a mutual understanding of, differences. Ackerman, Larmore and Habermas all offer versions of this position.[8] Thus, for example, Larmore and Habermas argue that the norms of rational discourse themselves provide the justification for political neutrality. Larmore suggests that the following 'universal norm of rational conversation' provides a justification for political neutrality:

> When two people disagree about some specific point, but wish to continue talking about the general problem they wish to solve, each should prescind from the belief that the other rejects, (1) in order to construct an argument on the basis of his other beliefs that will convince the other of the disputed belief, or (2) in order to shift to another aspect of the problem, where the possibilities of agreement seem greater. In the face of disagreement, those who wish to continue the conversation should retreat to *neutral ground*, with the hope of either resolving the dispute or by passing it.[9]

Politics provides that neutral ground for conversation. Given this conception of neutrality, public dialogue, if not the whole of political life, is a central component of it. Politics is a forum in which individuals are able to discuss competing conceptions of the good with the aim of coming to some consensus, either through convergence on a common view or arrival at mutual understandings of the opposing views sufficient to allow cooperation on common problems. For the political sphere to act as a forum, the rules of engagement for those entering into the conversation must be themselves neutral so that no conception of the good is disadvantaged within the public conversation. This dialogical account of neutrality is not standardly limited to the political sphere. The arguments within the political forum need themselves to be informed by a wider public dialogue: what pluralism primarily requires is a public space in which rational conversation can exist. Pluralism requires a space for rational dialogue and that in turn requires public space neutral between conceptions of the good.

This dialogical account of neutrality stands in opposition to a second non-dialogical account. In the non-dialogical defence of neutrality, the market, not the forum, becomes the central institutional form of neutrality. The most explicit and developed formulation of this position is to be found in Austrian economics. Like the dialogical conception, neutrality is introduced as a response to the pluralism of modern society. The market is an institutional framework compatible with, indeed required by, modern pluralism. Thus Hayek presents the market order of the 'Great Society' as a response to such pluralism:

> The Great Society arose through the discovery that men can live together in peace and mutually benefiting each other without agreeing on the particular aims that they severally pursue. The discovery that by substituting abstract rules of conduct for obligatory concrete ends made it possible to extend the order of peace beyond the small groups pursuing the same ends, because it enabled each individual to gain from the skill and knowledge of others whom he need not even know and whose aims could be wholly different from his own.[10]

The market is both amoral and arational. It allows individuals with quite different ends and beliefs about the good to cooperate with each other. Indeed through market exchanges actors might contribute to the realisation of ends to which they might be opposed.[11] Such cooperation occurs without rational dialogue or conversation about those ends. In exchange I do not engage in conversation. An actor informs others not by voice but by exit.[12] That the market is not a form of dialogue is central to the Austrian case for the free-market. The Austrians are standardly non-cognitivist about value. Beliefs about values do not answer to rational argument. The claim that they do is one of the fatal conceits of socialism. The market is a necessary institution in a pluralistic society just because there is no possibility of rationally resolving disputes about values. The alternative to market is either continual enmity and social discord or the resolution of difference by forcible imposition of one set of ends by the state.

What is the role of politics given this conception? Clearly it cannot be understood as a neutral forum in which rational dialogue between competing beliefs about the good can take place. Neutrality requires non-rational mechanisms, like those of the market, which involve no inspection of the ends individuals choose to pursue. The dialogical model of political neutrality is incompatible with the non-dialogical, and supports a quite different conception of social and political institutions. While the dialogical conception of neutrality cannot be used to support conversationally inert institutions like the market, the non-dialogical conception is incompatible with political institutions understood as conversational forums.

What form of political institution then does the non-dialogical perspective support? The answer, within the Austrian school, is to restrict the role of politics to setting the framework required for the working of the neutral, non-rational mechanisms of the market.[13] The only role of politics is to frame a set of abstract rules that make the catallactic order of the market possible. Those rules themselves must presuppose no particular set of beliefs about ends and the political has no role beyond codifying and enforcing them. It is on these grounds that the Austrians reject patterned or end-state accounts of justice. Procedures can be just or unjust and the state does have a role in codifying laws governing market procedures. However, end-states at which such procedures arrive cannot be described as just or unjust without introducing some particular conception of the good – be it one of merit or of need given some conception of human flourishing. Hence, any principle of justice that prescribes a particular pattern in the distribution of goods will be non-neutral both in effect and justification. The application of such a principle will involve the imposition of some contested set of values on others.

The Austrian view is not the only conception of the political which takes the neutrality of the market place as its starting point. The view that the market is a neutral framework for the cooperative realisation of whatever ends individuals happen to have is defended in a very different form within the neo-classical tradition of economics which has traditionally allowed a larger role for political intervention. A central feature of the Pareto-optimality criterion employed in neo-classical economics is that it is couched in terms of preferences and preference satisfaction. The neo-classical account of the market, in so far as it justifies the market, begins with the preferences individuals happen to have. The market is not understood as a procedure for cultivating desirable ends amongst individuals, but rather for efficiently satisfying those they have.[14] Ends and ideals are treated as wants and the market is neutral between them. As with the Austrians, that neutrality is non-dialogical. It does not promote any one end in preference to any other. The market is 'in principle unprincipled': 'In the modern liberal view, the socio-economic system is seen as amoral'.[15] And, again, like the Austrians, neo-classicals typically assume a non-cognitive view of values. Since no rational resolution of normative disputes is possible, the best that one can expect is the co-existence of the divergent ends that the market facilitates. Ends are treated as wants, and no judgement of their inferiority or superiority is allowed to enter criteria of efficiency.

The neo-classical approach has traditionally allowed for a much larger role for state activity than is allowed by the Austrians. Economic activity by the state is introduced as a means of solving problems of market failure – in particular in contexts of negative externalities and public goods. Moreover, the strict Pareto-optimality criterion is often modified further by the introduction of distributional constraints. However, any redistribution of primary goods by the state is to remain neutral with respect to the ends individuals pursue. Any distributional principle itself must be neutral.

While neo-classical analysis allows a greater role for politics, and while 'social' constraints are added to the economic, the conception of politics is itself market based. Politics is not a forum in which citizens engage in rational conversation about their ends. Politics rather becomes another method of aggregating whatever ideals people happen to have, without conversation or judgement on those ideals themselves. Ideals are to be treated as wants or preferences which are not open to rational dialogue. Politics thus becomes a surrogate market place in which substantive normative argument has no role and in which the main aim is to realise ideal market outcomes by other means. It is procedurally neutral between conceptions of the good.[16]

Dialogical and non-dialogical conceptions of neutrality are at odds in their responses to pluralism. However, they concur in arguing that classical perfectionist accounts of political and social institutions are incompatible with the plurality of different conceptions of the good life to be found in modern society. Given such plurality the classical account of politics is neither feasible nor desirable. Typical is the following comment by Larmore who, having rejected Aristotle's 'monist' conception of the good life, writes:

> The ideal of neutrality can be best understood as a response to the variety of conceptions of the good life. In modern times we have come to recognize a multiplicity of ways in which a fulfilled life can be lived ... The state should not seek to promote any particular conception of the good life because of its presumed *intrinsic* superiority, that is, because it is a *truer* conception.[17]

Liberal neutrality involves a rejection of the 'monism' of classical conceptions of politics. Against the background of modern pluralism, the classical account of politics will necessarily involve the imposition of a particular conception of public virtues, that modern history has shown to be at best authoritarian in its implications, at worst totalitarian. In the next section I reject this charge. I show that a classical conception of politics is compatible with pluralism.

2.2 Aristotle: self-sufficiency, plurality and the good life

Aristotle's *Politics* has been the major source of the classical conception of politics. For Aristotle the polis exists for the sake of the good life. It is notable, however, that Aristotle combines this doctrine with the claim that plurality is of the very nature of the polis, and a rejection of Plato's attempts to impose an 'excessive unity' on the polis via the common ownership of property and the abolition of the family.[18] I will not enter into a discussion of his defences of the family and private property here.[19] Rather, I focus on one general argument for the plurality of the polis which is independent of these – that from 'self-sufficiency'.

The argument runs thus:

> There is still another consideration which may be used to prove that the policy of attempting an extreme unification of the polis is not a good policy. The household is an institution which attains a greater degree of self-sufficiency than the individual can; and a polis, in turn, is an institution which attains self-sufficiency to a greater degree than a household. But it only attains that goal, and becomes fully a polis, when the association which forms it is large enough to be self-sufficing. On the assumption, therefore, that the higher degree of self-sufficiency is the more desirable thing, the lesser degree of unity is more desirable than the greater.[20]

This argument echoes an earlier discussion of the passage from household through village to polis:

> When we come to the final and perfect association formed from a number of villages, we have already reached the polis – an association which may be said to have reached the height of full self-sufficiency; or rather [to speak more exactly] we may say that while it *grows* for the sake of mere life [and so far, and at this stage, still short of full self-sufficiency], it *exists* [when once it is fully grown] for the sake of the good life [and is therefore fully self-sufficient].[21]

The end of the polis is the good life, and hence it is self-sufficient; because it is self-sufficient it must have an internal plurality. The argument as it stands is difficult to follow. To unpack it we need to give a more general account of Aristotle's view of what it is to live well.

Aristotle claims that *eudaemonia*, happiness or flourishing, is a self-sufficient and complete good.

> We regard something as self-sufficient when all by itself it makes a life choiceworthy and lacking nothing; and that is what we think happiness does. Moreover, [the complete good is most choiceworthy, and] we think happiness is most choiceworthy of all goods, since it is not counted as one good among many. If it were counted as one among many, then, clearly, we think the addition of the smallest of goods would make it more choiceworthy; [for the smallest good] that is added becomes an extra quantity of goods [so creating a good larger than the original good], and the larger of two goods is always more choiceworthy. [But we do not think any addition can make happiness more choiceworthy, hence it is the most choiceworthy.][22]

22

Happiness is self-sufficient and complete in that it contains all those goods pursued for their own sake. It is not one good amongst others, but rather includes all intrinsic goods. Since it contains all such goods – none more could be added – it is the most choiceworthy of goods. Happiness on this account is an inclusive good.[23] This inclusive conception of happiness presupposes that the component goods of human happiness are themselves internally plural. A flourishing human life contains a variety of intrinsic goods which cannot be reduced one to another.[24]

A human being is able to realise this complete and self-sufficient good only within the polis:

> Not being self-sufficient when they are isolated, all individuals are so
> many parts all equally dependent on the whole [which alone can bring
> about self-sufficiency]. The man who is isolated – who is unable to share
> in the benefits of political association or has no need to share because he
> is already self-sufficient – is no part of the polis, and must therefore be
> either a beast or a god.[25]

While within the household or village an individual can possess those goods necessary for 'mere life', in the polis they can realise those goods necessary for the 'good life'. Why? First, only in the polis can an individual realise the full range of those relationships which are constituents of human well-being:

> What we count as self-sufficient is not what suffices for a solitary person
> by himself, living an isolated life, but what suffices also for parents,
> children, wife and in general for friends and fellow-citizens, since a human
> being is naturally a political [animal].[26]

Given the kinds of beings we are, friends, family and fellow citizens are goods, and a person without them could not live a flourishing life. Second, these relationships make accessible to us a variety of goods that could not be realised alone or within smaller associations. My concern for the well-being of those for whom I care widens my own interests. This point deserves further elaboration.[27]

For any individual there are limits to the goods she can pursue. Individuals face limits of capacity, time and resources which impose on them practical choices in their pursuit of goods. An individual may not have the capacities to be successful in some pursuits – she may lack a musical ear, the voice for oratory, and so on. An individual who is capable of excellence in many activities – in music, mathematics, sport and carpentry – is rarely capable of realising excellence in all. Pursuit of one good will rule out accomplishment in others. Moreover, some groups of activities will make up a form of life that is incompatible with others: one may not be able to lead a life of contemplation and a life of action. Finally, the pursuit of such activities may conflict with the calls of other relationships. Such conflicts give rise to the practical dilemmas of individual lives. There is no algorithmic procedure in such cases – rational choice is made on the basis of judgement of one's particular capacities, the possibility of success, the relative merits of the goods of different activities, the pleasures each activity will bring, and so on. Choices may be more or less difficult. However, the limitations of individual lives force such choices upon us.

Choices are forced also on a particular society. However, the boundaries within which choices are made are wider. I cannot realise excellence in music, politics, carpentry, sport, etc. – *we* can. The goods realised by the polis are wider than those any member or household can realise. This greater range of the goods realisable within the polis enhances the lives of its members. Through my relations with others, I can have a vicarious interest in these goods. Consider the case of friendship: to have friends with a diversity of interests and pursuits extends me. In caring for the good of my friends, I care for the success of the projects in which they are involved, for their realisation of excellence in the activities they pursue. A friend 'shares his friend's distress and enjoyment'.[28] Thus in friendship the ends of another become one's own. Hence, while I may not be involved in such activities, I have a vicarious interest in the achievement of goods within them. My concerns are extended by those around me. While there are limits to the goods I can personally achieve, I can retain an interest in their achievement through others for whom I care. Hence, given relations of civic friendliness of a kind Aristotle assumes in an ideal polis, a community in which the largest number of goods can be realised will enrich the lives of all its members.

We are now in a position to understand Aristotle's argument from self-sufficiency against the excessive unity of Plato's ideal society. Humans can achieve a complete and self-sufficient good only within the polis. This in turn requires that individuals are able to enter a variety of relationships and pursue diverse and distinct goods. The pursuit of these particular goods will be itself a social enterprise that will take place within different associations. The end of the polis is not some completely separate good over and above these partial goods: its end is rather an inclusive end. Hence Aristotle's characterisation of the polis in the opening paragraph of the *Politics*:

> Observation shows us, first, that every polis is a species of association, and, secondly, that all associations are instituted for the purpose of attaining some good – for all men do all their acts with a view to achieving something which is, in their view, a good. We may therefore hold that all associations aim at some good; and we may also hold that the particular association which is the most sovereign of all, and *includes all the rest*, will pursue this aim most, and will thus be directed to the most sovereign of all goods. This most sovereign and inclusive association is the polis or the political association.[29]

The good that the polis pursues is an inclusive good: it contains all those goods sought in more particular associations. The polis has the comprehensive goal of realising the good of the 'whole of life'. On this view, the polis does not replace other partial associations, but is rather a community of communities containing a variety of associations realising particular ends.[30] It has the architectonic function of bringing order to and resolving conflicts between these goods, just as practical reason brings order to the pursuit of the variety of goods pursued by an individual through a lifetime. There are contingent limits on the goods any society can pursue and this entails that the practical conflicts beloved by Berlin and those who follow him still inevitably exist in public as well as individual life.[31] Just as in individual lives we must choose between different goods so also must we make social choices. Health may be a good, but so also are arts – and any community may have to give up resources for those with health needs for the pursuit of arts. How much any good should be realised at the expense of others in the end is a matter of practical judgement.

The proponent of liberalism may feel dissatisfied with the Aristotelian defence of pluralism outlined thus far. An objection might run as follows: Aristotle's account of the good life might be internally plural, it might allow for the flourishing of a variety of activities, but it remains just one conception of the good life which competes with others. Hence, a political society that was committed to the good life for its citizens would still be one which was incompatible with the co-existence of a plurality of ways of life and cultures. Thus Aristotelian pluralism remains illiberal.

This objection fails for reasons outlined below. However, it does reveal an important ambiguity in the way in which the term 'pluralism' has been employed in liberal arguments. The term 'value-pluralism' can have at least two distinct sets of meaning which are often conflated.

I   Value-pluralism can refer to one of a set of theses about *goods*.

    I.i   The pluralist holds that there are a plurality of intrinsic goods which are not reducible one to another.

    I.ii   Politically, the pluralist holds that the end of politics is the realisation of the plurality of goods.

        These two theses are themselves logically independent. One might for example hold that there are a variety of intrinsic goods, but that politics has the end of realising just one, e.g. civil peace.

II   Value-pluralism can refer to one of a set of theses about *beliefs* about goods.

    II.i   At a descriptive level the thesis is that there are a plurality of beliefs about what is of value.

    II.ii   At the meta-ethical level it is the thesis that no belief about values is superior to any other in the sense of being 'truer'.

    II.iii   At the level of political theory it refers to the liberal neutrality thesis that it is not the end of politics to promote one belief about the good because it is assumed to be superior.

It should be noted again that those three levels are themselves logically independent. For example, one might hold that one account of the good life is superior but deny that politics should be concerned with its implementation. Thus a dialogical defence of neutrality might reject II.ii, but defend II.iii on the grounds that neutrality at the political level is required in order to arrive at a proper judgement as to which belief about the good is superior. Moreover, it is clearly possible to consistently hold II.i and I.i and I.ii.

Aristotle's account of the good life and of politics is pluralistic in the first set of senses. The end of the polis is to promote the good life given a pluralist conception of the good life. Politics aims at the realisation of a variety of intrinsic goods. In defending these claims he rejects the meta-ethical claim that no belief about value is superior to any other, and the political claim that one belief about the good should not promoted in virtue of this superiority. Hence for the liberal committed to neutrality Aristotle's account remains illiberal, since politics should be neutral between all beliefs about the good: such beliefs might include, for example, both monist and pluralist views of the good life.

This reply clarifies the neutrality thesis – but in doing so it also weakens it. In the first place, neutrality between beliefs is not necessary to defend the co-existence of different ways of life and cultures, or, indeed, of different 'conceptions of the good' given the way that term is often employed. The much used phrase 'conceptions of the good' suffers from a misleading ambiguity. First, it is sometimes used to refer to individuals' 'life plans'.[32] Thus understood Aristotelian pluralism is committed to the co-existence of different conceptions of the good. The pluralism of the polis depends on different individuals pursuing different life plans each with its own distinct goods.

Second, 'conceptions of the good' is sometimes used interchangeably with 'forms of life' or 'ways of life'. Larmore, for example, in the passage quoted earlier, refers to 'the multiplicity of ways in which a fulfilled life can be lived'.[33] Again Aristotelian pluralism allows that different forms of life – say that of action and that of contemplation – can both have their own internal excellences and virtues.

Third, 'conceptions of the good' is sometimes used to capture differences between different cultures. While Aristotle himself views all cultural difference in terms of a departure from Greek excellence – the peoples of northern Europe have spirit but lack intelligence, those of Asia have intelligence, but no spirit, the Greeks unite the qualities of both[34] – that discussion, for all its undoubted problems, presupposes the possibility that different cultures have their own virtues. It is compatible with his position to allow that different cultures develop different excellences of character. Moreover, the distinctive practices of different cultures provide the settings in which standards of excellence and their realisation take place, and hence the precondition for individual achievement. Cultural diversity in the sense that it incorporates differences in artistic, culinary, sporting activities and the like is consistent with a suitably pluralistic conception of the good. Given a plurality of intrinsic goods, it is possible that different life plans, ways of life and cultures arrive at quite different bundles of goods which are still coherent and admirable.[35]

Cultures, however, are more than colourful activities. They incorporate beliefs about the ends of life, the social relations between and virtues of those of different genders, castes and classes, and so on. It is if 'conceptions of the good' is used in the sense of 'belief about what is good', that clear incompatibilities emerge between the general Aristotelian position outlined in the last section and that of the liberal committed to neutrality. The non-perfectionist liberal is committed to the co-existence of different beliefs about the good life and of different life plans, ways of life, and cultures that are informed by such beliefs. The Aristotelian position in contrast encourages diversity only in so far as it comes within its specific account of the good.

Should political and economic processes remain neutral between divergent beliefs and the forms of life associated with them? The defender of neutrality argues that, given pluralism, they should. As noted in the last section there are two quite different accounts of neutrality, the dialogical and the non-dialogical. In the following section I argue that the dialogical argument for neutrality fails. The position already presupposes a particular conception of the good. I then criticise the non-dialogical argument and show that an Aristotelian conception of economic life is not totalitarian and is compatible with a flourishing civil society.

2.3 Polity, household and market

The defender of dialogical neutrality responds to the existence of a plurality of conflicting beliefs about the good by insisting on a public space for conversation that is itself neutral between contested beliefs. There is a basic flaw in that response: to accept the constraints of public rational dialogue already presupposes a particular conception of the good which has long been itself contested. When Kant introduces the conception of public life as a sphere in which one has 'freedom to make *public use* of reason in all matters',[36] he is aware that it is contested, that it is at odds with some forms of social and religious life. Indeed *the* central issue between defenders of the enlightenment and their conservative critics resides in the question of how far traditions and ways of life should be open to rational reflection according to the 'universal' norms of rational discourse. For the conservative to require such reflection and discourse is already to betray a rationalist outlook that fails to appreciate the place of unreflective judgements and commitments in a well-ordered society. In a similar fashion some recent defenders of Islam in the UK have been rightly suspicious of placing their beliefs in the domain of public debate on the grounds that it induces reflection that has already undermined other faiths in post-enlightenment Europe: faith requires a central place for unquestioned authority and dogma. The appeal to the need for public rational discourse already presupposes a particular account of the good for individuals. This is not to criticise that account or the enlightenment value of autonomy that provides its foundation. It is to deny that politics understood in terms of a rational dialogue is neutral.

The ideal of politics as a forum for debate between conceptions of the good, and of non-political public life as the arena for such public use of reason is, then, quite compatible with perfectionist political theory. Indeed, a form of perfectionism is necessary to give it a proper foundation: a commitment to engagement in public dialogue already presupposes a substantive conception of the good. A forum requires substantive foundations.

The gulf between an Aristotelian conception of social and political institutions and the non-dialogical conception of neutral institutions looks much deeper than that between the Aristotelian and dialogical conception. Aristotelian perfectionism can readily be connected with the forum. The construction of a bridge to the market is more difficult. I discuss how it might be constructed in the last section of this chapter. The existence of that gulf is one of which Hayek is well aware. He self-consciously draws on it in defining the market as a non-economic institution, and that definition of the market lies at the basis of its neutrality. Hayek, at the outset of his non-dialogical defence of market neutrality, places markets in opposition to the economies:

> An economy, in the strict sense of the word in which a household, a farm or an enterprise can be called economies, consists of a complex of activities by which a given set of means is allocated in accordance with a unitary plan among the competing ends according to their relative importance. The market order serves no such single order of ends.[37]

The distinction that Hayek employs here is one that is drawn from Aristotle and which has been employed also by those critics of the market whose work is written in a broadly Aristotelian tradition.

In the *Politics* Aristotle distinguishes between two forms of acquisition, the economic and the chrematistic, the former being characteristic of the household, the latter of the market. The two modes of acquisition are correlative with two possible uses that articles of property can have: as items to be used – say a sandal to be worn – or as an item to be exchanged with others.[38] Economic acquisition, that of the household, considers acquisition only with respect to the object's primary use, as an object that satisfies a need. Objects thus employed constitute true wealth. In opposition to Solon, Aristotle asserts that this wealth has bounds: 'the amount of household property which suffices for a good life is not unlimited'.[39] The second form of acquisition, the chrematistic,[40] is concerned with the accumulation of the means of exchange, of currency: 'It is the characteristics of this second form which lead to the opinion that there is no limit to wealth and property'.[41] This form of wealth making is often confused with the first, but the two are distinct. While there is a limit to the accumulation of natural goods, namely the needs they satisfy, there is no limit to the acquisition of the means of exchange: 'There is no limit to the end it seeks; and the end it seeks is wealth of the sort we have mentioned [i.e. wealth in the form of currency] and the mere acquisition of money'.[42] Whereas exchange in the household is entered into only to acquire what is useful, the second form of acquisition becomes its own end.

Aristotle, in setting up the distinction between household and market, is not simply drawing a contrast between two sets of institutions and the ends they presuppose. He is also drawing a contrast between an objective and proper conception of the good life and a misconception. Solon's view, that there are no limits to wealth, is founded on a mistaken view of what it is to live well. It is to confuse mere living with living well. In their 'anxiety about livelihood' individuals forget their 'well-being'.[43] For this reason it is the household rather than the market which is to provide the model for political economy, since the polis is concerned with the acquisition of wealth for the good life, not for mere living.[44]

In Aristotle's work, economic institutions like political institutions exist for the sake of the good life. In the terms that Hayek takes up, he defends an economic model of the economy. This householding conception of economics, according to which economic life should be judged and organised according to a conception of the good, continues to be at the basis of the case for socialism, and some of the best writing in the defence of socialism bears a self-conscious Aristotelian heritage. Most notably it permeates the work of both Marx and Polanyi. The distinction at the heart of Marxian economics, between the use value and the exchange value of commodities, Marx explicitly takes from Aristotle. Likewise, Aristotle's distinction between economic and chrematistic acquisition is reintroduced in terms of the distinction basic to volume I of *Capital* between the circuit commodity-money-commodity from that of money-commodity-money.[45] The model of communism set up in opposition to commodity producing societies is that of a householding economy, an economy organised around the satisfaction of needs and the realisation of individuals' human powers.

In the work of Polanyi the influence of Aristotle's distinction between household and market is even more pronounced. The development of modern market society, the great transformation, is a story of the escape of the economy from the social and ethical limits: Aristotle's greatness lies in his anticipating the consequences of this disembedding of the economy from human ends:

> In denouncing the principle of production for gain 'as not natural to man,' as boundless and limitless, Aristotle was, in effect, aiming at the crucial point, namely the divorcedness of a separate economic motive from the social relations in which these limitations inhered.[46]

Hence Polanyi's comment that Aristotle's 'famous distinction of householding proper and money-making, in the introductory chapter of his *Politics* … was probably the most prophetic pointer ever made in the realm of the social sciences; it is certainly still the best analysis we possess.'[47] For Polanyi the aim of socialism is to make economic existence answerable to ethical goals in modern conditions. It represents 'the transcending of an industrial civilization through the deliberate subordination of the economy to the ends of the human community'.[48] Economic life must be constrained by a publicly agreed conception of the good life.

Hayek's defence of the market as a 'catallactic' and not 'economic' order is aimed against this Aristotelian householding conception of the economy. He is well aware of the Aristotelian heritage of modern socialism and deeply critical of it.[49] The 'economy' of common parlance is not and should not be an 'economy' in the strict Aristotelian sense of the term. It rather represents a network of economies, of households and enterprises, ungoverned by any order of ends. Hence, the case for the market is not that it realises some specific end or good, but rather that it is neutral between different conceptions of the good and specific ends of different agents and economic institutions.

The central argument against the householding model is that, given the pluralism of conceptions of the good characteristic of modern society, the householding model necessarily involves the imposition of some particular contested conception by coercive means. Hence the charge that it represents the road to totalitarianism and serfdom. While Hayek's worries that any interference in the market order is a step on this road might not gain widespread acceptance the claim that the free market is a necessary and ethically neutral institution in pluralistic societies is also widely held outside the Austrian school. Thus the claim that what is required in former totalitarian societies is a reinvention of civil society might be understood precisely as a need for the disembedding of the market from social and ethical limitation, for an economy that is 'in principle unprincipled': to subordinate the economy to introduce ethical and social ends leads to a 'dictatorship of needs'. Hence it might be argued that the whole Aristotelian heritage of socialism in the form defended by Polanyi and Marx needs to be rejected.

Does an Aristotelian conception of economics necessarily entail totalitarianism and the disappearance of civil society? One central part of an adequate defence of the Aristotelian position will be that autonomy is a central human good. Hence just as political institutions should be judged according to whether they develop in individuals the capacity and desire to formulate and pursue their own projects so also should economic institutions. It is incumbent on the critic of the market to show that a non-market economy can develop those capacities and desires, that, as Polanyi puts it, 'the passing of the market-economy can become the beginning of an era of unprecedented freedom'.[50] By the same token, the most effective defence of market institutions would not be to appeal to institutional neutrality between conceptions of the good but rather to develop a perfectionist liberal economics according to which the free market is a necessary condition for that good.[51] Once autonomy is recognised as a good, the argument between different economic systems can be debated within a common Aristotelian framework which recognises that economic life must answer to a conception of the good. The lines of argument that might be employed within that framework I discuss in the following chapter. The remaining part of this chapter has a more modest but related aim – to outline a conception of socialism which stays within the form of Aristotelian pluralism outlined in section 2.2, and to show that it does contain a response to the charge of totalitarianism and authoritarianism aimed at the householding conception of economics.

The lesser charge of 'authoritarianism' has been made not only against Aristotle's successors but also against Aristotle himself. Typical here is Mulgan. Mulgan accuses Aristotle of confusing two sense of 'polis': in the exclusive sense 'polis' refers to strictly political institutions, in its inclusive sense it refers not to 'one aspect of city-state society but the whole of that society, including both the controlling, "political" institutions and the other communities which they control'.[52] Mulgan suggests that the confusion between these sense of polis is results in an 'authoritarian' view of political institutions:

> It may be unexceptionable to say that the polis aims at total human good if the polis is thought to include all aspects of human society. It does not follow from this that the exclusively 'political' institutions of the polis should be directly concerned with the achievement of all facets of the good life, many of which may be left completely in the control of other institutions, groups or individuals.[53]

This charge depends on a particular interpretation of Aristotle's account of the 'supreme good' at which the polis aims. On Mulgan's interpretation that good is '*distinct* from those lesser goods or partial aspect of the good life which are met by the subordinate institutions and communities of the polis'.[54] Hence, when the polis in the 'exclusive' sense pursues the good life, it is understood to replace the subordinate societies: it 'includes all other ends' in the sense of directly pursuing them in the place of those societies. On this interpretation, the Aristotelian position becomes a precursor of the modern corporate state, including all other societies directly in its orbit.

This interpretation is flawed and presents a picture of Aristotle's political theory which is closer to the Platonic conception of the unified polis which Aristotle criticises than it does to Aristotle's own position. I noted in section 2.2 that Aristotle's pluralist conception of the good life entails a pluralist conception of the polis as the institutional framework in which the good life is realised. Against Plato, Aristotle argues that the polis is not a unified association that supplants all other partial societies. It is within other partial societies that individuals pursue that variety of goods that makes for a self-sufficient polis. The polis is an association of partial societies. To make this claim is not to confuse inclusive and exclusive senses of the polis. Rather it is to present a particular conception of the polis as an institutional framework in which the partial ends of partial societies are pursued in a coherent fashion. The end of the polis as the good life is not some other 'distinct' end beyond the ends of partial societies. It is rather an inclusive end which includes all intrinsic goods pursued in particular associations. Just as the individual's happiness is an inclusive good, which includes all intrinsic goods, so the polis's end is inclusive. The polis is the supreme community not in the sense of directly replacing all others, but rather in that of giving a proper order to the ends they pursue. The polis does not then directly take over the ends of partial associations. The proper place for the pursuit of the component ends of the good life remains those subordinate associations themselves. The polis rather brings coherence to them, having a role analogous to that of practical intelligence in ordering the goods of an individual life. The polis on this account is not authoritarian (although it cannot be denied that Aristotle's account of the polis does have, for other reasons, authoritarian features). It rather recognises the goods and autonomy of the subordinate associations of society.

This point is of significance for the defence of the householding conception of the economy. That economic life be subordinate to the realisation of the good life is compatible with a pluralistic and associational account of economic life, which recognises the importance of non-political institutions in a free society. The principles of socialist versions of that picture are to be found in the work of the guild socialists and some other less fashionable socialist theorists such as Neurath.[55] In this form the Aristotelian householding account of the economy does have relevance to recent debates on civil society, socialism and totalitarianism.

The rejection of the totalitarian regimes of Eastern Europe is often conceived of in terms of the 'reinvention of civil society'. However, the term 'civil society' is employed in a number of different senses. Two are of significance here:

(a) civil society refers to the market and
(b) civil society refers to associations that are independent of the state.

These two senses are often used interchangeably, in particular in critiques of Marx.[56] However, they are by no means the same nor necessarily partners – indeed, the opposite is true. The proponents of the free-market have fought on two fronts: against 'state socialist' incursions into the market on the one hand; and against associations – unions, professional associations and other combinations – on the other. It is often forgotten, for example, that Adam Smith wrote before any significant socialist movement – and his defence of commercial society is aimed as much against independent associations of producers as it is against state interference.[57]

Where totalitarianism is concerned, it is civil society in the second sense that is of significance, not the first. Through most of history markets have played a marginal role in economic life. An economy in which the unfettered market becomes *the* institutional framework for economic life is a recent phenomenon. However, for all that persons have suffered from tyrannical and oligarchical forms of government in the past, totalitarianism itself is a recent phenomenon. It is born of the disappearance not of the market, but of independent associations. The distinguishing feature of totalitarian movements is that they recognise no association or activity that is not subordinate to their own political ends – in Himmler's words 'there is no task that exists for its own sake'.[58] The possibility of such movements is itself founded on the loosening of other loyalties and associations in modern society, of the creation of the isolated individual. The market economy itself has been a major source of the loosening of such ties.

The critique of the market on the basis of a householding conception of political economy is not totalitarian. In particular it is not committed to the disappearance of partial associations. Rather, in the Aristotelian conception outlined above, it is through partial societies realising particular goods for their own sake that the good life is realised. A flourishing civil society made up of non-political associations is compatible with an economic life pursued for the sake of the good life.

2.4 Markets without neutrality

In this chapter I have examined the attempt to defend market economies by appeal to neutrality. This is not however the only move available to the defender of market economies. A second is to attempt to show that a bridge from market economies to perfectionist accounts of the human good can be constructed: while decisions in markets are primarily determined by shifts in prices, not by the demands of ethics, a society thus organised in fact does realise the best life for human beings. As I put it in chapter 1, it may simply be a paradox that the best life is realised in a society that does not make it its goal. It is a paradox that Marx noted in favourably comparing capitalist and pre-capitalist societies. Smith's invisible hand arguments can be understood as a way of making the some point.

There are broadly two ways an argument from markets to the human good might go: the welfarist, according to which markets are justified on the ground that they realise human well-being; and the perfectionist liberal according to which markets realise a central or the central good of human life, freedom or autonomy. These arguments form the object of the next six chapters. However, the nature of appeals to welfare and autonomy in recent defences of markets is somewhat complicated, for these appeals in turn can take either perfectionist or non-perfectionist forms. The non-perfectionist version of the welfarist position is that which appeals to a thin formal definition of well-being. Well-being is defined in terms of preference satisfaction, one justification being that the economist is not thereby committed to endorsing a particular conception of the good. The economist is neutral between them, showing merely that the market realises whatever condition of the good agents happen to have. Likewise, the appeal to freedom and autonomy is often one that claims neutrality: autonomy is a good in the sense that it is a condition of individuals being able to pursue their own conceptions of the good life. These neutrality based versions of arguments from welfare and autonomy need to be distinguished from the more substantive accounts. The substantive defence of the welfarist position argues that, on the basis of some particular conception of the good life, the market best realises the human good: Adam Smith, Jevons and Menger offer different versions of that position. The substantive version of the liberal position defends the market on the grounds that it fosters the development of the autonomous character, where that autonomy is seen as a component of the good life: J. S. Mill provides arguments of that kind. As will become evident, in their perfectionist versions, welfare and liberal justifications can converge: autonomy can and I believe should be seen as part of human well-being.

The existence of both perfectionist and neutral versions of the arguments from welfare and autonomy complicates the story I have to tell in the following chapters. There are two distinct components in my discussion of both. I will argue for the superiority of the perfectionist version of the argument over the thinner version that appeal to neutrality. However, I will also argue that there are problems even with the stronger perfectionist defences of the market economy.

3

ECONOMIC THEORY AND HUMAN WELL-BEING

Welfare arguments have been central to the defence of market economies. The market is an economic institution that best improves human well-being. The theme runs through economic theory from classical economists such as Smith through to modern neo-classical and Austrian schools. However, over the past century these welfarist defences of the market have exhibited a shift that is closely related to the move towards the political ideal of neutrality discussed in the last chapter. There has been a shift from arguments that employ a substantive conception of the human well-being that specify the content of what it is for humans to live well to arguments premised on purely formal definitions of well-being. That formal concept often comes under the name of utility understood in a technical sense as a preference ordering or structure. In this chapter I will examine the reasons offered for that shift and suggest that they are unsound. I argue that if one is going to mount a welfare defence of markets then the formal concept of utility that informs modern economic theory will not do. The work of this chapter is largely preparatory for the next in which I examine a corresponding shift in the structure of welfarist arguments for the market.

3.1 The meaning of welfare

If one picks up a book in modern neo-classical economics then one will find the concepts of welfare or utility defined in terms of preferences.[1] The economic agent of the textbook is characterised by a set of preferences rules. In particular, the agent is assumed to be rational in the sense that she has consistent preferences: her preferences are transitive, i.e. if she prefers a to b and b to c then she prefers a to c, if she is indifferent between a and b, and b and c, then she is indifferent between a and c.[2] The utility, welfare or well-being of the agent is taken to be a function of preferences. As Harrod put it: 'If an individual prefers a commodity or service X to Y, it is economically better he should have it'.[3] Welfare is characterised in terms of the satisfaction of preferences, the stronger the preference then, for that person, the greater the welfare improvement given its satisfaction. The strength of a person's preference for a good is measured by their willingness to pay at the margin for its satisfaction. The account of well-being or welfare is purely formal. It says nothing about the content of human well-being, makes no claims about whether it is pleasurable states that makes a person's life go well, or virtues of character, the satisfaction of need or whatever. On the entire debate about the nature of well-being that has been at the centre of discussion from the Greeks through to nineteenth-century economics, the modern welfare economist is silent.

This was not always true of economics. The welfare defences of markets in classical economists began from straightforwardly classical accounts of the nature of well-being. Smith for example is an objectivist about the content of well-being: to live well is characterised classically in terms of a set of external material goods and internal intellectual and moral excellences of character. His account is Stoic: the virtue of self-command with those of benevolence and justice form the central dispositions of character that make for the best life.[4]

The founding figures of neo-classical economics were hedonists. The concept of well-being or utility in Jevons is that of classical hedonistic utilitarianism: well-being consists in pleasure and the absence of pain. Jevons explicitly attempts to develop economics from Benthamite foundations: 'The theory ... is entirely based on a calculus of pleasure and pain: the object of economics is to maximise happiness by purchasing pleasure, as it were, at the lowest cost of pain'.[5] The strength of preferences for a good, measured by individuals' willingness to pay for their satisfaction at the margin, is an indirect measure of subjective states: 'it is from the quantitative effects of the feelings that we must estimate their comparative amounts'.[6]

The view that price is an indirect measure of subjective states is followed by Marshall and Pigou.[7] Both display survivals of this hedonism. The shifts in the definitions of utility in successive editions of Marshall's *Principles of Economics* III, iii, 1 reveals both its influence and the problems Marshall had with it. Utility is defined in terms of 'happiness' (first edition), 'pleasure affording power' (second edition), the 'benefit giving power' yielding 'satisfaction' (third edition) and 'total pleasure or other benefit' (fourth edition).[8] By the final edition, it is taken to be 'correlative to Desire or Want', but since 'desires cannot be measured directly' it is revealed in behaviour, in particular through the 'price a person is willing to pay for the fulfilment or satisfaction of his desire'.[9] However that measure is still taken to be an indirect measure of 'the affections of the mind' and these subjective states are taken to be constitutive of welfare. Pigou, in *The Economics of Welfare*, defends the same account of behaviour as an indirect indicator of expected satisfaction: 'it is fair to suppose that most commodities ... will be desired with intensities proportioned to the satisfactions they are expected to yield'.[10] Economic welfare consists in 'that group of satisfactions and dissatisfactions which can be brought into relation with a money measure'.[11]

In recent neo-classical welfare economics the relation between preferences and mental states disappears. The term utility is defined in terms of a preference ordering, such that if x is preferred to y then x has a higher utility function than y. Willingness to pay, which in Marshall and Pigou is understood as an indirect measure of well-being understood in terms of the possession of a subjective state, is used as a measure of preference rankings.

The shift to a formal definition of well-being apparent in the neo-classical tradition is also evident in the Austrian school. However, the move has been from an objectivist rather than hedonistic position. While Menger is remembered as a founder of Austrian subjectivism, his account of well-being is clearly objectivist, a point later Austrian critics such as Mises recognised. The account of human flourishing in *Principles of Economics* owes a self-conscious debt to Aristotle and the scholastics.[12] A real good is an object that has powers to contribute to human flourishing by satisfying a human need, is recognised to have the potential to so contribute and can be directed to do so.[13] This he distinguishes from an imaginary good, that is a thing that is thought to contribute to flourishing, but does not, either because the person has made a mistake about the good – it lacks the powers attributed to it – or an error about the nature of human flourishing itself, a mistake about needs. Imaginary goods occur '(1) when attributes and therefore capacities erroneously ascribed to things that do not really possess them, or (2) when nonexistent human needs are mistakenly assumed to exist'.[14] What makes a good a good is its real capacities to meet real needs. Such goods include not only material goods, but also relationships that are constitutive of human well-being, including those of friendship, hospitality, love and kinship.[15]

In the work of later Austrians this objectivism is rejected: there is a shift to a preference satisfaction account of welfare akin to that of recent neo-classicals. Bohm-Bawerk's defines a person's well-being as embracing 'everything that seems to him worth aiming at', a 'formal' definition endorsed by Mises.[16] Utility is defined 'as that which acting man aims at because it is desirable in his eyes'.[17] That account of well-being is implicit also in the welfare justification of the market offered by Hayek. The market is a condition for the 'general welfare' of individuals in society in virtue of allowing individuals to coordinate their activities so that each individual is able to pursue whatever their aims happen to be.

Within both neo-classical and Austrian traditions of economics, there has, then, been a marked shift in the definitions of well-being or utility from substantive accounts offered by the founders of the tradition to the formal accounts offered by later generations.[18] How are we to understand that shift? One response, more evident in the self-consciously positivistic economics of the 1930s than the 1990s, is to simply deny there is any relation between the formal concept of utility and the substantive concept of welfare.[19] If that line is taken then no normative immediate conclusions about welfare follow from the results of modern economics about the relation between ideal markets and utility. Without endorsing the positivist route to it, the conclusion is one with which I have sympathy: there is I think no direct relation between the formal concept of utility and welfare.[20] However, that conclusion is not now generally followed.[21] Austrian and neo-classical economic theory is taken to have direct welfare implications. Welfare is defined as preference satisfaction. It parallels a similar shift that has occurred within modern utilitarianism, from the classical hedonistic account to the modern preference utilitarianism.

Why is this so? There are two kinds of reasons that are offered for the shift. First, there are those that are broadly methodological in nature especially those concerning the 'subjectivist' revolution in economics:[22] in the following section I argue that these arguments are founded upon confusions. Second, there are those arguments that are founded upon more substantive worries about hedonistic or objectivist accounts of well-being, worries about both their adequacy or possible illiberalism: in sections 3.3 and 3.4 I argue that while the objections to hedonism are well founded a version of objectivism, properly understood, is defensible.

3.2 Subjectivisms in economics

The shift in accounts of well-being from substantive to formal definitions is sometimes characterised in both Austrian and neo-classical economics as part of the subjectivist turn in economics. The term is not altogether helpful. While there is a sense in which the formal turn can properly be characterised as subjectivist, the term 'subjectivism' is used as a name for a different set of claims that are logically independent of each other and which are illegitimately confused. Much of this section will be concerned with sorting them out.

3.2.1 Preference satisfaction, well-being and subjectivism

In what sense is a preference satisfaction theory of well-being 'subjectivist'? To get some initial clarification I want to start with a useful distinction made by Allen Wood between three different senses of subjectivism as an account of well-being.[23]

1 Subjectivity of content: well-being consists in having the right subjective states.
2 Subjective variability: the content of well-being may change from person to person. Different people can lead happy lives in different ways. What is good for you or makes you happy may not be good for me.
3 Subjective determination: the content of a person's well-being is determined by their desires or beliefs about what is good for them. What is of value for me is determined by what I value. What is good for me is determined by what I actually desire or believe is good for me.[24]

Wood claims, rightly I think, that if there is a modern shift towards subjectivism it is in the third sense, that of subjective determination. While the first two forms of subjectivism are found in both the classical and modern period, the third is distinctive of the modern.

Classical theories of well-being can be subjectivist in the first two senses. Epicurus offers the standard subjectivist theory of well-being as an account of content: to live well is to have the right mental states, those of pleasure and the absence of pain. Those like Aristotle who are objectivist about content, for whom to live well is to have or realise certain objective states of affairs – to have friends, to achieve certain intellectual and ethical excellences and so on – are subjectivist in the second sense. Aristotle allows for variability. What is good for one person may not be good for another: the food required for the physical well-being of Milo the athlete differs from that of the ordinary person.[25]

There is indeed a more general sense in which Aristotle's position allows of variability. What is good for us depends upon the kinds of being we are. The point is related to one very particular sense in which Menger uses the term sub-jectivism to describe his position. Menger describes his account as subjectivist in virtue of the fact that the properties of objects that make them goods are dispositional properties of objects to meet human needs and in that sense not 'an independent thing existing by itself'.[26] However, objectivist accounts of the prudential good from Aristotle through the scholastics all agree on this dispositional analysis of goods according to which the worth of an object is a passive power to meet human needs.[27] Menger, in characterising the position as subjectivist, is merely drawing attention to the fact that the powers in question cannot be characterised without reference to human needs.

Menger's point is of importance, however, for there is a confusion about the term 'objectivism' that underlies its prima facie implausibility to many. If 'objec-tivism' meant that what is good for a person is entirely independent of who and what that person is then it would be implausible. What is good for us depends on something about us, on what we are like. The point is central to the Aristotelian account of well-being. If we were angels, water and other material conditions of life would not be valuable to us. Neither if Aristotle and Aquinas are right would friends. But we are not angels. Given the beings we are they are valuable. What is of value to us cannot be independent of the kinds of being we are, and the capacities we have. That is compatible with the rejection of the subjective deter-mination thesis that what we desire or value determines what is valuable to us. On an objectivist account we cannot choose like that. Given the kinds of social creatures we are, no matter how much an individual might place a value on a life without ties of affection to others, his life cannot be led happily without them.

Competing classical accounts of the content of well-being, subjectivist and objectivist, all deny this subjectivism in the third sense of subjective determina-tion. None of them holds that what you desire determines what is good for you. They believe there is objective fact of the matter. The therapeutic aim of philoso-phy is to re-educate the desires for what is good. Typical is Epicurus who combines subjectivism about content with objectivism about determination. Whether you realise it or not, what is of value for you is states of pleasure. When you realise this you will be freed of anxieties that are founded upon errors about the good. For example, death and posthumous reputation really do not make a difference to how well your life goes and hence you do not need to be troubled by them. The classical authors aim to shape desires to those objects which are really good for the person.

How is the modern definition of well-being as preference-satisfaction or desire fulfilment to be understood? It is sometimes offered as an account of the content of well-being that is a competitor with hedonism or the objective list account.[28] However, interpreted in this way there is something odd about the theory of well-being for it is unstable and ultimately collapses into one of its competitors. The reason for its instability is that, as an account of content, it is empty. To this extent Mises is I think right in saying of the preference satisfaction account that it is a 'purely formal view of the character of eudaemonistic concepts ... treating them as indifferent to content'.[29] To define well-being in terms of desires, preferences, purposes or aims is not to specify a content. The content is given by the object of desire. If it is for a pleasurable state, then the theory reduces to a subjective state account of content, if for an objectively given state of affairs then it reduces to an objective state account. Hence preference satisfaction theories are not best interpreted as accounts of the content of well-being in the same field as the hedonistic and objective state approaches.

The theories are more plausibly understood as accounts of what determines the content. They are subjectivist in the third sense outlined. The thesis is that for any person, what that person values determines what is of value for them. The content is given by the preferences or aims of the person. The view reverses the Aristotelian account of the relation between desire and good, that 'we desire an object because it seems good to us'.[30] Mises indeed cites Jacobi's inversion of Aristotle: 'We originally want or desire an object not because it is agreeable or good, but we call it agreeable or good because we want or desire it'.[31] The point is sometimes made in the formal mode: a sentence of the form 'x is of value to a' is always reducible to a sentence of the form 'a values x'. What is of value to us is determined by what we value – the verb is prior to the noun. The statement of the position in the formal mode, however, points to an immediate problem with any simple preference satisfaction theory. There is a difference in the logical properties of the two types of sentences: 'x is of value to a' is extensional, i.e. if x is of value to a, and x = y, then y is of value to a; 'a values x' is intentional, i.e. it is not the case that if a values x and x = y then a values y'. 'Joseph is of great value to Martha' – unbeknownst to her he has assisted her through her education. Since Joseph is the local priest, it follows that 'the local priest is of great value to Martha'. But 'Martha values the unknown benefactor who has assisted her through her education' does not entail 'Martha values Joseph' or 'Martha values the local priest'. She may despise Joseph and loath the clergy. Whether or not something is of value to a person depends on the nature of the object, its capacities to contribute to the flourishing of a person. Whether an object is valued by someone depends upon the nature of the person's beliefs about the object.

This logical difference points to the central problem with the subjective determination thesis stated in its crude form, a problem which lies at the heart of both

40

neo-classical and Austrian defences of the market that employ it. It doesn't appear to allow for mistakes about what is of value. In its crude form whatever persons believe is good for them is good for them. Some versions of the desire-determination account of well-being will follow that move quite explicitly. Mises for example will not allow for any departure between what is good for a person and what person's actual values or desires. But that is clearly implausible and defies the common observation that people can get what they want and be worse off than before. However, it is possible from within a subjective determination thesis to allow for a departure between the satisfaction of actual desires and well-being by adding constraints on the competence and knowledge of the agent: what is of value for a person is what the person would desire or value when cognitively competent and fully informed. Hence Griffin's initial definition of utility: '"utility" is the fulfilment of informed desires, the stronger the desires, the greater the utility'.[32] I return to the sophisticated version in section 3.3. However, for the rest of this section I will focus, for ease of discussion, on the simple version of the subjective determination thesis: what I value or desire determines what is good for me.

A part of the reason for the popularity of the subjective determination thesis about welfare is the product of a confusion of it with quite distinct 'subjectivist' theses that have been central to modern economic thought. The confusions are particularly prone to be made in the Austrian tradition in which subjectivism is a ruling premise. Subjectivism does not only refer to one of three quite distinct claims about welfare. It can also refer to explanatory and ontological claims in economics; a more general meta-ethical claim about norms; particular methodological corollaries that are (mistakenly) taken to follow from those meta-ethical positions; or political positions that are also (mistakenly) inferred from the meta-ethics.

3.2.2 Explanatory and ontological theses

Subjectivism often refers to one of a number of substantive explanatory claims in economics. The epistemic versions popular in the Austrian tradition I discuss in detail in chapter 10. However, in its most basic sense subjectivism as an explanatory thesis refers to the claim that the exchange value of goods in the market is determined by the subjective value that a person puts on it. Objectivism in this context refers to the claim that the exchange value of goods in the market is determined by some non-subjective factor such as the costs of production or the amount of socially necessary labour time that goes into their production. Subjectivism in the explanatory sense is associated with the marginal utility theory of Menger, Jevons and Walras. The theory answers the problem posed by Adam Smith, and before him by Locke,[33] concerning the departure of the exchange value of an object from its use value. Using the examples of water and diamonds, Smith notes: 'The things which have the greatest value in use have frequently little or no value in exchange; and on the contrary, those things which have the

41

greatest value in exchange have frequently little or no value in use'.[34] The paradox appears to block the determination of exchange value of goods by their use value to individuals, rather than by objective factors such as 'scarcity' and hence the 'labour and expence' required to procure them.[35] The marginalist response to the paradox is well known. It employs the distinction between the marginal or incremental use value of an object for a person and its total utility. While the total utility of a good is irrelevant to its exchange value, exchange value is determined by marginal utility, the value placed upon some small incremental addition to one's consumption of the good. Now whether or not this theoretical move in the explanation of exchange value is sound or not, and that question I leave aside here, it is distinct from a subjectivist account of the determination of well-being. However the distinction is not always observed.

The confusion is illustrated vividly in Mises' criticisms of Menger. Menger combines a subjectivist answer to the explanation of exchange value – 'Goods always have a value *to* certain economizing individuals and this value is also *determined* only by those individuals'[36] – with an objectivist account of well-being which insists on a distinction between real and imaginary goods and values. For Mises this is inconsistent: the latter doctrine represents a residual objectivism from which Menger failed to liberate himself.[37] However, while Menger himself is not always clear in his terminology, his basic view is coherent. His objectivism about welfare, that as Mises misleadingly puts it, there exist an 'objectively "correct" scale of values',[38] is quite consistent with 'the subjective theory of value [which] traces the exchange ratios of the market back to the consumers' subjective valuations of economic goods'.[39] The explanatory claim about the determination of *exchange* value is independent of any substantive claim about what determines whether a good is of value to a person.

Subjectivism is also used by Austrian economists to characterise an ontological claim about economics as a social science that also goes back to Menger.[40] The claim is stated with particular clarity in Hayek's *Scientism and the Study of Society*. Against the physicalist programme advocated by Neurath, which aimed at the elimination of all terms that could not be given a characterisation in physical terms, Hayek argues, quite correctly, that the objects of the social sciences cannot be thus characterised. They are objects constituted by beliefs and 'ideas' that individuals have about them: 'Neither a "commodity" or an "economic good", nor "food" or "money" can be defined in physical terms but only in terms of views people hold about things.'[41] This hermeneutic thesis about the nature of social objects, that they are in part constituted by beliefs and social meanings, has its origins within the Austrian tradition in the work of Menger. Specifically Menger held that an economic good becomes such only given certain shared beliefs about the causal powers of the object. There is an epistemic condition that is part of what makes an economic good a good: an object that has causal powers that contribute to flourishing but is not recognised as having those powers is not yet, on Menger's account, an economic good. However, that claim is clearly independent of the stronger claim that what is good for an individual is simply

42

what that person believes to be good. More generally, Menger commits no inconsistency in combining a hermeneutic approach to the social sciences with an endorsement of the difference between what individuals believe to be a good and what is a good.

3.2.3 Meta-ethical subjectivism

Mises' criticisms of Menger illustrate another inferential error that leads to the subjective determination thesis that what is value for a person is determined by what they value. I refer here to the path from value subjectivism as the meta-ethical thesis. As a meta-ethical thesis subjectivism involves a form of non-cognitivism according to which values are ultimately a matter of will and not of judgement. Statements of value are not assertions that have a truth-value. Mises holds a particular version of meta-ethical subjectivism: values are a matter of choice and as such are not open to critical examination – 'the ultimate goals – the values or ends – at which action aims are beyond rationality'.[42] One interpretation of the subjective determination thesis about well-being might be that it is a particular and fairly peculiar version of meta-ethical subjectivism applied to the sphere of prudential value. However, while meta-ethical value subjectivism could take that form it clearly need not. Nothing in meta-ethical subjectivism commits its proponent to saying that it is up to each individual to legislate what is good for them. It is open for the meta-ethical subjectivist to make claims about the well-being of others that are inconsistent with an individual's preferences and their own account about what is good for them. Thus, for example, if Hume is a meta-ethical subjectivist, and the point is contentious, there would be nothing in that position that would not allow him to declare as he does that 'celibacy, fasting, penance, mortification, self-denial, humility, silence, solitude'[43] are qualities of a person of value neither for himself or for others. The subjective determination thesis can be resisted from within a meta-ethical subjectivist position.

3.2.4 Value freedom

Subjective determination of well-being is also independent of another claim that is often taken to be a corollary of a subjectivist meta-ethic, that is the methodological claim that economics, like other social sciences, should be 'value-neutral' or 'value-free', where, in its basic sense, this refers to the claim that ethical values ought to play no role in the appraisal of the empirical claims by the economist. Meta-ethical subjectivism is associated with the distinction between positive economics and normative economics. The reasoning that runs from one to the other runs something as follows: values do not answer to rational argument and, in particular, empirical evidence; whereas economics, as a science, ought to do so; hence, substantive ethical values should play no part in economics. I leave aside discussion of this argument, save to say that I believe the first premise to be false. Nor will I consider here the defensibility of the doctrine of value freedom.[44] Rather I want to consider the question of whether value freedom entails the subjective determination thesis.

The answer that it does is one of the major reasons for the shift to preference satisfaction accounts of well-being. In the Austrian tradition, Mises again is a source of the thought. The following passage is worth quoting at length in virtue of the variety of confusions it illustrates:

> Praxeology deals with the ways and means chosen for the attainment of such ultimate ends. Its object is means, not ends. In this sense we speak of the subjectivism of the general science of human action. It takes the ultimate ends chosen by acting man as data, it is entirely neutral with regard to them, and it refrains from passing any value judgement. The only standard which it applies is whether or not the means chosen are fit for the attainment of the ends aimed at. If Eudaemonism says happiness, if Utilitarianism and economics say utility, we must interpret these terms in a subjective way as that which acting man aims at because it is desirable in his eyes. It is in this formalism that the progress of Eudaemonism, Hedonism and Utilitarianism consist as opposed to the older material meaning and the progress of the modern subjectivistic theory of value as opposed to the objectivist theory of value as expounded by classical political economy. At the same time it is in this subjectivism that the objectivity of our science lies. Because it is subjectivistic and takes the value judgements of acting man as ultimate data not open to any further critical examination, it is itself above all strife of parties and factions, it is indifferent to the conflicts of all schools of dogmatism and ethical doctrine.[45]

Eudaemonistic concepts like happiness or utility are to be interpreted in a formalistic way since this assures value neutrality. The same thought is stated by Robbins, partially under the influence of Mises, and through Robbins it has had a strong influence within the neo-classical tradition.[46]

However, this shift from the doctrine of value freedom to the subjective determination thesis is a mistake. It has to be admitted that, given a commitment to value-free social science, the use of the concepts of 'welfare' or 'well-being' are a problem, for they are evaluative concepts and to endorse one concept of welfare over another is to take a position in an argument about values. However, there is a distinction that needs to be made between refusing to endorse one competing conception of well-being or the good for the purpose of an empirical study, and simply *defining* well-being or the good as being whatever the individual believes it to be. The former commitment to value freedom does not entail the latter preference satisfaction account of the determination of well-being. One can indeed do value-free empirical research concerning the relation between markets and some contested account of well-being without endorsing that conception: 'if one defines well-being as X, Y, or Z then the market leads to an increase or decrease or well-being'.

In the hands of Robbins the argument from value-freedom takes a more specific form: the rejection of the possibility of interpersonal comparisons of welfare in economics. The argument runs thus: for any agent, A, with a given budget, that agent's willingness to pay more for nth unit commodity X than mth unit of commodity Y is taken to show that that unit of X increases their welfare more than that unit of Y. However, one cannot assume for another individual, B, with the same budget who is willing to spend more on the mth unit of Y than is A on the nth unit of X, that unit of Y will produce a greater improvement for B than the unit of X for A, unless one assumes an 'equal capacity for satisfaction' across the agents. However, that assumption is taken to be a value claim, not one of fact that is open to empirical support. Thus Robbins writes:

> The assumption of the propositions which did not involve interpersonal comparisons of utility were assumptions which ... were capable of verification [by observation or introspection]. The assumptions involving interpersonal comparison were certainly not of this order. 'I see no means' Jevons had said, 'whereby such comparison can be accomplished. Every mind is inscrutable to every other mind and no common denominator of feeling is possible.' Would it not be better ... to acknowledge that the postulate of equal capacity for satisfaction *came from outside*, that it rested upon ethical principle rather than upon scientific demonstration, that is was not a judgement of fact in the scientific sense, but rather a judgement of value – perhaps, even, in the last analysis, an act of will.[47]

Robbins' argument should I think be rejected. It combines a disreputable philosophy of mind with a dubious theory of well-being. The disreputable philosophy of mind in the background here, expressed in the Jevons passage endorsed by Robbins, is the hedonistic psychology which conceives of pleasure as a 'feeling' engendered by an object or action. What is the 'feeling' engendered by reading a good novel?[48] It is only given such a picture that the subjective state is taken into the 'inscrutable' world of mind. The dubious theory of well-being is the subjective state account assumed by Jevons, Marshall and Pigou, which takes well-being to consist in having the right pleasurable feelings of satisfaction: since such feelings are subjective states their strength is not open to verification and hence, we cannot compare them across persons. While you and I may have identical incomes and I may be willing to spend more on my next beer than you are on your next novel, the pleasure I get from my beer cannot be compared with the pleasure you get from the novel. Moreover the theory of well-being is in error. Given an objective state account of well-being the problem does not arise – the quality of a person's life can be ascertained in how far that person is capable of realising those goods constitutive of human flourishing. This is not to say there may be problems in making such comparisons, for example, those stemming from the incommensurability of the goods involved and variability in the lives and needs of individuals. However, putatively inscrutable states of mind are not among them. Finally, a mistaken methodological corollary that is often drawn from Robbins argument, although it needs to be stressed not by Robbins himself,[49] is that the economist should avoid making interpersonal utility comparisons. This depends upon a failure to make the distinction between refusing to endorse, for the purposes of empirical enquiry, a principle, such as the equal capacity principle, and the denial that it have any role in one's empirical work. Even given a commitment to value freedom, the former does not entail the latter.[50]

3.2.5 Political neutrality

'Because it is subjectivistic and takes the value judgements of acting man as ultimate data not open to any further critical examination, it is itself above all strife of parties and factions, it is it indifferent to the conflicts of all schools of dogmatism and ethical doctrine.'[51] The sentence from the long Mises passage quoted above illustrates another common confusion concerning subjective determination. The term value-neutrality can be used to describe two distinct theses: a methodological thesis about the social sciences; and a substantive political thesis – the liberal thesis that public policy should be neutral between different conceptions of the good. The liberal thesis may give one grounds for assuming subjective determination as a working rule that what individuals' believe to be good be taken as what is good for them. However, while the idea of the value neutral economist is often married to the liberal thesis – the economist acts as an adviser 'above all strife of parties and factions' whose policy recommendations are neutral between conceptions of the good – this is a marriage between parties who have distinct identities. Nothing in value neutrality as a methodological claim commits one to liberal neutrality as a political ideal. Indeed to claim that it did would itself be incompatible with the methodological claim as Mises at least holds it.

A related inconsistency occurs in the long passage from Mises quoted in 3.2.4. The passage is remarkable in attempting to combine the theses that value judgements aren't open to rational appraisal and that economics is neutral between competing values and ethical doctrines, with the rational defence of a substantial normative position, utilitarianism.[52] The combination is attempted through the formal definition of 'happiness' as the satisfaction of desire. The position is simply internally incoherent.

Arguments for the subjective determination thesis by appeal to a more general subjectivist turn in economics are founded upon confusions. There are however independent and more substantive reasons for preference satisfaction accounts of well-being and against objective determination accounts. First, there are welfarist arguments for the superiority of sophisticated preference satisfaction theories able to meet objectivist objections to the cruder versions. These I consider in section 3.3. Second, there are liberal worries about the potential paternalism of objectivism and correspondingly its compatibility with autonomy and diversity. I respond to these in section 3.4.

3.3 Informed preferences and objective goods

In its crude form the subjective determination thesis identifies what is good for a person with what they believe to be good for them. Now that is not a straw person – there are real flesh and blood theorists, like Mises, who hold that position. Moreover, it is the position that is assumed in what I will call the direct welfare argument for the market to be discussed in chapter 4. But it is not a particularly defensible version of the subjective determination thesis for the reason noted earlier: it allows for no room at all for the possibility of making a mistake about what is for our good – and clearly we do. However, it is possible to hold on to that point in more sophisticated versions of the thesis. The sophisticated subjective determination thesis allows for the possibility of error by identifying the constituents of well-being not with what we in fact value, but with what we would value were we fully informed and competent to make requisite judgements.[53] There are plenty of things we value or desire which when fully informed about the object we would no longer value or desire. Well-being can be identified with the satisfaction of fully informed preferences. The position allows for error but still holds that whether something is good for a person depends on ultimately on what they would want or value. What is good for us is still determined ultimately by our preferences.

This account of the subjective determination of well-being is clearly much more plausible than the crude account I have criticised thus far. However, it remains I believe unsatisfactory. There are two roles that information can play in forming a preference for an object. First, information can serve to find whether an object that I currently desire in fact satisfies other given preferences. I have a preference for some food which unbeknownst to me is carcinogenic. Were I fully informed about the food I would no longer prefer it, for I have a settled preference for good health which has priority over my preference for gastronomic pleasure. This role for information is quite compatible with the informed preference account of well-being. However, informing a person can also act in a second way to form or reform her preferences. Education often is not a question of telling you about an object so that it fits current preferences, but altering preferences by pointing to features of the object that make them worthy of being preferred. Consider for example the issues involved in environmental economics about the relation between environmental goods, information and welfare. It is well recognised in the literature on economic valuation of environmental goods that changes in the quantity and quality of information one presents will alter the strength of a person's preferences for environmental goods. Generally the better the information the stronger the preference. But in these cases to introduce information is often not to provide better grounded beliefs to realise a given set of preferences: it is to alter preferences by developing our distinctively human capacities to respond to the natural world by pointing out features of an object that make them valuable.[54] I may have had no preferences at all for a flat muddy piece of ground by the sea. On education about salt marshes one may come to value it a great deal, and this education might make a large difference to my well-being: I walk by the coast with developed capacities to see and hear what is there. But here my well-being is not increased by allowing me to better realise some given preferences, but rather by changes in perception and knowledge to form new preferences. That is what education, both formal and informal, is all about.

Improvements in well-being come through public deliberation and education of our preferences, not simply through satisfying those we have. Welfare is increased not by fitting objects to current desires, but by forming those desires for their object. To refer to informed preferences in these case is not compatible with the subjective determination thesis. It is a disguised way of talking about objective determination. The point is summarised well by Griffin in his own presentation of the informed preference account of well-being:

> What makes us desire the things we desire, when informed, is something about them – their features or properties. But why bother then with informed desire, when we can go directly to what it is about objects that shape informed desires in the first place? If what really matters are certain sorts of reasons for action, to be found outside desires in the qualities of their objects, why not explain well-being directly in terms of them.[55]

There is a distinction to be drawn here, however, between the attempt to define well-being in terms of informed preferences and the attempt to give the epistemic criteria for good judgement about what is constitutive of well-being. The only criterion we have for a good judgement is that which would emerge from reasonable dialogue, informed by the well-constituted practical and cognitive practices, in conditions of social equality. To that extent something akin to an informed preference theory of well-being is right as an account of the criteria for a judgement of what is constitutive of well-being, although the concept of 'information' here is I believe a little too thin to be adequate.[56] To this has to be added the observation that individuals and social groups often have local knowledge of the material and cultural conditions and history which matters for a judgement about what would make their own lives go better. Moreover, at least some of that knowledge is practical knowledge which is in principle unavailable to others.

It may be that given a sufficiently sophisticated elaboration of a subjective determination thesis the main difference between it and an objective determination thesis is about how to interpret the criteria for good judgement about well-being – as constitutive of well-being or as an epistemic criterion. For that reason when it comes to content the two accounts can be expected to converge. Given the now well-rehearsed problems with hedonism and other subjective state accounts of welfare that convergence will be on something like an 'objective list' account. People's informed concerns for their own well-being are not limited to having the right mental states: we want friends, not just the pleasure of believing we have friends; we want real achievements, not just the pleasure in believing we have realised them. The sophisticated subjective determination thesis will come out with something like a 'desired objective list' account of the good.[57] Hence, while the sophisticated subjective and objective determination theses are distinct and the latter I believe the more defensible, the theory of content will be identical. The critical examination of the welfare arguments for the market to be discussed in chapter 4 could start without loss from sophisticated subjective determination.

3.4 Autonomy and diversity

There are two outstanding liberal worries that provide reasons for many to stick with a sophisticated subjective determination account which deserve some more detailed response. The first concerns autonomy. One major substantive motivation that lies behind the modern subjectivism concerns autonomy and it is related to one standard argument for markets, that it fosters autonomy. I discuss that argument in chapters 6 and 7. But some consideration needs to be given here to that criticism that objective determination of what is of value to us is incompatible with autonomy, that it entails some form of paternalism. Typical is Harsanyi who defends preference utilitarianism by appeal to the principle of Preference Autonomy: 'The principle that, in deciding what is good and what is bad for a given individual, the ultimate criteria can only be his own wants and his own preferences.'[58] Two points can be made in response. First, the claim depends upon a conception of autonomy according to which to be autonomous requires being the author not only of one's own projects but also of the standards by which they should be judged. That conception of autonomy is I believe indefensible and I criticise it in detail in chapters 6 and 7. Second, an objectivist account of well-being can sustain autonomy in a defensible sense. To live well requires autonomy. One argument for this is the Aristotelian position that runs roughly as follows. Human flourishing involves developing our characteristic capacities. Amongst other things we are beings with a capacity to judge what is and is not good for us and others of our kind. Given we have those capacities part of our good consists in their development and exercise. Autonomy is a good in virtue of that fact about us. Given the kinds of beings we are we need the space and opportunities to exercise our capacities of judgement. Were we beings of a non-rational kind, autonomy in the sense of exercising capacities of valuation and judgement would not, indeed, could not, be part of our good.[59]

A second substantive worry that provides the basis for the belief in a subjective determination thesis is the quite proper observation that there exist a variety of ways in which a good life can be lived. The worry is related to concerns about the forms of economic and cultural domination that occur both within existing national borders,[60] and globally across boundaries where it is assumed that one group has privileged access to the correct account of what the good life is about. I have already noted reasons for rejecting any such paternalism and for accepting at the level of epistemic criteria for the good life a convergence between objective and sophisticated subjective determination theses. Here I want to develop a little further a point noted earlier in the chapter that objective determination is quite compatible with subjective variability. One reason for this I have already discussed in detail in chapter 2 – that there are a plurality of goods that go to make up a good life, and there are a variety of ways in which these can be brought together in a particular life. Here I want to expand on two other reasons: first, the difference between the general and particular questions about the good life; second, the nature of humans as beings with a history.

In discussing well-being it is important to distinguish the general question, 'What makes human life go well?', from the more specific questions faced in practical deliberation, 'What would make the lives of this group of persons, this group of women, the members of this community, the life of this particular individual go well or better?' Any answer to the first question can and should be as Nussbaum puts it 'thick',[61] but 'vague ... in a good sense': an answer must allow of many different concrete specifications.[62] However, it must allow for variation without emptiness. An answer constrains possible answers to the second kind of question without determining them. If a theory of well-being rules out nothing it loses its critical value. It must allow, for example, that the social isolation of many of the old in modern western societies, and the cramping of the potentialities of women in many traditional societies are incompatible with their living as well as the material and cultural conditions available in those societies should allow. At the same time any theory that did not allow that personal relations between old and young can take quite different forms, or that there are varieties of skills and capacities that women can exhibit in different cultural settings would be quite mistaken. At a more individual level it is quite compatible with an objective determination thesis that the constituents of individuals' well-being depend on very particular facts about those persons – their particular circumstances, the particular relations they have to others, their tastes, the capacities and powers they have and so on. Moreover, for the reasons given that an individual, in general, has knowledge of such facts unavailable to others, she will normally be in a better position to make judgements about what will make her life go best.

This point about the multiple ways in which a good life can be lived still, however, does not I think capture the extent of subjective variability. The objective determination thesis is often associated with an 'objective list' account of the content of well-being. A list of goods is offered that correspond to different features of our human needs and powers – personal relations, physical health, autonomy, knowledge of the world, aesthetic experience, accomplishment and achievement, a well-constituted relation with the non-human world, sensual pleasures and so on – such that increasing welfare is a question of maximising one's score on different items on the list or at least of meeting some 'satisficing' score on each.[63] Now, this maximising picture of welfare increases and its more modest satisficing relatives is compatible with the kind of variability I have just outlined. The different items on the list can be satisfied in a variety of different ways, and the descriptions on the list much be such that they allow for different instantiations of the goods. However, while the appeal to such general values is I think part of the answer, the maximising or satisficing approach it suggests is unsatisfactory.

The appeal to an objective list misses the role of history and narrative in appraising how well a person's life goes. The importance of temporal order is already there at the biological level. In appraising the health of some organism, the path of growth and development matters, not just some static scoring system for the capacities it has. Once we consider the cultural and social dimensions of human life this temporal order has a stronger narrative dimension. Answering specific questions of how a person's life can be improved is never just one of how one can optimise the score on this or that dimension of the good, but how best to continue the narrative of a life. The question is 'Given my history, or our history, what is the appropriate trajectory into the future?' This is not to say there is just one possible trajectory, nor that there is any algorithm to determine it. Our history enables and constrains, but it does not determine. However, it moves us more away from maximising concepts and entails a more radical variability. It may be that from some static maximising perspective, the best course for a person would be to abandon the isolated farm on a fell that he has farmed for the past sixty years and which was farmed by his family before him, and to move to a retirement home. His material, social and cultural life might all improve. But given the way his life has been bound up with that place, that would involve a disruption to the story of his life. The desire to stay 'despite' all the improvements offered is a quite rational one. Likewise, for communities with their particular traditions and histories, what may be 'maximising' from an atemporal perspective, may not for that particular community.[64]

The worry about variability can take another historical form. It is sometimes argued that since humans are beings with a cultural history, which give rise to new and unpredictable forms of life, activities and objects of desire, the idea of any objectively determined standards is untenable. What is good is ultimately determined by the cultural preferences of an age.[65] The inference is in error. The denial of subjective determination is quite compatible with the rejection of the claim that the objective standards of the good are ahistorical and fixed. It is quite compatible for example with the kind of historicised Aristotelianism one finds in Kant, Hegel and Marx, which with Aristotle claims that it is in the exercise of human powers and capacities that is constitutive of human well-being, but argues that these develop historically and are not determined by some fixed biological fact: hence Marx's remarks contrasting the ancient fixed concept of wealth with wealth understood as 'the absolute working-out of [humanity's] creative potentialities, with no presupposition other than the previous historic development, which makes the totality of development, i.e. the development of all human powers as such the end in itself, not as measured on a *predetermined* yardstick'.[66] On this account there is an objective standard of well-being given by our human powers, but this is not a given standard. The view is one I would endorse, but only given major qualifications. Three in particular need mentioning. First, any reference to human powers needs to refer to the passive as well as the active powers of human beings. There is a danger in writers like Marx that it is the Promethean powers to actively 'master nature' that tend to be called upon, rather than the passive sensibilities to the natural and human world that are also the result of our cultural history.[67] Second, there is a danger in accounts like that of Marx to set history against biology, and to see our powers as completely open. There are features of our nature as biological beings that are fixed and put real limits on what counts as the development of our *human* powers. The desire to escape the human condition is a quite mistaken one: many of the worries that inform criticism of the technology of human life in the late twentieth century reflect I think a proper worry about what it is to be a human in an increasingly technological world.

Finally, there is a danger in talking of history in this context of assuming that later is better or assuming that history is the realisation of human development: that, as Kant formulates it, 'the history of the human race as a whole can be regarded as the realisation of the hidden plan of nature to bring about an internally ... perfect political constitution as the only possible state within which all the natural capacities of mankind can be developed completely'.[68] It may well be that earlier ages had powers and capacities that have been lost, and that we can enter into periods of decline. The enlightenment story of inevitable human progress looks less plausible today than it did in the eighteenth and nineteenth centuries. As a social ideal however, I see no reason to depart from it. Moreover, some of the advances in the material control of nature can foster that ideal. There is a tendency exhibited in many criticisms of 'Western materialism' and 'Western' models of development to spoil an argument by forgetting that the external means of happiness are significant: enough to eat, minimally decent housing, a roof that does not leak, security from violence, the means to cure illness. Discussions by green theorists of a spiritual turn on the (overestimated) virtues of 'voluntary poverty' often confuse it with the 'involuntary poverty' endured everyday by the poor.[69] Poverty, like hard manual labour, is a fine experience in one's leisure time. It has become much sought after as an exotic tourist spectacle. As an inescapable fact of a person's existence it is an evil.

4

THE MARKET AND HUMAN WELL-BEING

The claim that the market is an economic institution that best improves human welfare runs through economic theory from those of classical theorists like Smith through to those of modern neo-classical and Austrian schools. The arguments in those traditions are not, however, of a piece. The structures of the arguments are importantly different. The shift in the structure of the argument is closely related to the move from substantive to formal conceptions of the human well-being outlined in the last chapter. There has been a corresponding shift in the nature of welfarist arguments for the market, from indirect to direct arguments. The direct argument begins with a definition of welfare or well-being as preference satisfaction and justifies the market as an institution that best ensures that the preferences of individuals are satisfied. The exercise of consumer choice in the market acts directly as a means by which welfare is increased. However, given a conception of well-being that allows for a departure between preference satisfaction and human well-being, no such direct route from markets to well-being is possible. Any welfare argument would necessarily be more indirect. The most insightful and credible of such arguments are those of classical economists such as Smith, according to which commerce increases welfare despite satisfying many of the preferences that drive accumulation rather than because they do. In this chapter I argue that if there is a welfare defence of the market that has any plausibility it is the older indirect and substantive argument. However, it entails that there is a deep tension within market societies between the motive forces of economic growth and any unintended welfare benefits, that entails at least the need for boundaries to markets or more strongly the need for non-market economic institutions.

4.1 Direct welfare arguments

Welfare arguments for the market are at the heart of the neo-classical tradition of economics. As I noted in the last chapter, neo-classical economics has its roots in utilitarianism. Historically, the welfare problem it sets out to solve is that stated by Jevons:

> The problem of economics may ... be stated thus: *Given, a certain popu-*
> *lation, with various needs and powers of production, in possession of*

certain lands and other sources of material: required, the mode
of employing their labour which will maximize the utility of the
produce.[1]

The market is to be shown in this welfare justification to be the institution that
solves that problem. The modern neo-classical departs from Jevon's problem of
maximising utility in a number of ways including the following. First, as discussed
in the last chapter, the concept of utility has shifted for a hedonistic account to a
preference satisfaction definition. Second, the problem the modern neo-classical
claims to solve is weaker than that of Jevons. Those modern neo-classical economists who take Robbins' strictures against interpersonal comparisons in welfare to
heart do not claim to prove that markets maximise well-being. Rather they claim to
show that in certain 'ideal' conditions the market will issue in a state of equilibrium,
defined as a state in which, so long as individuals' preferences and productive resources remain the same, any departure from that state will involve a welfare change
for the worse for some party, in the sense that a previously satisfied preference will
no longer be satisfied. An ideal market issues in a Pareto-optimal outcome that is a
state S_1 such that there is no state S_2 such that someone prefers S_2 to S_1 and no one
prefers S_1 to S_2. An ideal market is roughly one in which:

1   All agents are fully informed at no cost.
2   There are no 'transaction costs' – costs of enforcing property rights and con-
    tracts, bringing goods to markets, and so on.
3   Agents are rational in the sense that their preferences are internally consist-
    ent, in particular that they satisfy transitivity – if a person prefers A to B and
    B to C then she prefers A to C.[2]
4   The market is perfectly competitive – there are no externalities, i.e third party
    effects on the satisfaction or dissatisfaction of individual's preferences that
    are not taken into account in market exchanges, and relatedly there are no
    'public goods', that is goods which are such that the action of some or all of
    a group is a necessary and sufficient condition for the good, the action of a
    few insufficient, where the action is a cost to each, the good is available to all
    including non-contributors and none can be excluded from the good.

The claim that ideal markets yield Pareto-optimal outcomes is a modest one in
two senses. First, Pareto-optimality is a weak condition of 'optimality': it says
nothing about the total amount of welfare in a society or about its distribution.
Second, as Hahn notes it is a possibility theorem:[3] it says that free markets in
some fairly unlikely looking conditions can issue in Pareto-optimal outcomes. It
does not show that actual markets do yield any such outcome. The defence of
actual markets it offers is that given that markets are sufficiently like ideal markets, they will meet well-being 'efficiently'. Hence it justifies state intervention
in markets where there are departures from ideal conditions, that is where there
exist 'market failures' – where there exist negative externalities, public goods that

markets could not provide and so on. The state here intervenes to realise the welfare improvements that 'ideal' markets would have produced.

The problem of economics that Jevons introduced and which much, although not all, of neo-classical economics has subsequently addressed is a static problem: it assumes certain givens, productive powers and preferences, and defines a state in which utility is optimally met. The problem is very different from that which was the object of classical economics. The classical economist was concerned much more centrally with the dynamics of commercial societies, of the reasons for the growth of the productive powers of labour within that order and, in the Ricardian and Marxian version of the theories, with the ultimate limits to such growth. Thus, for example, Smith's *Wealth of Nations* begins with the problem 'Of the Causes of improvement in the productive Powers of Labour, and of the Order according to which its Produce is naturally distributed among the Different Ranks of the People'.[4] Its aim is to explain why, in commercial society, 'the general welfare of society' increases despite the decrease in the number engaged in productive labour.[5] Smith's arguments I discuss later in this chapter. Its structure is different from that offered by the neo-classicals. It is also different from that of the Austrians, for all the Austrians stay closer to the classical version of the 'economic problem'.

The place of welfare in the arguments of the Austrian tradition has always been less clear cut than in both classical and neo-classical. There is a libertarian strain within the tradition which allows welfare to be overridden given a conflict with liberty. However, there is a strong welfarist component within Austrian economics. The market is the economic institution that best serves human well-being. Moreover (as I noted in the last chapter), with the exception of Menger, the Austrian tradition has followed the same kind of account of well-being as preference satisfaction found in recent neo-classical economics. Bohm-Bawerk's definition of a person's well-being, as embracing 'everything that seems to him worth aiming at', is explicitly endorsed by Mises and something like it is implicit in the work of Hayek.[6] In the work of Mises this is employed to serve in a utilitarian justification of the market. In the work of Hayek the situation is complicated by Hayek's own explicit attacks on utilitarianism as a form of constructive rationalism that fails to acknowledge the consequences of human ignorance consequent upon the division of knowledge in society.[7] However, Hayek still employs a broadly welfarist justification of the market: 'the maintenance of a spontaneous order is the prime condition of the general welfare of its members'.[8] It serves to realise them in virtue of allowing them to coordinate their activities in the realisation of whatever their ends happen to be:

> In this sense the general welfare which the rules of individual conduct serve consists of what we have already seen to be the purpose of the rules of law, namely that abstract order of the whole which does not aim at the achievement of known particular results but is preserved as a means of assisting in the pursuit of a great variety of individual purposes.[9]

The abstract order of rules that govern the 'Great Society' of free markets allow individuals with quite different ends and their own local knowledge to coordinate their activities with each other. The structure of Austrian welfare argument is different from that of the neo-classicals and closer to that of the classical economists. It rejects the static problem from which the neo-classicals began. The Austrians assume that resources and preferences are always changing and ignorance is a starting point. Hence the concept of ideal markets is irrelevant. Nor is it clear that Pareto-optimality is really an appropriate measure of economic efficiency given the existence of constantly shifting preferences and resources. In place of the static problem of the neo-classicals, the Austrians retain the more dynamic set of problems that informed classical economics. The welfare justification proceeds not by reference to the realisation of an equilibrium on the basis of given preferences, information and resources, but in the more dynamic concept of coordination processes which allow the plans of actors to be mutually adjusted on the basis of constantly changing preferences, information and resources. The concept of plan-coordination processes replaces the concept of equilibrium.[10] What it still shares with recent neo-classical as against the classical economics is the concept of welfare itself understood as the satisfaction of preferences or purposes and a picture of welfare improvements occurring through the satisfaction of consumer preferences in the market.

Both recent neo-classical and recent Austrian economics employ a direct welfare justification of markets. Well-being is defined in terms of preference satisfaction and the market is, in different ways, presented as an institution that best realises the satisfaction of consumer preferences and hence improves welfare. As direct justifications of the actual market economies that exist, the basic point is that these economies satisfy the preferences of consumers. In support of this claim is the empirical evidence of the long-term growth of incomes, such that consumers are, on the whole, increasingly able to satisfy a larger array of their wants, from producers who, to compete on the market, attempt discover and satisfy those wants. It is against this historical background of growth, albeit uneven, in the satisfaction of consumer demand that recent neo-classical and Austrian economics draw some empirical strength.

Now there are a variety of distributional points that one might want to make here about market economies in criticism of these claims. These I will not pursue here. Rather I want to pursue another well-known empirical problem that this direct justification throws up. The empirical problem is this – that with all the increase in the variety of goods and services that consumers are able to buy, there is no corresponding reported increase in perceived satisfaction. The total amount of welfare understood as preference satisfaction over dissatisfaction appears to be remarkably static in modern market societies. There appears to be little evidence of any growth in the gap between preference satisfaction and dissatisfaction. As Lane notes:

> In a variety of cross-cultural studies it has been found there is virtually no relationship between the level of national income and life satisfac-

tion, happiness or person's ladder scaling of his life position. Historical studies agree. Over time, as national income increases happiness or life satisfaction remains constant.[11]

Now there are caveats to be made here.[12] It is true for example that the obverse holds: a decrease in income is associated with a decrease in perceived life satisfaction. However, the picture of life in modern society that emerges from studies paints a remarkably Hobbesian picture of agents endlessly satisfying one desire after another and never finding rest. Like the fisherman's wife of the folk tale, they move progressively from hovel to palace without any decrease in dissatisfaction. The assumed positive relationship between markets and well-being understood as preference satisfaction is not confirmed by empirical evidence. For reasons I outline below it does not follow that there is no relation between increased welfare and increased wealth. There may be an indirect relation. However, the direct route outlined looks far from plausible.

Why is there no relationship? One important part of the answer is that offered by Hirsch. Many of the goods that people seek in the market are positional goods, that is goods and services whose worth to a person is affected by the consumption of the same goods and services by others. A standard example of a positional good is the exotic tourist destination – its value depends on there being few others who have read and acted upon the same 'off the beaten track' guidebook. Another is educational qualifications in so far as they are valued as a means to employment – their value depends on their exclusivity. To the extent that the objects sold on markets are positional goods – and as we shall see if Adam Smith is right then nearly all objects sold are positional goods – it follows that in markets the promise to each individual that a good will make them better off will not be realised, since collective consumption of that good will mean that no one will be better off.[13] Each individual makes an individual choice for a good that is affected by the same choice by others. Increased income and consumption is not matched with any increase in life satisfaction:

> [I]t is ... questionable whether the road to a carefree society can run through the market economy, dominated as it is by piecemeal choices exercised by individuals in response to their immediate situation. The choices offered by market individuals are justly celebrated as liberating for the individual. Unfortunately. individual liberation does not make them liberating for all individuals together.[14]

However, to make this criticism points to a further problem with the whole nature of direct argument from markets to welfare. A central problem lies in the very account of well-being offered in the first place. To define well-being in terms of satisfying preferences appears to disallow the everyday observation that getting what you want need not make you happier. It all depends on what your wants are. Want satisfaction leads to welfare increase only if you have the right wants. Any direct argument for markets appears to rely on an implausible account of human well-being as the satisfaction of actual preferences that I criticised in the last chapter. However, this does not show there is no relation between well-being and markets. Once the want-satisfaction account of welfare is abandoned, it no longer follows in any straightforward way that the failure to lead 'satisfied' lives in markets means they do not increase welfare.

The possibility of a gap between want satisfaction and welfare improvements was one that the earlier figures in the neo-classical and Austrian traditions did allow. As I noted in the last chapter, within the neo-classical and Austrian traditions of economics, there has been a marked shift in the definitions of well-being from substantive accounts offered by the founders of the tradition to the formal accounts offered later generations: from hedonistic or objectivist definitions of well-being to definitions in terms of preference satisfaction. One consequence is that a set of problems about the relation between well-being and markets that earlier economists took seriously has disappeared from view.

In the neo-classical tradition, the position of Jevons, Marshall and Pigou shares with classical hedonism the view that people's preferences can depart from what is really good for them. People can desire things that will not give them 'satisfaction' understood as a mental state, and fail to desire things that will. Hence there is no direct route. However, the indirect route is one that employs only a minor detour from growth to satisfaction. The argument from the market to welfare improvements runs roughly as follows: the market fosters the growth in 'economic' welfare, that is that part of welfare that can be 'bought under the measuring rod of money' and there is a presumed but unproven assumption that the growth in economic welfare will tend to increase total social welfare, including those parts of well-being that cannot be measured by money – 'there is a presumption – what Edgeworth calls an "unverified probability" – that qualitative conclusions about the effect of an economic cause upon economic welfare will hold good also of the effect on total welfare'.[15] The argument allows that the presumption be proved false. The apparent problem with this version of the indirect argument is that it looks like it has. The empirical argument raised against the direct argument still has considerable power against the hedonistic version of the indirect argument. There appears to be little relation between growth in economic welfare and growth in reported 'satisfaction'.[16]

A similar problem arises with Menger. While Menger assumes an objectivist account of well-being which allows for a gap between preference satisfaction and well-being that is wider than of the hedonists, his own argument largely relies on the preference satisfying features of the market. Menger's position depends on a general enlightenment confidence in the growth of knowledge both of the world and human needs which is such that preference satisfaction in the market founded upon that knowledge will lead to the growth in welfare. It is blind to the problems about the relation between markets and welfare improvement outlined above. To gain insight into that problem one needs to turn to the classical economists.

4.2 Indirect welfare arguments

The most sophisticated welfare defences of the market are those to be found amongst classical economists who employ classical objective state accounts of welfare. In such theories, the material conditions of physical well-being, the social and cultural conditions for the development of human excellences, such as the capacity for autonomous choice and the possibility of cultural accomplishment, and conditions that foster proper social relations are the indicators of human well-being. The relationship between commerce, the growth in productive powers and the development of the central goods of human life takes the centre of the argument. It needs to be noted that, once one moves towards an objective state account of well-being, the relationship between satisfaction, dissatisfaction and well-being becomes more complex than that assumed in basic preference satisfaction accounts. Indeed, the fact that there is no increase in preference satisfaction over dissatisfaction no longer entails immediately that there is no increase in welfare. Not all dissatisfaction is a sign of a life that has taken a turn for the worse. Indeed, it can indicate the opposite, that a person is exercising capacities that are part of what it is for a life to be improving. Consider a pianist, who starts being greatly satisfied with her initial developments, but who, as she continues to develop technically and artistically, becomes ever more critical of her performance. Her increasing dissatisfaction is a symptom of increasing accomplishment. Or again consider the contented slave, wage earner or housewife who become discontented with their lot: it is better for them that this is so and not just in virtue of other possible improvements this might bring. This is an old point. As Mill notes, it is better for the person to suffer the dissatisfactions that a developed emotional and intellectual life bring than to accept satisfaction in their absence. More generally, there may be features of life in modern society that are genuinely improvements in welfare. The cultural options that are open to people in modern society are welfare gains even if they issue in no change in levels of satisfaction. The same is true of material improvements: in the story of the fisherman's wife, there is some point in the passage from hovel to palace at which well-being was increased. Once one drops a subjectivist or preference satisfaction theory of welfare, there is no relation as such between increasing dissatisfaction and decreasing welfare. Rather, the story is reversed. The account of well-being given will entail a distinction between different kinds of dissatisfaction: those that arise from mistaken preferences and desires and those that arise in the pursuit of what is good.

When one goes back from the formalism of modern economics to the substantive discussions of the good found amongst the founders of classical economics one finds an acute awareness of the complexities of the relationship between commerce and welfare that anticipate in a different idiom the problems that Hirsch addresses. In particular Smith offers a sophisticated indirect defence of the market as a welfare fostering institution that has a plausibility that recent discussions lack. The plausibility of the argument lies in the fact that it is premised on the claim that commercial society increases welfare not because of the manner in which it satisfies consumer preferences but despite the way it does so.

Smith is an objectivist about the content of well-being: to live well is characterised classically in terms of a set of intellectual and moral excellences of character. For Smith the preferences that drive consumption and accumulation in commercial society are by and large preferences which are such that their satisfaction does not increase well-being but rather furnishes anxiety. They are preferences founded on mistakes about the constituents of a good life. The drive for growth is not founded upon desires for objects of use but upon vanity. It is in the desire to be noticed through objects of display, in the 'numberless artificial and elegant contrivances', the frivolous baubles through which individuals attempt to draw attention upon themselves.[17] On this account, that the growth of goods that meet consumer preferences should result in no increase in satisfaction is to be expected. Desires driven by a concern for appearance 'cannot be satisfied, but seem to be altogether endless'.[18] The economy of commercial society is driven almost entirely on Smith's account by desires for what are in Hirsch's terminology 'positional goods'. The empirical evidence against the preference satisfaction theory of well-being I cited earlier is quite what one would expect.[19] Nor for Smith is the dissatisfaction of the kind that indicate any genuine accomplishment. The 'vain and insatiable desires' that drive the growth of commerce are inimical to human happiness. Smith's account of the 'character of the individual, so far as it affects his own happiness' is 'as I have just noted' classical, influenced in particular by the Stoics. The Stoic virtue of self-command alongside those of benevolence and justice form the central dispositions of character that make for the best life.[20] The virtues are exhibited in 'industry and frugality',[21] in independence and self-reliance, and in the preference for 'secure tranquillity' not only over the 'vain splendour of successful ambition' but even over 'real and solid glory of performing the greatest and most magnanimous actions'.[22] Given that the desire for appearance is founded upon a mistake, the satisfaction of the driving preferences of commercial society cannot of themselves lead to well-being but the reverse, to anxiety and unhappiness.

However, the error is a happy one:

> It is this deception which rouses and keeps in continual motion the industry of mankind. It is this which first promoted them to cultivate the ground, to build houses, to found cities and commonwealth, and to invent and improve all the sciences and arts which ennoble and embellish human life.[23]

The metaphor of the 'invisible hand' makes its appearance in this context, referring to the indirect and unintended link between 'the gratification of ... vain and insatiable desires' and 'the distribution of the necessaries of life' across the whole population.[24] The material and cultural means of proper happiness are then an unintended consequence of the action of commercial society. Through the growth of division of labour founded in the exchange relations of commercial society in which 'every man ... becomes in some measure a merchant',[25] the growth in productive powers of labour brings with it growth in 'the necessaries and conveniences of life' for the labourer and his social independence. Moreover, in 'the middling and inferior stations of life', the virtues that are constitutive of the good life are fostered: 'the road to virtue and that to fortune ... are ... very nearly the same'.[26] 'The habits of oeconomy, industry, discretion, attention, and application of thought' are cultivated from the pursuit of self-interest.[27]

There is much in Smith's account of the relation between markets and well-being that is open to criticism. The particular tables of virtues he offers will look unconvincing to those of us unpersuaded of the truth of Stoicism. The empirical claims he makes about the relation between virtue and economy are open to question. However, leaving these details aside here, the general indirect strategy certainly has strengths that the direct argument lacks. The general strategy of arguing that the market has indirect and unintended consequences in the development of the arts and sciences, the character of a person as well as the material conditions for human flourishing, all has some plausibility. If there is a welfare argument for the market it is of the kind that Smith offers. It is true that commercial society offers material and cultural options that were unavailable in pre-commercial societies. A version of the indirect argument is echoed in Marx's critical praise of commercial society. Thus Marx notes that pre-commercial societies look more humanistic than commercial society. Within such societies

> the question is always which mode of property creates the best citizens. Wealth appears as an end in itself only among the few commercial peoples ... who live in the pores of the ancient world ... [T]he old view, in which the human being appears as the aim of production ... seems to very lofty when contrasted to the modern world, where production appears as the aim of mankind and wealth as the aim of production.[28]

However, it is within the market economy that the human powers are developed: hence the reference to the 'universality of human needs, capacities, pleasures and productive capacities etc., created through universal exchange.'[29] The kind of historicised Aristotelianism that Marx and Hegel present is a response precisely to the way in which, for all the losses, modern commercial society creates new powers and potentialities for human beings. As a story of the move from pre-modern to modern market societies it has some plausibility. While there are losses in well-being in transition, especially in the sphere of social relations, there are gains. Any criticism of commercial society needs to recognise and build upon the real improvements in human life that commercial society brought, aiming to realise the potentialities that have developed within commercial society.

However, while the Smithian defence has strengths it also entails a deep and enduring conflict within commercial society, between the forces that move accumulation and the indirect welfare benefits that are consequent upon it.[30] The existence of the possibility of this form of conflict was one recognised from within the republican political tradition which informs Smith's work: it is expressed in terms of a twist in the traditional story of the republican virtues undermined by the luxury it eventually creates through its conquests. The new version of the traditional tale was articulated by Montesquieu:

> the spirit of commerce brings with it the sprit of frugality, economy, moderation, work, wisdom, tranquillity, order, and rule. Thus as long as this spirit continues to exist, the wealth it produces has no bad effect. The ill comes when an excess of wealth destroys the spirit of commerce.[31]

The theme is echoed in Smith,[32] and has been a recurring theme since concerning the 'depleting moral legacy' of commercial society, that is the idea that late market societies depend on a pre-commercial or early commercial moral legacy which the market itself undermines.[33] The story is one version of the tale of capitalism failing due to its own inner nature. Now, the truth of that claim I leave aside here. It may be that the institutions of capitalism are much more robust than these pictures suggest. However, whatever the truth or otherwise of the causal story, it points to a real tension in the indirect welfare argument. In so far as welfare is an achievement that is not only indirect but also achieved despite the driving forces of the market, it entails a deep lying instability of that achievement. There is, if the argument works, a tension within the market that it at the same time promotes arts and sciences, cognitive and practical practices that foster human well-being and the virtues that are constitutive of it while at the same depending upon and encouraging a character and set of institutions that are incompatible with the flourishing of both practices and virtues. The position points to a constant tension that is inherent in market economies, between the drives that push it forward and any unintended beneficial consequences it might have.

The market, as Smith and other classical economists recognised, is corrosive of the conditions of human well-being. That corrosion I discuss in the following chapters of this book. The forms of commitment that are constitutive of personal relations are incompatible with the contractual relations of the market order. While, in comparison with pre-market societies, it creates conditions of social independence, it also loosens social bonds and loyalties that are also part of what makes possible an autonomous character. Social identity and the narrative order of a human life that is one condition of it are disrupted by market relations. The norms of recognition associated with the market are incompatible with those required by the internal order of the sciences, arts and crafts. The capacities and skills that are developed within individuals' working lives and which are central to their social esteem and a major constituent of their well-being are undermined by the drives to accumulate in market societies.[34] The norms of property that are presupposed by markets are incompatible with the public nature of the sciences and arts. The market is compatible with the good life only to the extent that it is hedged and bounded, such that non-market associations and relations can flourish. In so far as the market has a tendency to extend its boundaries it is corrosive of the conditions for human well-being. Commercial society may call upon not just a depleting moral legacy but a depleting legacy in those conditions that foster human well-being. The indirect welfare argument for the market entails that commercial society always contains within it the source of its own corruption, that the drives that push the growth of markets, for positional goods and baubles are also drives that undermine the unintended beneficial consequence. At the very least it is an argument that carries with it the claim that markets need boundaries. More radically, it may be that, for all the development of human capacities commercial society allowed, the realisation of human well-being now requires a non-market economic order.

5

AUTONOMY, FREEDOM AND MARKET

In the next four chapters I consider arguments for the market that appeal to a cluster of values around liberty. The market is often defended as a sphere of freedom, of voluntary uncoerced contracts between free and independent agents who can shape their own lives. This liberal argument is central to the Austrian school and is implicit in the anti-paternalistic arguments in the neo-classical tradition discussed at the end of chapter 3. In examining this line of argument, I focus on what looks the strongest case for it, namely that which asserts a relationship between market institutions and autonomy. I leave aside here, for reasons of space and not cogency, traditional socialist objections, recently revived by feminists: that contracts in markets are often only formally voluntary acts between free and independent agents – the relations between the agent often in substance involve real asymmetries of power; that labour contracts, even if they are born in the Eden of free contract, are a route to significant unfreedoms, since in buying labour power the buyer gains rights of direction.[1]

Arguments for markets from liberty and autonomy can take either neutrality-based or perfectionist forms. Thus the appeal to freedom and autonomy is often one that calls upon neutrality: liberty and autonomy are goods in the sense of being conditions for individuals being able to pursue their own conceptions of the good life.[2] The appeal can also call upon perfectionist arguments: the dispositions of character that form the virtues constitutive of the autonomous person – the powers to reason for oneself, to be self-reflective, to act as the author of one's own life – form a central component of the good life. Political and social institutions should be such that they develop those virtues, and undermine the opposing vices of heteronomy – passivity, self-abnegation, deference to authority. Both kinds of appeal to autonomy are evident in liberal defences of market institutions. Indeed there is often slippage between them that goes unnoticed.

In the first section of this chapter I clear some of the basic conceptual ground for discussion of the relation between autonomy and markets. I do so by looking in detail at the arguments of Hayek, in which many of the different uses of the concept of freedom and autonomy and the tensions between them are apparent. I argue that it is the perfectionist appeal to autonomy that is the more promising for the liberal defender of the market. In the second section I outline the nature and problems with that appeal. These will be developed in detail in chapters 6 and 7.

5.1 Autonomy, freedom and neutrality

Hayek might look an odd theorist to begin a discussion of the arguments for the market from autonomy. He is standardly presented as defending a purely negative conception of liberty which is taken to be distinct from the concept of autonomy which is identified with the 'positive' conception of liberty.[3] That presentation is encouraged by Hayek himself who presents his account of freedom as a purely negative account and in opposition to a 'positive' conception. In its 'negative' sense liberty refers to the absence of constraints on doing what one wants, where constraint is characterised as intentional interference by other persons. The market is thus a sphere in which individuals have negative liberty: they pursue their aims without the intentional interference of others even if their actions might be constrained by unintended outcomes. Hayek clearly does define political liberty in that sense: freedom is defined as 'the state in which a man is not subject to coercion by the arbitrary will of another or others'.[4] Furthermore, in defending liberty in that negative sense, he rejects the 'positive' conception of liberty according to which freedom is to be defined in terms of the power or capacity to act in pursuit of one's aims: thus he attacks both Commoner and Dewey for spreading

> an ideology in which 'liberty is power, effective power to do specific things' and the 'demand for liberty is the demand for power', and their equation of the absence of coercion with merely 'the negative side of freedom', 'to be prized only as a means to Freedom which is power'.[5]

Hayek, with other negative theorists, rejects this position insisting upon the distinction between liberty and the conditions for its exercise.

The debate between the positive and negative theories thus defined follows well-worn paths which I will not pursue here.[6] Rather I want to focus on the prior question: why should it be thought to be good that one has liberty in the 'negative' sense?

The question takes us back to the debates concerning neutrality and perfectionism in political theory. There are two different kinds of answers that the liberal might make. The first is to appeal to the political principle of neutrality. On this account freedom is not itself a basic value, but rather a condition of the procedural neutrality of political and economic institutions between different conceptions of the good. If those institutions are to be neutral, then there must be no intentional constraints on an individual's pursuit of her values or wants, provided these do not interfere with the similar pursuit of these by others. On this account, freedom itself cannot be understood as a basic value to be pursued by political and economic institutions, since that itself would be to deny the principle of neutrality. A corollary of this view is that there should be no constraints on the kinds of contracts individuals enter of the kind that Mill, for example, proposes with respect to slavery contracts, since any such constraint would involve the imposition of some conception of the good. If individuals prefer the peace and contentment of slavery to the difficulty of making their own choices, then so be it: let them enter a contract for slavery.[7]

Mill's position rests on a more substantive foundation. The possibility of making free choices unconstrained by others is of value in virtue of its consequences for the character of the individual. For individuals to be the authors of their own characters, it must be the case that they have projects which are their own, which they enter into out of choice and not out of compulsion. This view underlies Mill's defence of participatory democracy, his defence of liberty in the sense of a sphere from which physical and moral coercion is absent, and his defence of the market economy. All are of value since they give individuals the scope to make choices between different projects and ways of life, and hence they develop the moral character.

These two answers to the question 'Why negative liberty?' map on to the two kinds of appeal that are made to the concept of autonomy in discussions of liberal institutions, the neutralist and the perfectionist. Here a major ambiguity needs to be noted in standard accounts of the debate between 'negative' and 'positive' liberty. The debate is a more tangled affair than is often assumed, since there is not one positive conception in the literature, but two, and these are often conflated. The first is that of Dewey, that liberty is the power, including the enabling conditions, that allows an agent to realise her goals. The second concept of 'positive liberty', logically distinct from that of Dewey, is that introduced by Berlin:

> The 'positive' sense of the word 'liberty' derives from the wish on the part of the individual to be his own master. I wish my life and my decisions to depend on myself ... I wish to be the instrument of my own, not of other men's acts of will. I wish to be a subject, not an object; to be moved by reasons, by conscious purposes, which are my own ... I wish, above all, to be conscious of myself as a thinking, willing, active being, bearing responsibility for my own choices and able to explain them by references to my own ideas and purposes.[8]

Positive liberty thus characterised is a form of autonomy or self-determination. The two concepts of positive liberty are logically independent. Indeed it is just this logical independence of the two positive concepts that Hayek often asserts when contrasting 'negative' and 'positive' liberty.

Consider the following claim: 'Whether or not I am my own master and can follow my own choice and whether the possibilities from which I must choose are many or few are two entirely different questions'.[9] Hayek draws attention to real distinctions here. However, he miscounts. He distinguishes not two, but three questions.

1   'Whether or not I am my own master': the question concerns positive liberty
    in Berlin's sense, that is, whether or not I am an autonomous person, who has
    the powers and dispositions of character that allow one to formulate my own
    values, plans, etc.
2   'Whether or not I ... can follow my own choice': the question concerns the
    limiting or impeding conditions on the exercise of my capacity to choose –
    for Hayek, whether or not the 'negative' conditions for the exercise of those
    powers obtain the absence of coercion.
3   'Whether the possibilities from which I must choose are many or few': the
    question, as Hayek develops his answer to it, becomes one about the exist-
    ence of enabling conditions on the exercise of powers of choice, that is,
    whether the 'positive' conditions for the exercise of those powers are present
    – the 'powers' external to the individual, such as material means, that are
    required to realise autonomous choices.

Hayek claims that an answer to 3 should not count as an answer to the question
'What is it to be free?' The existence of enabling conditions, such as the material means to satisfy choices, should not form part of the concept of liberty: it is
this point he is making when he contrasts his account of liberty with that of
Dewey.

The ambiguity in Hayek's position and that of a number of other radical liberals concerns the first two questions. Hayek miscounts since he treats the first and
second questions as one and the same. They are however distinct. Whether or not
one has the dispositions and powers to be one's own person is distinct from
whether or not one is coerced by others: there is a difference, for example, between people who are enslaved but have developed the capacities and desires to
formulate their own life plans, and those who are enslaved and have neither the
capacities nor the desires of the autonomous agent. Hayek tends to assume that
'to be one's own master' is simply a procedural matter of being uncoerced. For
this reason, his defence of negative liberty and his defence of autonomy are never
distinguished and the positive component of Hayek's concept of liberty goes
unnoticed.

Hayek does appeal to a positive conception of liberty in Berlin's sense of the
term, although he does use neither that term nor 'autonomy' in doing so.[10] Thus
consider the following account of the value of freedom:

> Man, or at least European man, enters history divided into free and un-
> free; and this distinction had a very definite meaning ... It meant always
> the possibility of acting according to his own decisions and plans, in
> contrast to the position of one who was irrevocably subject to the will of
> another, who by arbitrary decision could coerce him to act or not to act
> in specific ways. The time-honoured phrase by which this freedom has
> often been described is therefore 'independence of the arbitrary will of
> another'.[11]

The value of being free from the coercion of others is precisely that it allows one to be free in the positive sense that Berlin outlines. To be free is to ensure that my 'decisions to depend on myself' to be 'the instrument of my own, not of other men's acts of will', to be my own master, to be 'moved by reasons, by conscious purposes, which are my own'.[12] However, Hayek elides self-determination with the negative conditions for its exercise, the absence of the constraints due to the intentional acts of others – 'independence of the arbitrary will of another'.

Hayek's defence of market neutrality in terms of autonomy has its foundation in this elision of the two concepts. Hayek appeals to the Kantian notion of respect for persons in his defence of the market as a neutral institution: neutrality is a condition for the recognition of the autonomy of others.

> The recognition that each person has his own scale of values which we ought to respect, even if we do not approve of it, is part of the conception of the value of the individual personality. How we value another person will necessarily depend on what his values are. But believing in freedom means that we do not regard ourselves as the ultimate judges of another person's values, that we do not feel entitled to prevent him from pursuing ends which we disapprove so long as he does not infringe the equally protected sphere of others.[13]

For Hayek, all agents construct their own scale of values, and the failure to recognise the exercise of this capacity to construct one's own values is a failure to respect the person: 'A society that does not recognise that each individual has values of his own which he is entitled to follow can have no respect for the dignity of the individual and cannot really know freedom'.[14] The market is justified as an institution precisely because it does allow individuals to follow their own values and hence is consistent with 'respect for the dignity of the individual'.

Thus goes the argument. It works, however, by reducing autonomy to a procedural matter of having choices. It fails because it treats having choices and possessing the powers of the autonomous agent as identical. More generally, appeals to autonomy to found neutral institutions assume a minimal account of autonomy – anyone able to choose has it – and treat this as a gift – something we simply have in virtue of being adult human beings. The question only arises about the conditions for its exercise – and these are given by absence of coercion. The question Hayek implicitly raises concerning the conditions for the development of the autonomous character disappears. This position not only is unsatisfactory in itself, but also hides a deeper commitment to autonomy that animates the work of Hayek and a number of other libertarian defenders of the market.[15]

Hayek independently values the development of a certain kind of character understood in a more substantive way, of the free person who is able to think and value for themselves. Moreover, there are passages which are open to a perfectionist interpretation: the market is understood as a condition for the development of the autonomous character, not just for the exercise of her capacities. Consider the following defence of the absence of coercion by the will of others: 'Coercion is evil precisely because it thus eliminates an individual as a thinking and valuing person and makes him a bare tool in the achievement of the ends of another'.[16] The passage is open to two interpretations. The non-perfectionist interpretation is that coercion is evil because it fails to recognise a person as the 'thinking and valuing person' he is. The second is the more literal and perfectionist interpretation, that coercion is evil because it 'eliminates' that person, that it undermines individuals' capacities and powers to formulate their own values and thoughts and renders them dependent and servile. On the second interpretation, Hayek's defence of negative liberty is that it is a condition for autonomous persons whose values, beliefs and decisions are their own and not others. The argument thus construed belongs to that of a long line of perfectionist arguments presented by liberal theorists, of whom J. S. Mill is the most prominent example, which defend negative liberty, and the market economy as a sphere of negative liberty, as a condition for the development of autonomous character. On this view the dispositions that go to make up the autonomous character are not just givens. They require particular conditions for their development, and amongst these are economic conditions. Whereas in pre-commercial society individuals define themselves in terms of their particular role or station, and are discouraged from developing powers of independent thought, in modern market societies individuals are forced to define their lives for themselves and to think for themselves. That this is the case is a virtue of commercial societies. That perfectionist theme runs as an undercurrent in Hayek's writing. It forms the stronger case for the market.

5.2 Autonomy, perfectionism and the market

Much recent liberal writing has turned from its recent flirtations with neutrality back to its perfectionist roots: liberal political and economic institutions are defended on the basis of the character of the persons they foster. A perfectionist account of autonomy is often invoked.[17] In keeping with that move, the market, as a liberal institution, has been defended in more explicit terms for fostering the development of the autonomous person. The point is made with characteristic clarity by Gray:

> the virtues elicited in market economies are those of the autonomous agent – the person ... who is self-possessed, who has a distinct self-identity or individuality, who is authentic and self-directed, and whose life is to some significant degree a matter of self-creation.[18]

The autonomous character is one who displays some measure of independence in the exercise of her faculties of judgement, decision and action. There are at least three large problems with any straightforward attempt to defend markets and the

extension of free markets in terms of the development of the autonomous character. The first two are recognised by Gray himself. They concern the value and
conditions of autonomy. Very briefly they are these:

1   The value of autonomy   The value of autonomy requires the existence of
     valuable options over which autonomous choices can be made. There are
     weaker and stronger ways of understanding this claim. The weak version
     goes that autonomy is of little value if there are restricted options available.
     The stronger version, defended by Raz, claims that such options are a neces-
     sary condition for autonomy: autonomy is in part constituted by the exist-
     ence of significant options. To use Raz's examples, neither a man in the pit
     whose choices are limited to when to eat enough to exist and to sleep, nor the
     hounded woman, whose life is solely a struggle to avoid the carnivorous
     animal who hunts her, can be said to be autonomous: the man in the pit has
     only trivial choices, the hounded woman only horrendous choices. Autonomy
     requires a variety of adequate options.[19] This, the argument runs, requires
     boundaries on the extension of markets. The existence of such options re-
     quires the existence of educational, cultural, familial and associational spheres
     in which the projects and relationships that constitute the valuable options in
     persons lives can be pursued. These are undermined if they are colonised by
     markets, either directly by being transformed into commodities that are sub-
     ject to sale in the market, or indirectly by being subject to the norms and
     meanings of the market. Hence, autonomy requires, at the very least, the
     restriction of the entry of the market into those non-market spheres.[20]
2   The conditions for the autonomous character   Even if it were to turn out to
     be the case that the market was a necessary condition for the development of
     autonomy, it is not sufficient. Autonomy requires individuals who have the
     capacities to exercise rational judgements and choices and those capacities
     require non-market domains of informal and formal education, and material,
     cultural, familial and working conditions that develop the capacity for self-
     determination which a free market will fail to deliver. The point is central to
     Taylor's social thesis – that individuals need a structure of social relations in
     order to develop the capacity for self-determination.[21]

Both of these points are I think right and both will be developed in the following
chapters. However, my discussion will focus on a third point of dispute that is
implicit in classical discussions of the market but rarely made explicit, that is
between different conceptions of autonomy itself. Consider Gray's characterisation of the autonomous character. It has the immediate virtue of recognising the
plurality of the dispositions that go to make up the autonomous character. For
analytical purposes one can distinguish the two central sets of dispositions that
characterise the autonomous person. First, the autonomous person has 'a distinct
self-identity or individuality' in the sense of determining in some significant way
her own character; she is standardly contrasted with the person whose identity

is given by external circumstance, who finds herself defined in terms of some pre-given or other-determined role or character. Second, the autonomous person displays self-authorship in the sense that her judgement and choices are her own, that she is able to rely on her own capacities of thought and decision: she is standardly contrasted with the person who displays excessive dependence on the authority of others, who is acquiescent to the judgements and choices of others. The autonomous person is one 'who has a distinct self-identity or individuality' and is one 'whose life is to some significant degree a matter of self-creation'. I want to suggest that as we unpack these concepts a little the relationship between the market and the autonomous character is much less clear cut than many liberal defenders and socialist critics of markets suggest.

The problem lies in a particular misconception of autonomy which is popular both amongst liberal defenders of the market and some of their leftist critics. The misconception is founded in one-dimensional contrasts between autonomous and non-autonomous persons which I have just illustrated in the last paragraph: autonomy is a virtue that to be defined in opposition to one vice – heteronomy. With respect to self-identity the opposing vice is standardly understood as that of being defined by others, of having an identity forced upon one from which there is either no possibility or, worse, no desire to escape. With respect to self-creation or self-authorship, the opposing vice is that of being excessively dependent on the authority of others. That the vices of heteronomy are vices I fully accept. However, any simple contrast of autonomy with heteronomy is liable to blind one to other vices which equally undermine autonomy. To use the Aristotelian terminology, the virtues of the autonomous character need to be contrasted not only with vices of deficiency, but also those of excess.[22] Self-identity requires not just the absence of definition by others alone, but also settled dispositions that go to make up the existence of character. Self-authorship can take the excessively individualistic form which understands its scope to include the very standards by which the self and its works is to be judged: the resulting excessive self-conceit is as much opposed to autonomy as excessive dependence.

The existence of these vices standardly goes unrecognised. Worse, a feature of much recent discussion of the concept of autonomy, especially in discussions of the relation of markets and autonomy, is that the concept is given an elaboration which celebrates not the virtues of autonomy but these vices. It is so when it applauds the self who plays with identity and the individual who stands as the authentic author of his own values. The proper response to this conception of autonomy is not, as Gray has done in more recent works, to abandon the ideal of the autonomous character.[23] It is rather to give a more defensible characterisation of that character and the conditions it requires and to point to the errors of the misconceptions. However, in doing so it turns out that the relationship between markets and autonomy is less happy than is standardly supposed. Markets are liable to undermine the autonomous character, and if recent accounts of the 'post-modern condition' are true, they are succeeding in doing so. In the following chapters I develop an account of this unhappy relation between markets and autonomy in detail. In chapter 6 I focus on the relation of autonomy and identity. In chapter 7 I take up the problems concerning the relation of autonomy to authority.

6

AUTONOMY, IDENTITY AND MARKET

6.1 Autonomy, character and identity

In a minimal sense, to be autonomous is to have projects that are one's own, that define one's identity. In so far as John Stuart Mill can be said to defend autonomy as an ideal, it is this component of the ideal that is central. While Mill never employs the term 'autonomy' itself, his description of what it is to have a character provides a classic version of what it is to be an autonomous person in this sense:

> A person whose desires and impulses are his own – are the expressions of his own nature, as it has been developed and modified by his own culture – is said to have a character. One whose desires and impulses are not his own, has no character.[1]

For Mill to have an identity is to have a character, to have desires and projects that are one's own. As with much else in Mill's discussion of liberty, the point is clarified in *The Subjection of Women*. Consider the following comment on the position of women: 'All the moralities tell [women] that it is the duty of women, and all the current sentimentalities that it is their nature, to live for others; to make a complete abnegation of themselves'.[2] In so far as she sacrifices her own projects always for others, a woman sacrifices her sense of her having her own identity, of her having a life which cannot be overridden by the demands of others. Mill's point here is echoed in the justifiable complaints made by women tied to the service of others, that they have no life of their own. The point is an important one of general import for other institutional constraints on the development of one's own projects.

The relation of freedom to the possession of an identity also forms a strong normative core of the negative conception of liberty. Consider again a passage from Hayek quoted in the last chapter:

> Man, or at least European man, enters history divided into free and unfree; and this distinction had a very definite meaning ... It meant always

73

the possibility acting according to his own decisions and plans, in contrast to the position of one who was irrevocably subject to the will of another, who by arbitrary decision could coerce him to act or not to act in specific ways.[3]

The unfree on this account have no life of their own. Their projects are those of others, their acts proceed from the will of others. Whatever the differences between socialist and liberal I take it that they do not lie, or at least should not lie, in this criticism of coercion. Indeed the same points often arise in criticism of wage labour as a form of self-abnegation. Consider Weil's comment that wage labour which involves obedience to others whose projects are alien to oneself is akin to a kind of death.[4] Periods subject to the arbitrary will of others are periods in which life is deferred and time arrested: 'He who is subject to the arbitrary is suspended on the tread of time; he has to wait ... for what the following moment will bring him. He does not dispose of his moments'.[5]

There is, however, a strong interpretation that liberals sometimes put on the concept of autonomy understood as individual self-formation. This strong interpretation is captured in the liberal view of the self as it is portrayed by its communitarian critics. According to that portrait, liberal political theory presupposes that a view of the self unencumbered by commitments to other individuals, communities, traditions, projects and conceptions of the good. It assumes a strong interpretation of the autonomous self: the autonomous individual is understood to be she who can stand outside any and all of her attachments, who always acknowledges the possibility of choice between them: 'From the standpoint of modern individualism I am always what I choose to be. I can always, if I wish put into question what are taken to be the merely contingent social features of my existence.'[6] In MacIntyre's version of the critique, the liberal self has its sociological counterpart in the self portrayed by Goffman as the peg from which are hung different roles in different contexts: 'the self is reduced to a "ghostly I" ... flitting evanescently from one solidly role-structured situation to another'.[7] Against this portrait of the self the communitarian asserts that an agent's identity is constituted by specific commitments and ties, and that she enters the ethical world individuated by these:

> we all approach our own circumstances as bearers of a particular social identity. I am someone's son or daughter, someone else's cousin or uncle; I am a citizen of this or that city, a member of this or that profession; I belong to this clan, that tribe, this nation ... I inherit from the past of my family, my city, my tribe, my nation, a variety of debts, inheritances, rightful expectations and obligations. These constitute the given of my life, my moral starting point. This is in part what gives my life its own moral particularity.[8]

The question of how fair the communitarian characterisation of liberal political theory is when offered by this or that theorist I will not pursue in detail. It certainly misses the mark if aimed at Mill's account of what it is to have a character – 'a person whose desires and impulses are his own – are the expressions of his own nature, *as it has been developed and modified by his own culture*' (my emphasis). It may hit home against later liberals, like Rawls, and there are other components of Mill's thought which may render it a proper target of criticism. To the extent that liberalism does presuppose a strong interpretation of the autonomous self who is able to lift herself free from all or any of her loyalties and can choose who to be as if picking from an open menu possibilities, then it is properly rejected.

However, the problem with communitarianism or at least some versions of the doctrine, such as that of MacIntyre, is that they appear to embrace an indefensible form of heteronomy in which individuals find themselves simply defined by a history and tradition from which no proper distancing is possible. It is one thing to reject a picture of the self who free floats trying on different identities at will. It is another to defend a self who unreflectively embraces that historical constitution they find themselves born into. The theory is insufficiently appreciative of the gains of modern society, of its opening up to individuals the possibility and capacity to reflect upon the projects, communities and ties that are constitutive of their lives.

A stronger and more significant point can be made here. The justifiable core of communitarian criticism of liberalism is quite compatible with the value of autonomy understood as a condition of having an identity or character. Indeed it provides us with an account of what autonomy in this sense involves and a diagnosis of what is wrong with the 'unencumbered' account of the virtue. The person who could move in and out of commitments has no clear identity or character at all. The commitments and loyalties to other persons and projects that make up a person's life, that make it her own life, could not exist in the person who with ease could move out of them. The person who shifted his ties to projects, to a community, to ideas and values, with the ease with which an individual change clothes with the changing fashions lacks an identity. They are in Mill's sense characterless.

A similar point can be made of recent feminist criticisms of liberalism from the perspective of 'an ethic of care'.[9] With the communitarian, the ethic of care stresses the centrality of commitments to particular others as the starting point of ethical responses and this is often associated with a rejection of the primacy that liberalism places upon the autonomous moral agent. Typical is Baier who remarks thus of the place of the value of autonomy in women's lives:

> A certain sort of freedom is an ideal, namely of thought and expression, but to 'live one's life in one's own way' is not likely to be among the aims of persons whose every pleasure languishes when not shared and seconded by some other person or persons. 'The concept of identity expands to include the experience of interconnexion'.[10]

However, as with the communitarian, in accepting a particular misconception about autonomy, the ethic of care is in danger of rejecting values that have been central to feminist thought. It is simply not true that the desire to 'live one's life in one's own way' is not important to those many women who find themselves trapped within a tight set of relations to man and children, nor that 'the experience of interconnexion' is always a positive one. It is worth setting Baier's Humean rejection of the modern 'obsession' with autonomy besides Mill's criticism of those moralities and sentimentalities that insist that women

> make a complete abnegation of themselves, and ... have no life but in their affections. And by their affections are meant only ones they are allowed to have – those to the men with whom they are connected, or to the children who constitute an additional and indefeasible tie between them and a man.[11]

Mill here is to be preferred to Hume. The simple rejection of the value autonomy supports a sentimental picture of the family and the woman's place within it that celebrates in the name of interconnection the very self-loss that has long been a proper object of feminist criticism of the way that a woman's life is defined purely in relations to others.

To say this is not, however, to reject much that lies behind feminist criticism of autonomy, its criticism of a contractual model of human relations, and the importance it gives to particular relations and commitments to others. However, the criticism is misdirected. It accepts a particular misconception of the autonomous agent that is being assumed. Autonomy is defined in a contractual or a 'playful' manner such that to have an autonomous character is to be able to slip off any or every commitment one has and move into another. That picture of autonomy is a proper object of criticism. Vices are turned into virtues. However, autonomy, in the sense of having an identity of one's own, requires serious commitments which are noncontractual in their nature. If I could seriously turn around to my children and say tomorrow 'I've decided not to be a parent any longer and I'm off', or 'The contract finishes at 16 – after that forget it', I would be displaying not character in the Millian sense but a lack of those commitments that are constitutive of character. To say this is not to deny the conflicts which exist between the different projects and commitments that make up a life. I may be a parent but I am also lots of other things. I do want 'to live my own life in my own way'. So should a mother. She is not just a mother but a person with other independent projects that are or should be central to her life.[12] The point here is that any conflict between them is a serious conflict about the kind of person I will be: 'playfulness' and references to contracts are out of place. It may be that a woman finds she can no longer exist in particular relations to companion or children. I take it is a sign of an autonomous person who has an identity that, particularly in relation to children, this is a struggle, and not something towards which a playful attitude is at all appropriate or which can be understood as a termination of a merely contractual relation.

To have an identity involves moving in a mean between two conditions: on the one hand, allowing oneself to live a life for and defined by others, without reflection; on the other, of living a life as if it consisted of endless choices, in which one could in the post-modern jargon 'play' with different identities. To live that second life would no more be to live a life of one's own at all, than would an unreflective life bequeathed to one by some tradition and lived entirely for others. There is a real danger that the liberal, in attempting to properly reject the life undetermined by oneself, celebrates a life that lacks any determinate form at all. Hence the power of the communitarian and feminist criticisms of liberalism. However, these are misdirected if aimed against the value of autonomy as such.

6.2 Autonomy, identity and the market

What is the relation of markets to the development of the autonomous character? One of the undoubted historic achievements of commercial society was the liberation of individuals from particular roles and social positions. On this basis both defenders and critics of market societies have asserted a relationship between markets and autonomy: autonomy, understood as the possession of an independent identity, is a condition that modern market societies have developed to a peculiar degree. The theme is central to the early defence of commercial society. In the work of Smith it appears in the language of independence. In precommercial society, riches are employed directly to command those who supply goods and services. In commercial society riches are employed to buy goods and services from workers who are 'all more or less independent' of the wealthy and beyond his direct command.[13] Commercial society fosters social independence.

The theme that commercial society frees individuals from ties to others is taken up and elaborated in nineteenth-century liberalism. That freedom is taken to define modern social life. The theme is developed thus by Mill:

> For, what is the peculiar character of the modern world – the difference which chiefly distinguishes modern institutions, modern social ideas, modern life itself, from those of times long past? It is, that human beings are no longer born to their place in life, and chained down by an inexorable bond to the place they are born to, but are free to employ their faculties and such favourable chances as offer, to achieve the lot which may appear to them most desirable. Human society of old was constituted on a very different principle. All were born to a fixed social position, and were mostly kept in it by law, or interdicted from any means by which they could emerge from it.[14]

The market is a central component of that peculiarly modern condition. The freedom to engage in projects and enter contracts uncoerced by others is taken to be part of what develops a person capable of determining his or her own life. Free market institutions are the condition of self-determination. Choices in the market are the kin in the economic sphere to those offered in the political sphere through democracy and the private sphere by the principle of liberty. Each set of choices develops the moral character whose impulses and desires are her own. Moreover, market competition provides a spur to the making of choices that counters that passivity which Mill takes to be the normal condition of humans.[15]

That markets develop autonomy is not a claim peculiar to the liberal. It is also accepted by critics of the market. Thus Marx notes, one of the historical achievements of the fully developed system of market exchange has been to destroy relations in which individuals are 'imprisoned within a certain definition, as feudal lord and vassal, landlord and serf, etc., or as members of a caste etc. or as members of an estate etc.'[16] For Marx, the market is not merely a condition of alienation, but also for the liberation of individual from particular social roles, and is hence an historical condition of that full social individuality that is to develop within communism.[17] Likewise in the work of Hegel, while the Kantian and Romantic accounts of autonomy are rejected, the development in modern civil society of a reflective character is taken to be an achievement: while the individual's identity is constituted by ties to the community and its culture, that constitution is in Hegel's picture of modern society not that of the unconsidered and involuntary acceptance of station that is the condition of pre-modern society.[18]

However, while it may be granted that the rise of commercial society did liberate individuals to particular social positions and roles, the relationship between markets and autonomy is less clear cut than this traditional picture supposes. As I noted above, autonomy requires not just the absence of definition by others, but also conditions for those settled dispositions and commitments that are components of what it is to have a character. The autonomous person needs to be contrasted not only with the individual with an unreflective identity typical of pre-modern society, but also with the person whose life lacks any determinate shape, who views different commitments and loyalties as constantly open choices from which exit is continuously possible. Because autonomy is contrasted merely with heteronomy, celebrations of the market, by both its friends and critics, often fail to acknowledge the ways that the market can undermine autonomy, by producing conditions for the characterless who lacks an identity.

The objection to the market on the grounds that it undermines autonomy in this second way draws on two ancient observations about the market economy made by both its defenders and critics. The first concerns its dynamic nature, its constant tendency to change. The market is often feted for its dynamic nature. Typical for the Austrians is Hayek's claim that the market is a condition of progress where 'progress is movement for movement's sake':[19] the very notion of a condition being better or worse simply does not arise 'since our wishes and aims are also subject to change in the course of the process'.[20] The market is progressive simply in virtue of encouraging the new. Hence the Austrians make much of the way the entrepreneur constantly discovers new desires and products that satisfy them and of the way that the market mobilises labour. This theme of the market dynamism is an old one and again is often accepted by its critics. Thus Marx's well-known celebration of the revolutionary nature of the bourgeois society:

The bourgeoisie cannot exist without constantly revolutionising the in-
struments of production, and thereby the relations of production, and
with them the whole relations of society ... Constant revolutionising of
production, uninterrupted disturbance of all social conditions, everlasting uncertainty and agitation distinguish the bourgeois epoch from all
earlier ones. All fixed, fast-frozen relations, with their train of ancient
and venerable prejudices and opinions are swept away, all new formed
ones become antiquated before they can ossify.[21]

Such celebrations of market dynamism sit uneasily, however, with the claim
that the market is a condition of autonomy: some of the forms of change it describes
are not conditions for an autonomous character able to form her own identity, but
those for the dissolution of any settled identity. To say this is not to assent to the
conservative's claim, echoed in some recent communitarian writing, that change
and identity are incompatible, that, as Oakeshott puts it, 'change is a threat to
identity, and every change is an emblem of extinction'.[22] Some change is a mark
not of extinction but of development, and as such forms part of what it is to have
an identifiable character.

To have a character is to be the subject of a life that has some narrative unity,
which is such that it is possible to tell a coherent story of its unfolding: of child-
hood through to adulthood, of the realisation of projects and of failures that
changed one's view of what is important, of the creation of the new from the old,
of the development of relations with particular other individuals, parents, children, colleagues, and friends. Change, as such, including radical change, is compatible with identity: it is a condition of what it is to have a character.[23] While the
accidental and fortuitous is a necessary part of any such narrative, change is
incompatible with identity where it consists of a series of disconnected changes,
such that a life can be described only as a series of unrelated episodes punctuated
by arbitrary interruptions, where one can no longer talk of the internal development of a person's character. To have an identifiable character which forms the
subject of a coherent life requires some forms of stability and certainty about the
future. It is difficult in conditions of 'everlasting uncertainty and disruption' in
which 'new formed relations become antiquated' before they solidify. Likewise
some of the very conditions that the defender of the market offers as conditions
of autonomy, the constant development of new and previously unknown desires
by the entrepreneur, the mobilisation of labour, its movement for movement's
sake can be conditions which undermine character.

These problems of identity are made more acute given the truth of a second
ancient observation concerning commercial society which has more direct significance to issues of character. I refer here to the claim, present in Rousseau and
taken up by writers as different as Smith and Marx, that in commercial society
identity becomes a matter of appearance which is divorced from the qualities a
person actually has. For Rousseau the market is a sphere of deception: 'To be and
to appear to be, became two things entirely different; and from this distinction

arose imposing ostentation, deceitful guile, and all the vices which attend them.'[24] The translation of Rousseau here is that of Smith, and this distinction between being and appearance lies at the heart of Smith's account of commercial society. It is not from the desire for goods with practical purpose that the impulse to acquire riches has its source but vanity:[25]

> For to what purpose is all the toil and bustle of this world? what is the end of avarice and ambition, of the pursuit of wealth and power, and preeminence? Is it to supply the necessities of nature? The wages of the meanest labourer can supply them … From whence, then, arises that emulation which runs through all the different ranks of men, and what are the advantages which we propose by that great purpose of human life which we call bettering our condition? To be observed, to be attended to, to be taken notice of with sympathy, complacency and approbation, are all the advantages which we can propose to derive from it. It is vanity, not the ease, or the pleasure, which interests us. But vanity is always founded upon the belief of our being the object of attention and approbation. The rich man glories in his riches, because he feels that they draw upon him the attention of the world.[25]

For Smith, the pandering to concern for appearance consequent on the divorce of appearance from real character is at one and the same time the source of the improvement of land, industry and the arts,[26] and of the corruption of the moral character.[27] The same ambivalence is found in the work of Hume, who while he defends commercial society as a condition of material and cultural development, in his more Stoical moments is equally critical of the concern for appearance as against the development of character. Hence, for example, his criticism of the sacrifice of 'the invaluable enjoyment of a character, with themselves at least, for the acquisition of worthless toys and gewgaws'[28].

Marx in his early work is the heir to this line of criticism of the market. Alienation involves in part a divorce of appearance and real character. Typical are his arguments in the section on money in the 1844 manuscripts: 'The properties of money are my, the possessor's properties and essential powers. Therefore what I *am* and what I *can do* is by no means determined by my individuality'.[29] The market separates character in the sense of real dispositions, skills, and relationships an individual has, from the social identity I have defined through the marketable goods I can buy.

An important consequence of an identity given by the appearances that commodities create for one is that it is constantly changeable in a way that real dispositions are not. Dispositions of character, skills to be exercised in work and other practical activity, the capacities of judgement both theoretical and practical take time and commitment to develop and time to fall into disuse. The virtues and vices that make up a character are not subject to immediate decisions and choices. They are gained and lost through habituation. If my social identity is merely a set of appearances then it is an identity that to a large extent I can acquire and cast off as I choose. Who one is is no longer a matter of projects and one's individual capacities to realise them and more a question of appearances and the capacity one has to buy them. Appearances are alterable in a way that capacities, dispositions and skills, whose development requires time and commitments, are not. Appearances are often ephemeral, something one is able to take on and put off as one has the money to do so. There are of course limits: character is sometimes written into physical appearance. Hence the element of truth in Orwell's dictum that 'at 50, everyone has the face he deserves',[30] although, given the advances in cosmetics, it is even here increasingly the face he can afford. Character in the sense of a set of self-determined dispositions that constitute an identity is not necessarily fostered by the market. Rather, to the extent commercial society encourages the purchase of the surrogate of appearance, it is undermined. The market is not necessarily an ally of the autonomous character.

Both these ancient observations on markets, that they constantly revolutionise relationships and goods, and that they tend to tie identity to appearances that one can buy, are asserted by some theorists to have special significance in contemporary society. Those who believe we are in a post-modern condition take that condition to be characterised, in part, as a world in which appearances and images become that which is bought and sold. The post-modern world is described as one in which 'the very memory of use-value is effaced' in which the 'original consumers' appetite for a world [is] transformed into sheer images of itself'.[31] Hence it is a condition in which identity 'is constituted theatrically through role play and image construction. While the locus of modern identity revolved around one's occupation, one's function in the public sphere (or family), postmodern identity revolves around leisure, centred on looks, images and consumption'.[32] Since it is focused around images that identity 'tends to be unstable and subject to change'. While both modern and postmodern identities are taken to be reflective, post-modern identities 'switch with changing winds of fashion'.[33] Post-modern individuals, one is told, have playful attitudes to their identity: they no longer seriously engage with the projects that define them. So the story goes.

How far it is true that any of this is a new and special feature of the contemporary world is a moot question. Given that the claims about the post-modern world are mere variations on ancient themes I find it difficult to believe that a substantively new phenomenon is at large. The claim that commodities are bought not for use value but for reason of appearance is defended by the earliest theorists of commercial society, Smith and Hume: the eighteenth-century salon is not different in that respect from the late-twentieth-century shopping arcade. What is different is perhaps something of the scale, variety and technology of the image construction, and the systematic way in which this is harnessed for the sale of commodities. That markets sell appearances is a more clearly developed phenomenon in the contemporary world than it might have been in earlier stages of the market. However, the question of how far we have entered a new social stage I leave aside here. My concern is rather a normative one, about the way in which this post-modern world is defended.

Much of the description of the post-modern world is at the same time an exercise in celebration. One central component of that celebration is applause for the disintegration of the self under the title of the 'death of the subject'. In celebrating 'the death of the subject', the post-modernist invokes a standard set of criticisms of the subject as described by Descartes or Kant. Many of these criticisms have little import of themselves. For example, outside the peculiarities of the French intellectual tradition, few ever seriously accepted the Cartesian picture of the self; hence, to be told of the non-existence of the Cartesian self is no great event. The significance of the attack on the subject is not its putative theoretical target, but the actual subjects in the world whose identities are under threat. The subjects of our everyday encounters in the world are not Cartesian cogitos or Kantian transcendental egos. I have yet to meet either. Rather we encounter embodied individuals who have an identity in the sense of having a character – a set of settled dispositions born of deep commitments to lasting projects and relationships which organises one's experience of the world. What the post-modernist celebrates is the market's unsettling of the condition in which such an identity is possible. Hence the unlovely figure loved by the post-modernist, who plays with his identity, who takes pleasure in the different identities offered in the market place, who loves the arcade and the different images and appearances that can be bought there, who loves the new and the ephemeral. The figure it celebrates is a recent version of the heroic romantic image of the autonomous self creator who in fact is no self at all.

Even those who are ambivalent about the development of the 'post-modern condition', such as Jameson and Kellner,[34] display in their positive remarks the confusions about autonomy and the conditions for its existence noted above. They assume a simple contrast between autonomy and heteronomy, and hence infer that the disappearance of the constraints on 'self-construction' is a source of liberation and autonomy. Kellner, for example, after noting the possibility of 'increased social conformity' goes on to refer to 'positive potentials of this postmodern portrayal of identity as an artificial construct' referring to the way in which it 'suggests one can always change one's life, that identity can always be reconstructed, that one is free to change and produce oneself as one chooses'.[35] The familiar romantic account of autonomy is appealed to here and it is open to the objections noted above. Individuals who could always reconstruct their identity whenever they chose to do so would simply lack any sense of what it is to have the commitments to projects and others that constitute what it is to have a character. What is being described here is not an autonomous individual, but rather one who lacks any sense of self and whose life lacks any narrative form.

The market's relation to autonomy in the sense of having one's own identity is more ambiguous than either liberals or socialists commonly suppose. It is true that the spread of market liberated many individuals from being tied by birth to some particular role or status. It eradicates many of the pre-modern conditions of heteronomy. However, the disappearance of those conditions is not itself sufficient for the existence of the autonomous character. Autonomy is not just the absence of heteronomy and the conditions that foster that character. Autonomy requires also settled dispositions and commitments that define what it is to have a character and hence the conditions in which these can develop. The market tends to undermine those conditions. Both post-modern leftism and the New Right celebrate not conditions of the autonomous self, but for the demise of identity. They are able to paint its demise in happy colours in virtue of sharing a misconceived account of the autonomous person. That misconception concerns not just questions of identity, but also of the relation of autonomy and authority. To this relation I now turn.

7

AUTONOMY, AUTHORITY AND MARKET

7.1 Markets, autonomy and authority

A central theme that runs through defences of the market is an anti-paternalistic one. Markets allow people to make their own choices in the consumption of goods and the shape of their lives. Critics of markets are liable to be accused of a variety of sins of paternalism and elitism, of believing that a few know better. This argument, if taken in a perfectionist direction, appeals to a second group of virtues that go up to make the autonomous character, those concerned with independence of judgement and action. The virtues are normally characterised through a contrast with those vices of heteronomy that involve an absence or abandonment of one's own power of judgement and decision and a corresponding dependence on the authority of others. The autonomous person is not thus reliant on the authority of others. She is neither gullible nor deferential to authority, but displays proper suspicion of those who call upon her to act or believe on authority. The autonomous person is able to rely on her own understanding and decisions in shaping her life. She does not need the guidance of others.

Autonomy in this sense is the central value of the enlightenment. It is expressed in the ideal of maturity that Kant took to define the enlightenment project:

> Enlightenment is man's emergence from his self-incurred immaturity. Immaturity is the inability to use one's own understanding without the guidance of another. The immaturity is self-incurred if its cause is not lack of understanding, but lack of resolution and courage to use it without the guidance of another. The motto of the enlightenment is therefore: Sapere aude! Have courage to use your own understanding ... For enlightenment of this kind, all that is needed is freedom. And the freedom in question is the most innocuous form of all – freedom to make public use of one's reason in all matters.[1]

Heteronomous characters in this sense are those who lack maturity, who are willing to let their own judgement and understanding be guided by others and lack the capacity, desire or courage to exercise them for themselves. With this basic sense of autonomy as maturity in using one's own judgement I have no argument. This enlightenment ideal of the individual who is suspicious of authority in both thought and action is one I will defend. Correspondingly there are good reasons to be suspicious of paternalism. I also endorse, with some qualifications that I outline later in this chapter, Kant's view that the public use of reason is a condition of enlightenment in this sense.[2]

However, like the concept of self-identity, this use of the concept of autonomy is open to strong interpretations concerning the scope of self-authorship and the extent to which one can reject authoritative standards. These, for all their radical appearance are incompatible with the value of autonomy. On the strong interpretations the individual is taken to be independent of any authority save that of her own reason, conscience, or will. The autonomous person makes no call on others beyond herself as to the way her life will be lived. She relies only on her own private judgement. This strong interpretation is open to one of two elaborations, the rationalist and the aesthetic. On the rationalist version of this account the autonomous self is the rational self who submits only to the universal principles of reason. On the aesthetic version even these principles of reason appear as constraints on the freedom of the authentic agent: the free agent is the free creator of the standards with which she will appraise her projects.

Both versions of this strong elaboration appear in defences of the market. They appear most visibly in the guise of the sovereign consumer and the claim that any limits on the scope of consumer sovereignty is a form of paternalism. It is in these terms that many on the libertarian right defend the extension of markets to cultural and educational fields that hitherto have been exempt from market norms. In this project they have been abetted by post-modern radicals who embrace the strong aesthetic versions of the concept of autonomy and see any authoritative standards as social power constraining the autonomy of individuals. Hence the convergence from post-modern left and libertarian right on the defence of consumer culture. In this chapter I suggest that this strong conception of autonomy, in either rationalist or aesthetic forms, should be rejected. It describes neither something attainable by ordinary mortals,[3] nor an ideal for which one should have admiration were it to be realised by the extraordinary. Correspondingly, the arguments for markets and their extension that are founded on these elaborations should be rejected. In section 7.2 I will focus on what is wrong with the strong interpretations of autonomy. In sections 7.3 and 7.4 I examine its use in defences of the market.

7.2 Autonomy: reason, aesthetics and morality

The rationalist elaboration of autonomy is often traced back to Kant's moral philosophy, in which the autonomous agent, the moral agent and the rational agent all turn out to be different descriptions of the same person. Autonomous agents are the moral legislators who govern their wayward inclinations by universal laws that pass the tests of rationality. The strong conception of autonomy that has been elaborated from this Kantian position is exemplified by Wolff, in his *In Defense of Anarchism*.

> The responsible man is not capricious or anarchic, for he does acknowledge himself bound by moral constraints. But he insists that he alone is the judge of those constraints. He may listen to the advice of others, but he makes it his own by determining for himself whether it is good advice. He may learn from others his moral obligations, but only in the sense that a mathematician learns from other mathematicians – namely by hearing from them arguments whose validity he recognizes even though he did not think of them himself. He does not learn in the sense that one learns from an explorer, by accepting as true his accounts of things one cannot see for oneself. Since the responsible man arrives at moral decisions which he expresses to himself in the form of imperatives, we may say that he gives laws to himself, or he is self-legislating. In short, he is *autonomous*.[4]

Autonomous people, like mathematicians, accept only that which they are able to affirm according to their own reasoning or experiences: they do not rely on the testimony of the explorer of lands they have not explored or cannot explore themselves. Thus goes the heroic rationalist elaboration of the concept of autonomy.

The parallel between the autonomous agent and the mathematician is badly chosen. First, it is simply false that mathematicians normally learn from others by checking the validity of their proofs. Sometimes they may do so, and sometimes a proof will be corrected by peers. However, it is often the case that one mathematician will simply accept a result proved by others on the grounds that they are competent mathematicians unlikely to make mistakes. Still more is this the way that natural or social scientists will learn from their mathematical colleagues. They have not only limits of time, but also of capacities and abilities to follow the proofs of theorems they employ.[5] Ordinary citizens to a still greater extent have to deal with their reliance upon the testimony of scientists on topics of public policy. We are all, whether mathematicians, scientists or citizens, forced to accept the testimony of explorers in intellectual landscapes to which we have not and could not have access. We apply our reason not to the validity of their proofs, but to judgements about their competency, reliability and credibility as explorers of those lands. We could do nothing else and we are not at fault in so doing. It is quite in order for us to believe propositions for which we do not and could not know or state the reasons in its defence. That the source of the belief is trustworthy will suffice.

Second, to learn mathematics in the first place already presupposes the acceptance of authoritative utterances of others. One does not learn mathematics by checking the validity of one's teachers' proofs. Indeed, one can do that only when one has been trained in a practical sense to distinguish good and bad arguments, between arguments that are valid and those that are not. Any process of education, be it in mathematics, the sciences, the arts, in language or in morals depends on the acceptance of the authority of others. There is a sense in which all teaching is authoritative (and this is quite different from its being authoritarian) and all learning requires the acceptance of epistemological authority:

> The acceptance of authority is not just something which, as a matter of fact, you cannot get along without if you want to participate in rule-governed activities; rather, to participate in rule governed activities is, in a certain way to accept authority. For to participate in such an activity is to accept that there is *a right and a wrong way of doing things*, and the decision as to what is right and wrong in a given case can never depend *completely* on one's own caprice.[6]

One learns mathematics from school to university by following standard cases of good proof and calculation, adopting exemplars of good inference, and accepting correction from an authority when one goes wrong. Such epistemological authority is not a luxury that one could do without, preferring one's own understanding. One can exercise one's own understanding only given authoritative education. The capacity for the kind of appraisal of the advice or arguments of others that Wolff outlines is possible only given a background of authority.

To thus defend certain forms of authority is not to advocate any irrationalism or authoritarianism, nor to deny autonomy its value. It is to reject a particular rationalist conception of autonomy, which denies that there is ever an occasion for accepting claims on testimony or authority. In its place one has a less heady picture of the autonomous person. She is able to reason well for herself, but knows when her own reason is insufficient; she is not credulous nor willing to accept all and any propositions put to her by putative authorities; she is able to judge whose testimony is reliable, whose is not; she knows when and how to be suspicious – she is versed in the practical art of suspicion.

The skills required of the autonomous person are not, on this account, merely those of the good logician – although these may be a significant component. They are those of the person who knows when and where it is reasonable to trust claims that call on authority. One basic component to this practical art of suspicion is the distinction between authority that is founded on competence and that answers to standards independent of the person, and authority that is founded on mere power, status or wealth.[7] The latter are never sources of competence nor grounds for deference. To defer to a person on the basis of his wealth and power is a peculiar form of heteronomy that goes under the name of sycophancy. The association of know-ledge with power and wealth always give good reason for suspicion: the 'they would say that' strategy is a proper part of the practical craft of suspicion. The putative conflict between autonomy and authority is primarily a misstatement of the conflict between autonomy and wealth and power: one of the problems of modern market societies to which I return below, is that legitimate authority is compromised by association with wealth and the social power it confers.

To make these claims is, however, to accept the distinction at the heart of the enlightenment project presented by Kant, the distinction between social authority and epistemological authority, between the authority conferred on a person in virtue of their institutional or social position, and that which is consequent upon appeal to impersonal standards independent of institutional position. Consider the imperatives to which Kant objects in outlining the enlightenment ideal: 'I hear on all sides the cry: *Don't argue!* The officer says: Don't argue, get on parade! The tax-official: Don't argue, pay! The clergyman: Don't argue, believe!'[8] Given an imperative 'Do X' there are two kinds of answers that might be made to a response 'Why?': (1) because I am your officer, your tax collector, your clergyman, paying you, etc.; (2) because it would be the right thing to do, the best thing to do, because it is a valid inference etc. The first set of responses make essential reference to the individual's occupancy of a particular institutional position or status. If it turned out that the individual did not have that position, or that the addressee was not within the range of the person's institutional authority, then the imperative is infelicitous. On its own terms there is no backing for its authority. The second set of responses are not of this kind. They make no essential call on institutional positions of authority, but, rather, on standards independent of institutional positions and status. The felicity of the speech act calls only on impersonal standards. A feature of the imperatives that Kant criticises is that they are the first institutional kind. Their felicity is essentially founded upon institutional authority, not on any standards independent of those positions. I take it that part of Kant's point here is that to defer to the judgement of another simply in virtue of a person's institutional position is never defensible: it is to forgo one's ability to judge for oneself. The only good grounds a mature individual has for deferring to the judgements of other persons is that there are good reasons to believe that they meet standards independent of those persons.

To this point needs to be added a second point that also forms part of Kant's account of enlightenment. The appeal to standards independent of the person's institutional position is not yet enough to give reasons for rational acceptance of the authorativeness of her pronouncements. The standards to which appeal is made may themselves be in disorder. If a person trained in the ways of astrology makes predictions about my future I reject them not because I am suspicious of his institutional position, nor because I think he is incompetent in applying the standards of his discipline, but because I believe that the discipline itself is in disorder. There are conditions that a community of enquiry must meet if its claims are to be ones that demand our assent. One of those conditions is a non-authoritarianism within that community itself. Not only is authorativeness distinct from authoritarianism, but also it is ultimately incompatible with it. This point provides a way of restating the core of Kant's position concerning the relation between autonomy and the public use of reason. The sophisticated defender of the enlightenment position might accept that one cannot always directly apply one's reason to claims made by others. There may be occasions in which trust in authoritative utterances is justifiable. However, one needs some reason to believe that the practice in which authoritative teaching is made is itself in order. Justifiable assent to epistemological authority is possible only if one has grounds for believing the authority in question could be redeemed in public argument within the relevant community of enquiry. Where the possibility of public dialogue and argument is absent one has good reason to believe something is amiss.

The root of a great deal of modern relativism lies in a refusal to recognise the difference between authority grounded solely in institutional position and authority grounded in standards independent of such positions to which rational assent is possible. There is a widespread anti-enlightenment view that all epistemological authority is simply a disguised way of enforcing social power. The prevalence of this anti-enlightenment view has its basis in an aesthetic version of the strong interpretation of autonomy which has its origins in the romantic reaction to the rationalist picture of the autonomous agent. On this view reason itself is a constraint on the free action of autonomous agents. Even in Wolff's favoured realm of reason, mathematics, it is possible to find expressions of that view. Consider the following remark on quaternions by William Rowan Hamilton, a nineteenth-century mathematician who belonged to the Romantic movement and wrote (bad) poetry about his discoveries: 'The train of thought is curious, almost wild, but I believe that the mathematical chain has kept the wings of fancy from soaring altogether out of bounds.'[9] The idea that reason and proof are chains that keep wildness and imagination within bounds is a common theme of the romantic movement. The universal laws of reason on this view are themselves constraints on the autonomous agent. The free agent is bound by no standards save those he creates himself: he is an artist of his own life deciding both the shape and colour it will possess, and the standards appropriate for appraising the work he produces.

The version of this aesthetic elaboration of autonomy which has exercised great and unfortunate influence on recent post-modern thought is that of Nietzsche. For the Nietzsche of the post-modernist (and I leave aside here the issue of how closely he resembles the historical person) the model of the autonomous individual is that of the person who gives aesthetic shape to his existence:

> To 'give style' to one's character – a great and rare art! It is practiced by those who survey all the strengths and weaknesses of their nature and then fit them into an artistic plan.[10]

Individuals are to see themselves as their own work of art who develop what is unique in them. We are to 'become those we are – human beings who are new, unique, and incomparable'.[11] This picture of the sovereign artist lies at the basis of Nietzsche's rejection of the Kantian account of the autonomous agent. The autonomous agent and the rational moral agent are prised apart. Hence the welcome for 'the *sovereign individual*, like only to himself, liberated again from the morality of custom, the autonomous and supramoral individual (for "autonomous" and "moral" are mutually exclusive), in short the man who has his own independent, protracted will.'[12] The 'free man' has 'his *measure of value*'[13] that is his own and not others. He does not submit his life to universal laws of the kind that Kant offers, but rather to laws that are entirely his own: 'The profoundest laws of preservation and growth demand the reverse of Kant: that each of us should devise *his own* virtue, *his own* categorical imperative.'[14] This picture of the self-creating free spirit applies as much to the sphere of science and reason as it does to morality. All views of the world are perspectives that are the product of particular interests and locations in the world. What is left of the rationalist concept of autonomy is contained in the concept of genealogy – our understanding of the way the past has created us so as to escape its domination of us so to allow the creation of new values.

The Nietzschean aesthetic response to the rationalist version of autonomy is central to recent post-modernism: the sovereign Nietzschean aristocrat makes a sorry reappearance as the consumer who is able to 'play with his identity'. As a source of criticism of epistemological authority it enters the scene through Foucault. It lies at the heart of the view that all forms of epistemological authority in all discourses are but 'regimes of truth' through which power is exercised.[15] While in one of his final essays 'What is Enlightenment?', written in response to Kant's essay of the same title, Foucault claims to refuse the '"blackmail" of the Enlightenment', the choice for or against rationalism,[16] his own position is largely an elaboration of a Nietzschean critique of Enlightenment rationalism, with genealogy playing much the same residual role that it does in Nietzsche. The position denies the existence of the distinction drawn above between social and epistemological authority.

The aesthetic account of autonomy has still less to be said for it than does the rationalist position. One of the errors of that position is precisely the kind of misconceived conception of autonomy that underlies it, one which assumes an ethic of complete self-authorship, that ends in either an 'aesthetic of existence' which treats one's life as a work of art – forgetting that art too has its standards and disciplines – or in the celebration of insanity. The position is a *reductio ad absurdum* of the picture of the autonomous person from which it begins. The autonomous person is independent, self-reliant, and versed in the practical art of suspicion. However, she is not thereby someone who can stand outside of any intellectual discipline, who alone could think entirely for herself. One who did that would be either angel or idiot.

Much of the attractiveness of both rational and aesthetic misconceptions about autonomy lies in the way it is specified simply in terms of a contrast with heteronomy. However, as I have already noted in the last chapter, the concept of autonomy is misleadingly characterised if it is contrasted only with the vice of heteronomy. Just as in the case of autonomy as a condition of identity, so also as a condition of self-reliance, it needs to be contrasted also with an opposing vice: the vice might be termed that of excessive self-assertiveness. In the realm of intellectual matters, the autonomous person stands opposed not only to the heteronomous character, the gullible or credulous who accepts unthinkingly the opinions of others, but also to the sceptic who refuses to rely on the testimony of others where it is rational for him to do so, who is intellectually arrogant and exhibits 'unhesitating reliance on [his] own acuteness and powers of reasoning'.[17] Hence Kenny's apt account of rationality as a virtue which is a mean between the vices of credulity and scepticism.[18]

These points about intellectual autonomy have a wider significance. It is not just in intellectual and normative matters that one must rely on the skills and judgements of others. One does so when one rides on the bus, goes to the doctor, has one's roof fixed, entrusts one's children to the care and education of others and so on. In all such matters, there are not merely heteronomous vices of the gullible, of the person who accepts without explanation whatever the doctor says, but also the vices of the overly self-confident, who is convinced that there is no skill which cannot be mastered. To trust one's doctor in judgements about diet is not, *pace* Kant or Wolff,[19] to forfeit one's autonomy. Rather one exercises it in considering whether one's doctor is trustworthy. Likewise education in practical matters relies on authority: apprentices need to accept that there is another who is able to judge and perform better than themselves, who is able to correct.

This said there is a widespread assumption that in one practical sphere, the sphere of ethics, it is different: here one has a special responsibility to be self-authors of a strong kind. With the view that we have special responsibility in the ethical and political spheres I have no argument. The demand that in such matters one cannot simply defer to dogma uttered by some authority *may* be a peculiarly modern enlightenment view, but if it is then it is one that deserves our assent. However, this demand is often confused with a much stronger claim that this requirement to be independent of authority needs to be much stronger, that it demands that we be self-authors in a strong sense. Ethical autonomy is tied to a subjectivist theory of value. This is a mistake. The assertion that we have special responsibility in ethical and political spheres is quite consistent with the assertion that claims within those spheres answer to standards of appraisal that are independent of ourselves. Our special responsibility consists in care in reasoning, sensibility and perception, and not care in creation.

One reason for the attractiveness of subjectivism to many of the market's liberal defenders lies in a putative connection made between certain versions of subjectivism about values and autonomy. The subjectivist claim that values are ultimately a matter of decision and will, not of recognition, draws much of its power from a romantic picture of ourselves as strong self-creative beings, who choose not only the central projects of our lives, but also the standards according to which they are to be judged. On this view, the kinds of parallels that Wolff draws between intellectual and ethical autonomy go awry because our freedom in matters of ethics is stronger than that of the intellect. Ethical matters do not answer to independent standards in the same ways as the factual. To assert the existence of standards independent of ourselves is to deny that we are free and autonomous beings.[20] This account runs through the implicit model of autonomy defended by Hayek that I outlined in chapter 5.[21]

The putative connection between value subjectivism and autonomy should be rejected. It is quite compatible with moral autonomy that one accepts and acts in accordance with standards that are independent of oneself, which one does not choose but rather recognises. Thus, whatever else might be said for or against cognitivism about norms, it is quite consistent with the value of autonomy. The cognitivist can accept that one has special responsibility in ethical and political matters to think through issues for oneself. What distinguishes the cognitivist is the account she gives of what that responsibility consists in. It consists in an obligation to use both cognitive and perceptual powers to arrive at right judgement. Respect for a person's autonomy consists not in simply allowing them to pursue whatever scale of values they happen to have chosen, but in the recognition that they also have those capacities that allow for rational appraisal of their values. Hence, the appropriateness of public argument on normative matters. It allows that one's best efforts may not be enough, that one has made a mistake and is open to correction. There are standards and facts independent of oneself that have a bearing on the conclusions one should reach. In saying this, it allows of the possibility in normative matters as in intellectual matters of the vice of excessive self-confidence and self-assertiveness. It is a sign of the grip of the strong conception of autonomy that a proper appreciation of the limits of one's capacities is seen as abnegation of ethical responsibility.[22]

The claim that one has special responsibility in ethical and political matters can be understood not as a consequence of ethical principles being a matter of decision, but in virtue of a recognition of the proper limits of expertise in such spheres. Two points are of importance here. First, the capacities for ethical and political judgement are capacities that are quite universal in the sense that they are capacities of judgement that any rational individual can develop, given the right conditions, through participation in public deliberation of common matters.[23] Second, we have special reasons to develop such capacities. Ethical or political beliefs engage with one's life in a way that say beliefs about physics, or aesthetics in the sphere of the plastic arts, need not. They permeate the shape a person's life takes. Ethical beliefs demand not just theoretical assent but also practical assent.

7.3 Perfectionism, paternalism and markets

Problems about the relation of autonomy and authority tend to enter arguments about markets as issues of market boundaries. Even amongst some of the market's traditional defenders, limits are placed on markets where the goods in question answer to authoritative standards that are independent of the desires and tastes of the consumer. Thus J. S. Mill offers it as a proper reason for the departure from *laissez-faire* policies:

> Now, the proposition that the consumer is a competent judge of the commodity, can be admitted only with numerous abatements and exceptions

... There are ... things, of the worth of which the market is by no means a test ... This is peculiarly true of those things which are chiefly useful as tending to raise the character of human beings. The uncultivated cannot be competent judges of cultivation. Those who most need to be made wiser and better, usually desire it the least, and if they desired it, would be incapable of finding the way to it by their own lights.[24]

Mill's arguments in this passage are perfectionist in form. Since it is the function of political and social institutions to 'raise the character of human beings', there are goods which cannot be left to preferences expressed in the market. It is those preferences themselves that are to be cultivated. The argument is applicable to a variety of spheres – wider than Mill realises. However, the Millian argument is most often called upon in defence of cultural and educational spheres from market interference. Mill himself employs the position to demarcate education as a non-market arena.

Mill's position has been echoed, for example, in recent debates around incursions by markets into university research and education.[25] These have taken many forms including not only the direct involvement by commerce in universities, especially in scientific research, but also the spread into universities of norms and institutional forms characteristic of commercial society.[26] Property rights on the products of intellectual research are increasingly being defined in terms of the norms of markets.[27] Forms of quality assessment and control borrowed from management techniques in the commercial world are being applied to teaching and research. Universities increasingly are under pressure to 'market' themselves to their prospective 'customers'.[28] The traditional roles of educator and educated are being redefined in contractual terms. The teacher is redefined as facilitator who provides not an education but a service or product; the recipient is no longer a student but a customer or consumer. In debates about this market colonisation of previously protected spheres, the Millian form of argument is sometimes invoked.[29]

However, this kind of argument is more likely to find itself a home in conservative political thought than it is in either liberal or socialist traditions. The reason is that it is liable to strike either as deeply inegalitarian and paternalistic: it assumes a distinction can be made between two classes of people, the 'cultivated' and the 'uncultivated', and it asserts that the former can decide for the latter what their wants should really be. Now while that kind of position is one that a traditional conservative might be willing to accept, it is also one that runs counter to the enlightenment thought that mature individuals are ones who are able to think for themselves and do not submit to the 'authority' of others who claim cultivation. It appears to be incompatible with the character ideal of the autonomous person. Mill appears here not as a proponent of autonomy but as the paternalistic defender of elite culture.

Can the perfectionist defence of non-market spheres be defended against these charges that it is incompatible with the value of autonomy? There are a number of points that are standardly made in reply. First, the problem of autonomy faces in more directions than this defence of the market suggests. The argument is partly one about who has autonomy and not with whether or not any one has autonomy. The independence of educational and cultural spheres from markets is a question itself of autonomy, of those within particular practices and institutions to pursue particular projects and activities independently of 'consumer' choices. There is no reason why the projects that individuals have as the 'consumers' of certain products should have priority over the projects they have as providers. Indeed, the opposite is true for two reasons noted in chapter 5. First, the capacities and dispositions of character that are constitutive of autonomy themselves need the existence of spheres of education in which preferences are ordered and in which independent capacities of critical thought can develop. Second, the existence of valuable options over which choices can be made likewise requires the protection of educational, cultural and associational spheres from the market. To these needs to be added a third point of special relevance here, that much of the criticism of the perfectionist argument relies upon a strong misconception of autonomy I have criticised in this chapter.

Many recent defences of the extension of market choices assume that any invocation of 'privileged' judgements founded upon reference to 'authoritative' standards itself commits one to paternalism. The objection is founded upon a strong conception of autonomy that itself reflects scepticism about the existence of authoritative standards. The objection itself can take stronger or weaker forms depending on just how far scepticism about the existence of authoritative standards is allowed to go.

The weaker form is that which relies on the rationalist account of autonomy, combined with an account of what the sphere of reason is. This will allow restrictions on markets where genuine 'knowledge' is concerned, but not where one is concerned only with non-cognitive values. Typical of this weak position is James Buchanan, who will allow something like Mill's arguments for the sciences, but not for the liberal arts. Since positive science seeks empirically grounded truth about the world, and since truth has an authority upon us that is independent of our preferences, and since the discovery of such truths depends on the freedom of trained scholars to pursue their own lines of research, scientific disciplines have a proper set of boundaries protecting them from markets and the preferences of its consumers.[30] Such boundaries are not, however, permissible for the liberal arts. To the perfectionist defence of the liberal arts in terms of its cultivating 'higher qualities' Buchanan responds thus:

> 'The making of higher-quality men' – this familiar high-sounding objective has an appealing and persuasive ring. But we sense the emptiness once we think at all critically about definitions of quality. Who is to judge? By whose criteria are qualities to be determined?[31]

For Buchanan, the perfectionist appeal is empty because, in the case of the liberal arts, unlike the sciences, no authoritative standards exist. Individuals have their 'own standards of evaluation', their own preferences, and it is the job of the universities to answer to them. Buchanan's argument here is based upon a value-subjectivism in ethical and aesthetic matters which is standard in both neo-classical and Austrian economics. Since values here are a matter of preference they should be left to consumer preference. The value of autonomy requires such consumer sovereignty. Autonomy is a matter of decision and will, not a matter of judgement.[32]

Liberal economic theory has traditionally kept spheres in which the norms of reason hold sway as protected domains of authoritativeness in which the Millian rejection of consumer sovereignty has a place. The limited sphere of protection for the sciences has come under fire from the recent sceptical moves about science that inform post-modern and social constructionist accounts of scientific knowledge: the main impact of recent science studies has been to raise a sceptical challenge to the whole notion of the authoritativeness of norms in science. In the cruder versions scientific truth itself is bought into the realm of preference – truth is merely a matter of preference in belief. Hence, the boundaries Mill defends between market and non-market spheres disappear.

What both the neo-liberals on the right and the post-moderns on the left play upon here is an egalitarianism about judgement. Where they differ is in the scope of Buchanan's questions about 'definitions of quality': who is to judge? By whose criteria are qualities to be determined? For the sceptic about science, it is not just the 'culturally cultivated' who are acting in a paternalist fashion when they impose their standards on all. So also are the 'scientifically cultivated' when they impose their own particular knowledges on others and silence other voices, the voices of those who have 'local knowledge' that lacks the authority of science. The paternalism of the scientist is undermined by scepticism about science's cognitive authority. There is no independent authority to either culture or knowledge. Hence both represent a form of power that lacks justification. Thus, in recent post-modern leftism, especially that influenced by Foucault, all forms of epistemological authority in medicine, science and other disciplines are understood as themselves forms of power. The upshot is a still more radical defence of the sphere in which individual preference cannot be challenged. Hence the degree to which social constructionists have appealed to market models of science.[33] Hence also the odd alliance in defence of the market and consumer culture between the New Right and the post-modern left.[34]

This attack on authoritative standards as incompatible with autonomy is mistaken in both its weak and strong forms. It is not internally coherent and it does not hit an objectionable target. The incoherence of the position lies in the ways in which the criticism of the standards implicitly relies on the authoritativeness of the very standards rejected. Thus Buchanan calls upon not only science to defend his position but also values, and he does not simply state them as personal preferences, but as judgements for which argument is offered in their defence. Likewise, the sceptics about science call upon the very standards of argument in support of their claims about which they express scepticism. In both cases, this is not merely a local difficulty that could with care be avoided. They could not do otherwise. The very activity of argument calls upon standards independent of the speakers.

More important here the criticisms depend precisely on the strong misconceptions about autonomy that I have criticised in this chapter. They assume that any acceptance of the authoritative claims of others exhibits the vice of heteronomy. This position is false for the reasons I have outlined. It describes an ideal of self-sufficiency that is neither attainable by the ordinary nor desirable if found in the extraordinary. The picture of the autonomous agent it invokes displays not a set of virtues, but of vices.

7.4 Autonomy, trust and social equality

One may be left however with a suspicion that justice has not been done to the worries that underlie the accusation of paternalism aimed against positions like Mill's. While the kind of position that Mill defends is not incompatible with autonomy in virtue of invoking authoritative standards that are independent of the preferences of consumers, there may still be problems with it. Does it have other features that render it incompatible with autonomy properly understood?

Clearly, there are accusations which, if Mill was guilty, would show his position to be incompatible with autonomy. For example, if it was the case that he assumed that certain particular privileged groups defined by some social or biological property – economic class, gender, ethnicity, etc. – have a special capacity to make authoritative assertions about what is better and hence can justifiably override the preferences of others, then the position would be straightforwardly paternalist in an objectionable sense. It would assume that the capacities that are constitutive of autonomous self-direction are not potentially open to all. However, Mill is not open to this charge. His defence of the universality of education and of participatory democracy are premised on the claim that given such conditions there is no restriction upon who can realise an autonomous character. His position is not open to any such straightforward objection.

There is, I believe, a variant of this objection that does have some power. His account of restrictions on markets does appear to assume an aristocratic ideal of the 'cultivated' who are in a position to know what is in the best interests of the 'uncultivated'. It is of a piece with his claim in *On Liberty* that democracy require that the 'sovereign Many ... let themselves be guided ... by the counsel and influence of a more gifted and instructed One or Few',[35] with his support for the notion of an intellectual 'clerisy', and also with his distinction between the higher and lower pleasures in his essay *Utilitarianism*. The proper worry about his paternalism is founded in the way in which the distinction between the 'cultivated' and 'uncultivated' is itself drawn. The way in which he draws the distinction betrays a particular set of assumptions about what cultivation consists in which reflects a particular class perspective. Moreover his background worry is that of the cultured being swamped by the uncultivated manual working classes. Now to say all this is still not as yet to make the criticism of the substantive assumptions he makes about values. There has always been a strong form of egalitarian socialism that has been critical of class societies because they excluded the worker from the good life the aristocrat leads.[36] There can be no straightforward inference from a claim about the social origin of a set of beliefs about what is good, to claims about the goods themselves. It might be that those who possess social wealth and power possess also the real goods that these bring. The position becomes objectionable where the particular perspective of a social elite is itself a distorted one that is blind to important sources of value.

There are independent reasons to assume that Mill does draw the distinction in a way that systematically ignores certain forms of human excellence. The problem lies the intellectualist account of human cultivation he assumes. The problem is not the value he places on the goods of high culture – they are goods – but in his blindness to the value of other pursuits. In his discussion of the limits of consumer judgement, and his related and more famous distinction between the higher against lower pleasures in *Utilitarianism* he identifies the higher with the intellectual and the lower with the bodily and physical. He reveals no real appreciation of excellences in craft, in manual skills or in the social skills required in the family and wider ethical and political communities. The skills of parenting, of the artisan and agricultural worker, of the organiser of labour are all left out of his account. A proper conception of human cultivation needs to be much wider than Mill's. Correspondingly, his arguments about the limits of the market apply also to these skills: preferences need to be shaped by practices encountered, and not those practices by raw preferences.

This move also makes best sense of the defensible component in the recent postmodern and social constructionist critiques of science. There is a real residual power in recent criticism of the elitism of scientific expertise and the defence of local knowledges against science. Scientism, the view that only science can give knowledge, and the corresponding denial of local and practical knowledge, is a proper object of criticism. But this requires putting a proper value on such local knowledge, of giving it its proper epistemological authority where it is due. The problem with the generalised scepticism that is exhibited in critical analyses of science is that by denying the possibility of *any* epistemological authority it undermines those very proper examples of local knowledge it aims to defend.

The acceptance of the existence of standards of human excellence, of authoritative standards of truth in sciences, of distinctions between what is good and what is not in practical spheres, is compatible with a rejection of what is objectionable in Mill's position. The recognition of excellence in a variety of spheres opens up Mill's argument for an egalitarian elaboration that entails greater constraints on markets than he allows. The move is contained in the following argument from Tawney:

> Progress depends, indeed, on a willingness on the part of the mass of mankind – and we all, in nine-tenths of our nature, belong to the mass –

97

to recognize genuine superiority, and to submit themselves to its influence. But the condition of recognizing genuine superiority is a contempt for unfounded pretensions to it. Where the treasure is, there will the heart be also, and, if men are to respect each other for what they are, they must cease to respect each other for what they own.[37]

There are three important features of Tawney's argument that need bringing out in more detail.

First, Tawney identifies the problem that is the source of much of the problem of the relation of autonomy and authority in modern commercial society. The problem of authoritativeness in existing societies is largely that those with power, wealth and status often have special powers to call upon authoritative judgement: they have special access to cultural goods; they possess the ability to buy the employment of those who have the training to make authoritative utterances – industries and governments both have their scientific spokespersons; and they define through their powers what is to count as authoritative. The conflation of social power and epistemological authority undermines the conditions of autonomy by undermining conditions of trust. The problem of autonomy is largely one of political epistemology, of determining the institutional frameworks of trust. The most favourable condition for rational acceptance of the authoritativeness of others is where there exists equality in wealth, power and status. Inequality in our capacities of judgement provides the starting point for an argument for social equality.[38]

A second welcome feature of Tawney's inegalitarian argument for social equality is that he combines respect for inegalitarianism about judgement with humility about the scope of his own. There is a tendency in those who believe in some 'genuine superiority' to think that they, and not others, have it. Admirers of Lenin's theory of the vanguard party always see themselves as part of the vanguard and not the led; sympathetic readers of Wilson's *The Outsider* always announce that they are outsiders, not one of the crowd; those who follow Nietzsche always consider themselves potential supermen, not as members of the herd.[39] And those who, like Mill, talk of the superiority of the 'more highly gifted and instructed One or Few' see themselves as one of the Few not of the Many. One of the qualities of Tawney's argument is that he does accept his own limitations, that in accepting the existence of genuine superiority he does not deny that for most of the time he belongs to those who must submit themselves to its influence. The invisibility of such relations of trust in others is a consequence of its ubiquity.[40] Everyone for most of their lives relies on acceptance of the competencies and skills of others, and relies on the existence of spheres in which those competencies can develop. Those skills depend upon associational and educational spheres that cut across market and state boundaries – of doctors, nurses, engineers who belong to networks of association through which those practices are sustained.

One of the great defects of market society lies in the way that it privileges the choices of 'consumers' over the skills of 'producers'. It does so not only between individuals in their different roles, but also within individuals' own lives where their life in work is forced to be subordinate to that in consumption.[41] The problem is not that producers should not answer to consumers. They should. It is false to assert, as does for example MacIntyre, that the excellences exhibited in any practice 'can only be identified and recognised by the experience of partici- pating in the practice in question.'[42] Some excellences are like this, but not all: cooks may criticise each other, but in the end as Aristotle put it, 'the diner – not the cook – will be the best judge of a feast.'[43] It is not the answerability but the way in which producers must answer that is the proper source of criticism.

To reject the market model of the answerability of 'producer' to the 'con- sumer' is not to say the recipient or user of a service should have no voice. The problem with the market model of the relationship is precisely with the way in which the 'consumer' is supposed to 'voice' their responses. Thus take the stand- ard argument in defence of the market – that it puts consumers in charge. The market's claimed informational virtues, central to Hayek's epistemic defence of the institution which I discuss in chapter 10,[44] lie in part in the way that consumer choice determines the outcome of production: consumer sovereignty assures that information is passed back to the producers. However, the information is passed back without dialogue. The market informs by 'exit' – some products find a market, others do not. 'Voice' is not exercised.[45] This failure of dialogue is cel- ebrated by Hayek: the market communicates, through the price mechanism, only that information which is relevant to the coordination of the plans of actors.[46] However, the failure of a dialogue represents an informational failure of the market, not a virtue. There are a variety of practices, from architecture and build- ing, through cultural practices like the arts, through to the cognitive practices of the university, that are in order where a dialogue exists between producer and the user. Where it exists the preferences of the user are not uninformed preferences, but preferences educated by contact with the practice. The producer in turn needs the critical comment of the educated user. There are contexts in which such rela- tionships exist, but they exist alongside markets and in virtue of boundaries to the market. The market, as Hayek notes, does distribute information. As I show later, it also blocks a great deal. The kind of feedback it provides from users, the 'consumer', to producers issues in no educative dialogue. The educative dia- logue exists not *through* the market, but where it survives in modern society, *alongside* the market in protected spheres.

However, the problem is one of not only education here but also power. The fact of mutual interdependence points also to the intractability of the problem of trust. Trust in the scientist, the nurse, the doctor, the builder, the farmer and so on are both part of life and inescapably a possible source of problems. Even given equality in wealth and institutional power, there is no reason to assume that authoritativeness should not be a vehicle of social power. The defence of self-governing associations that foster the internal standards of particular prac- tices – to which I am sympathetic – has to be tempered with the recognition that such associations can be conspiracies of professional power.

There are two major kinds of institutional responses that can be made to the problems of trust: contractarian and deliberative. The contractarian response hedges individuals and association by contractual obligations and targets which they are to meet, and to which they can be held to account for failing to do so. The approach has major failings. The spread of contractual relationships itself undermines the conditions of trust. Contract itself relies on the background of trust. Without conditions of trust, we live in a Hobbesian world, in which covenants without swords are mere words. Hence, the appeal to sanction and pre-emptive action to avoid sanction. The contractarian approach also distorts the workings of the practices themselves: contracts require explicitly stated conditions to be met, and hence the practice is directed towards objectives that can be explicitly stated. However, all practices involve ends and accomplishments that are embodied in and learnt in the course of skilled practice and procedure and which are not open to articulation. Indeed, this is the very source of the problem of trust. Hence a contractual framework of the kind exhibited in the increasingly audit culture of modern societies undermines the proper pursuit of those practices. I develop this point further in chapter 10.

The deliberative response places associations within the context of a framework in which the reliability of judgements is open to examination of citizens through deliberative institutions. This approach often calls upon a Kantian model: deliberative institutions are embodiments of the public use of reason that Kant takes to define the enlightenment project. The citizen displays maturity by subjecting the judgements of practitioners to critical scrutiny. However, this model of the answerability of practices to deliberation has difficulties for reasons outlined in this chapter: there are necessary limits to the citizens' maturity in matters outside their competence. This may seem to point to an impasse on the issue of answerability. There is however an alternative Aristotelian model of the public use of reason that does provide a defensible account of a deliberative model.[47] The model of the citizen's jury that has some current currency is illuminating here. It is a feature of juries that they do not for the most part if at all consider the truth or falsity of evidence directly, but the trustworthiness of those who present it. Thus it is with the citizens' jury: often, it is the character of those on whose testimony we call, their capacity to speak on the issue in question, their reliability independence and disinterestedness that is at issue. The model provides the best we can hope for in the institutional dimension to answerability. However, such formal institutional arrangements are artefacts that require for their operation economic and cultural arrangements for trust. For the reasons Tawney notes, conditions of social equality are a central constituent of those arrangements.

The third feature of Tawney's position that deserves reiterating is that it relies on a distinction between equality in the social, economic and political standings of individuals and groups on the one hand and equality in the appraisal of the worth of judgements, goods, cultures, and achievements. Tawney not only keeps these two senses of equality distinct but also holds that one reason for advocating equality in standing is that it allows for proper appraisal of the differences in worth of judgements, goods, cultures and achievements. Both the implicit distinction and the relation between them deserve further elaboration. They do so just because the failure to recognise them lies at the basis of much of which is wrong in recent liberal and post-modern thought. The conflation of the different senses of equality often emerges in the demand for equality of recognition, where the concept of recognition is used to describe a stance towards both the standing and appraisal of individuals or groups. The use of the concept of recognition to fudge the distinction is widespread.[48] In the following chapter I focus on one particular influential use of the concept to defend modern liberal market economies as the ultimate historical solution to the struggle for recognition, that of Fukuyama.

8

THE POLITICS OF RECOGNITION

The concept of recognition has recently returned centre stage to political and ethical argument.[1] In radical social theory this has often been associated with a cultural turn in which issues of power and inequality in the sphere of political economy have been put aside for a politics of identity and recognition in the cultural sphere.[2] However, in liberal political thought this is not the case. Rather, the concept of recognition has been used in a broadly Hegelian defence of the market economy: the market is justified as a sphere in which individuals receive proper recognition. The most influential version of that Hegelian argument is that of Fukuyama. My purpose in the following is to show that it is flawed. I do so by turning Hegel back against Fukuyama. Fukuyama employs a market model of recognition that Hegel himself had properly criticised. This flawed market model of recognition has a more general significance, permeating recent discussion of recognition in recent social theory. Its rejection gives us good reason to reassess the significance of the associational dimensions of economic life that were lost to Fabian and parts of the Marxian traditions of socialism.

8.1 Recognition: identity, authority and equality

The respect which we feel for wisdom and virtue is, no doubt, different from that which we conceive for wealth and greatness; and it requires no very nice discernment to distinguish the difference. But notwithstanding that difference, those sentiments bear a very considerable resemblance to one another. In some particular features they are, no doubt, different, but, in the general air of the countenance, they seem to be so very nearly the same, that inattentive observers are very apt to mistake the one for the other.

(A. Smith *The Theory of Moral Sentiments* (Indianapolis, IN:
Liberty Press, 1982) I.iii.3.3)

One can demand recognition not only for one's moral worth, but for one's wealth, or power, or physical beauty as well.

(F. Fukuyama *The End of History and the Last Man*
(London: Hamish Hamilton, 1992) p. 182)

Fukuyama's recent influential book *The End of History and the Last Man* presents history as the manifestation of a single great desire: the desire for recognition, *thumos*. The transition to modern society is struggle between two formally distinct forms of this desire, *megalothymia*, the desire to be recognised as superior to other people, and *isothymia*, the desire to be recognised as the equal of other people. The former is associated with the aristocratic ideal, the latter with modern democratic capitalist societies. The standard account of the transition to modern society as a shift from status to contract is reworked as a shift between modes of the desire for recognition. It picks up the Hegelian picture of modern civil and political society as spheres which, through contract and citizenship, a person's standing as someone is mutually recognised. In this realisation of universal mutual and equal recognition, the struggle for recognition that moves history has been completed. Hence the claim that in modern liberal market societies we have arrived at the end of history. Fukuyama's diagnosis of modern societies' remaining problems is Nietzschean – that of the last person who arrives at the end of history. The last person lacks the aristocratic impulse to excel: the desire for glory is defeated by the pursuit of material acquisition. The unresolved 'contradiction' of liberal democracy lies in the fact that the attempt to replace *megalothymia* with rational consumption cannot succeed. Human beings will not accept that condition. They will reject the status of being last men: 'they will rebel at the idea of being undifferentiated members of a universal and homogeneous state.'[3]

Fukuyama's account of history as the story of the struggle for satisfaction of a single desire, the desire for recognition, is an extended exercise in inattentiveness to distinctions. The desire for recognition, *thumos*, becomes a primitive of human psychology, specified only in terms of whether it is for equality or superiority – *isothymia* or *megalothymia*. A central distinction that Fukuyama glosses over in contrasting *isothymia* and *megalothymia* is that between concepts of 'standing' and the concepts of 'virtue'.[4] By 'standing' here I mean roughly the social, political and economic position, class or status a person has within a community: freeman and slave, lord and serf, husband and wife, citizen or noncitizen, and so on. By 'virtues' I mean the excellences that individuals have and display where these are understood in their widest sense to include not only excellences in moral character – kindness, courage, good judgement, humility and so on – but also excellences in practices – of the scientist, artist, teacher, athlete, parent and so on. There is a formal difference between concepts of standing and of virtue. The concepts of virtue are normally modifiable by terms of more or less. One can be more or less courageous, wise, kind, and so on. In contrast concepts of standing are not normally thus modifiable. They ascribe a status you either have or do not have. To make these distinctions is not to deny that there are not a complex set of relationships between the two sets of concepts. In traditional societies, the standing of a person is often in part constituted by a set of virtues peculiar to it: hence, the traditional distinctions in the virtues demanded of women as wife and mother and those demanded of men as husbands, fathers and citizens. Likewise, it is possible to have a standing in a particular community, for example in an occupational association, in virtue of meeting some set of skills in a trade. However, to describe the relationships between standing and virtues them is not, as Fukuyama does, to identify them.

Fukuyama's account of the move to modern society as a transition to *isothymia* from *megalothymia* confuses these two sets of concepts. The passage from pre-modern to modern societies, understood as a move from 'status' to 'contract', has involved a shift in the standing of agents: from a system of differentiated political, social and moral standing defined by roles, each with its distinct bundles of virtues, rights and obligations, to undifferentiated standings defined in terms of rights and duties that an individual has under some general description – as 'citizen' or 'person'. Individuals are in this sense understood, formally at least, to be members of a community of equal standing. The liberal social and political order is defined by the existence of a class of rights that are held by individuals as persons whatever their particular qualities – to vote, to enter associations, to enter into contracts and so on. The struggle for such rights is, as Fukuyama claims, in part a struggle for recognition. Hence, where they are won, as they were recently by the majority of the population in South Africa, their significance is more than instrumental. They have value in virtue of granting to individuals recognition that they are someone. They are recognised as having standing that is equal to that of others. Much of the traditional socialist and feminist criticism of liberalism has concerned issues of standing – of the restricted domains in which the community of equal standing exists and the formal nature of that equality. While in the realm of politics and market exchange individuals are related to each other as members of single status communities, as citizen or contracting agents, in the sphere of production they meet as capitalist and wage worker, in the domestic sphere as husband and wife. And in politics and market exchange, formal equality in status exists alongside substantive inequality of powers. In respect to standing, the struggle for recognition has not ceased. Its boundaries have shifted.

What, however, is presupposed by such debates is a claim that the recent emphasis on 'difference' in radical politics has obscured. The objective of a political community of equal standing has its basis in the humanist thought that whatever the differences that might exist in achievements and virtues, human beings share certain universal powers which deserve to be recognised: by powers here I refer both to active powers, in particular the primary powers to develop skills and capacities, including powers of theoretical and practical reason and the capacity to shape one's own life, and what the scholastics called passive powers, to feel pain and pleasure, to suffer humiliation and the like. Acceptance of the existence of such powers is quite compatible with difference. For example, the forms which humiliation can take are diverse and differ across gender, culture, and class. However, the capacity to feel humiliation is a universal one, and to meet other humans and not to be aware of that possibility of humiliation is to fail to recognise them as subjects to whom respect is owed.

Fukuyama's diagnosis of the problems of modern society, the contradiction between *megalothymia* and being 'undifferentiated members' of a 'universal and homogeneous' community, confuses recognition of standing with recognition of virtues. There is no conflict of the kind that Fukuyama assumes between the two forms of recognition. One can recognise someone as a person in a community of equal standing, and then make distinctions about that person's virtues. There is no conflict between saying that various individuals are a great pianist, a poor footballer, an ambitious and dangerous politician, a coward and so on and at the same time ascribing them an identical standing in a political or economic community with all others. Equality in democratic rights in a community is quite consistent with inequality in excellences. A community that is not differentiated in the standing of members is consistent with a community that is differentiated in the particular virtues that an individual can exhibit. Rather it is the case that, as Tawney notes in the argument outlined in the last chapter, the existence of equality in standing is a condition for the proper appraisal of a person's virtues. Proper differentiation in virtue and homogeneity in standing are not just compatible: the former requires the latter.

If one turns to what Fukuyama says about *megalothymia*, a second and related inattentiveness to distinctions is evident, one that is closer to the kind that Smith notes. Fukuyama assumes that *thumos*, the desire for recognition, is an end in itself. Individuals desire recognition for recognition's sake. Given this account, *megalothymia*, the desire to be recognised as superior, itself takes the form of simple recognition for its own sake. Hence Fukuyama introduces his account of the desire thus:

> [T]here is no reason to think that all people will evaluate themselves as the *equals* of other people. Rather, they may seek to be recognized as *superior* to other people, possibly on the basis of true inner worth, but more likely out of an inflated and vain estimate of themselves. The desire to be recognized as superior to other people we will henceforth label with a new word with ancient Greek roots, *megalothymia*. *Megalothymia* can be manifest both in the tyrant who invades and enslaves a neighbouring people so that they recognize his authority, as well as in the concert pianist who wants to be recognized as the foremost interpreter of Beethoven. Its opposite is *isothymia*, the desire to be recognized as the equal of other people. *Megalothymia* and *isothymia* together constitute the two manifestation of the desire for recognition around which the historical transition to modernity can be understood.[5]

The desire of pianists for recognition of their talents is treated in exactly the same way as the desire of tyrants for recognition: both manifest the same desire in different spheres – the desire for recognition as such.

The account of *megalothymia* that Fukuyama presents is of a peculiar self-absorbed form of the desire for recognition. The desire to excel in some pursuit is treated as a desire to be noticed. Now this clearly is possible. The desire for recognition as such might drive pianists in their pursuit. What they want is fame and the art is simply the route to its achievement: if another route were available that would do. The art is parasitic on the desire. However, this desire for recognition for its own sake is a peculiar one. To desire recognition is not normally to simply desire to be noticed, but to desire confirmation of the worth of excellences independent of recognition. Recognition is parasitic on objective goods. Hence Aristotle's proper rejoinder to those who desire for honour as a final good:

> [T]heir aim in pursuing honour is seemingly to convince themselves that they are good; at any rate, they seek to be honoured by intelligent people, among people who know them, and for virtue. It is clear, then, that in the view of active people at least, virtue is superior [to honour].[6]

Recognition is a good in so far as it involves the confirmation by others who are believed to be competent to judge the goods which an individual has achieved, not by anybody. The concert pianist demands recognition not from the crowd in the local public bar for a good tinkle on the ivory, but from those who understand classical music and are able to discern what a good and poor interpretation of Beethoven would sound like. To be recognised by someone who one believed to be incompetent to make a judgement, someone like myself for example, would be of no value. Pianists seek recognition to endeavour to confirm the independent worth of their achievement. The desire is not reducible to the simple desire to be noticed. Nor is it the manifestation of the same desire as that of the tyrant, who wants simple confirmation of brute force, not of worth.

This Aristotelian point runs through the work of Smith[7] and Hegel. Indeed it is notable here how far Fukuyama moves away from his own Hegelian roots. Hegel's account of the need for mutual recognition, in his discussion of the master–slave relationship, plays on an Aristotelian point: that recognition counts only from beings whom we recognise to have a worth. The master's desire for recognition from the slave is self-defeating because it is not from a being that he recognises as having worth. The self-defeating nature of the desire has a good Aristotelian foundation. It is self-defeating in virtue of the fact that recognition is parasitic on other goods. Recognition is required to confirm my self-worth as a being with powers of rationality and the capacities to stand above and shape particular desires. It is only from beings that I recognise as themselves having such powers and capacities that recognition counts. It is because recognition of self-worth is demanded, not being noticed *per se*, that one-sided recognition will not do.

8.2 Recognition, markets and associations

It is in virtue of this parasitic nature of recognition on prior goods that Hegel ultimately rejects an individualised market economy as satisfactory as a means of recognition even within civil society itself. A notable feature of Fukuyama's account of Hegel is that, while Fukuyama is clearly committed to a defence of the associational spheres of modern society and a rejection of an individualistic 'Anglo-Saxon' model of liberalism, Hegel's discussion of corporations, the associations of skill in civil society that educate and protect their members, disappear from his account.[8] However, for Hegel, the corporation matters as a sphere of recognition in part precisely because it maintains a link between recognition and the possession of a set of competencies one has in a practice. Recognition is situated within a community of skills. As a member of the corporation a person's capability is 'a *recognized* fact'. His membership of the corporation is 'evidence of his skill ... that he is somebody'.[9] This Hegel contrasts with the member of civil society who is a member of no association of skill: '[H]is isolation reduces his business to mere self-seeking ... Consequently, he has to try to gain recognition for himself by giving external proofs of success in his business, and to these proofs no limits can be set'.[10] Hegel's distinction between the two modes of recognition points to two important features of recognition which is not tied to some independent good, but which is concerned solely with appearance. First, it is a competitive good in a possessive 'self-seeking' sense, not a good that can be held in common in a community. Second, it is a good the pursuit of which is a never ending struggle of the Hobbesian kind: there are no limits in its pursuit. The two features are related.

Good appearance divorced from any independent good is a pure positional good. There is no standard available other than one's comparative standing to others. Recognition of worth in contrast is not a pure positional good. It is something one can have in virtue of meeting standards that are independent of one's comparative standing. One can be a competent boat builder, carpenter, philosopher, rock climber or whatever and be recognised by others as competent, as a person with skills and achievements of a particular standard that gives one a standing within a community of art or skill. At the same time one can recognise other individuals as achieving excellences within a practice without this being of necessity competitive. I can admire the achievements of others. Moreover, their achievements extend the practice and in this sense benefit the whole community.[11] They are not a threat to my self-respect or self-esteem: my own performance is measured against standards of competence to which I aspire. Those who assume self-esteem is a purely positional good confuse it with vanity.[12] That worth is not a pure positional good also places limits on its pursuit that do not exist for the pursuit of appearance as an end in itself. For any practice the achievement of a certain level of performance is that – an achievement recognised by standards independent of the mere fact of recognition itself. With appearance as an end in itself this is not so. Each attempts to stand above the crowd to be noticed and, since all strain upwards, none is satisfied. All desire to stand higher.[13] As Hegel has it, there are no limits to the external proofs of success. Fukuyama misses all this in the Hegelian account. He describes a self-obsessed account on the level of appearance that Hegel explicitly rejects.

Fukuyama's self-obsessed account of recognition and his confusion of the desire to be noticed and the desire to be recognised exhibit a peculiar market model of the desire for recognition that is common in recent writings on recognition. This mistaken market model is illustrated well by the account of recognition offered by Walzer in *Spheres of Justice*. Walzer also treats the quest for recognition as a separate sphere detached from others, which, once the differential status of premodern society disappears, takes its modern form of self-obsessed individuals competing for admiration as an end in itself:

> Since he has no fixed rank, since no one knows where he belongs, he must establish his own worth, and he can do that only by winning the recognition of his fellows. Each of his fellows is trying to do the same thing ... The competitors speculate on the market, intrigue against near rivals, and bargain for power, spend money, display goods, give gifts, spread gossip, stage performances – all for the sake of recognition. And having done all this, they do it all again, reading their daily gains and losses in the eyes of their fellows, like a stockbroker in his morning paper.[14]

What Walzer describes here is a struggle for recognition that takes place entirely at the level of appearances, in which to there is no distance between recognition for looking good and for being good. Individuals do not seek recognition to confirm their independent worth: their worth is their appearance.[15] Appearance is something that is vied over by competitors in a market. The idea of independent worth disappears.

This market model of recognition permeates social psychology and sociology. Consider for example its use as a rhetorical device in the deflationary social constructionist accounts of science. Woolgar and Latour for example present scientific activity as a competition in professional credibility:

> Scientists are investors in credibility. The result is a creation of a *market*. Information now has value because ... it allows other investigators to produce information which facilitates the return of invested capital. There is a *demand* from investors for information which may increase the power of their own inscription devices, and there is a *supply* of information from other investors. The forces of supply and demand create the *value* of the commodity.[16]

Not only the problems that scientists work on but also what counts as 'good work' and what in the end becomes scientific knowledge is determined by the market in credibility, by investment in recognition by others in the community. The intent of the model is deflationary. The notion of standards of worth independent of appearance, of scientific truth and valid argument disappear. All that is left is the outcome of a market competition over appearance. Science is described in the image of a commercial society in which appearance and real worth are divorced. Worth is appearance. The plausibility of the model depends almost entirely on the rhetoric of Hobbesian realism, of a battle for glory, which must be 'true' since it describes the worst of all possible worlds.

As I noted in chapters 5 and 6, it is the divorce of appearance and character in commercial society that for Adam Smith is at the same time both the driving force to accumulation and the cause of the corruption of the moral sentiments. Its corrupting influence lies in part in the confusion of different forms of recognition.

> The disposition to admire, and almost to worship, the rich and powerful, and to despise, or at least, to neglect persons of poor and mean condition, though necessary to establish and to maintain the distinction of ranks and order of society, is, at the same time, the great and most universal cause of corruption of our moral sentiments. That wealth and greatness are often regarded with the respect and admiration which are due only to wisdom and virtue; and that the contempt, of which vice and folly are the only proper objects, is often most unjustly bestowed upon poverty and weakness.[17]

The distinction that Smith draws here between recognition of wisdom and virtue and recognition of wealth and power is one to which recent writing on recognition has been blind. Writers like Fukuyama, Walzer, Latour and Woolgar are examples of 'the inattentive observers' whom Smith quite properly criticises in the passage that opens this chapter. However, the problem is not mere inattention, but the nature of commercial society to which attention is paid.

8.3 Social equality and associational socialism

Tawney's argument for social equality (discussed in the last chapter) is essentially an inversion of that which Smith makes. Whereas for Smith the confusion of different forms of recognition is the price that must be paid for the maintenance of distinctions of ranks, for Tawney, the disappearance of 'the distinction of ranks and order of society' which wealth and power support, is a condition for proper recognition where it is due, for the powers and virtues that individuals possess. Without that equality of wealth and power, the inattentiveness to the distinctions between what is and is not a proper object of respect will persist. Smith's complaint about the universal cause of corruption in the moral sentiments is transformed into an argument for social equality.

This apparently inegalitarian line of argument for socialism is not peculiar to Tawney. The same point is central to Marx's criticism of commercial society for divorcing appearances, which can be bought, from the powers of character a person possesses. Whereas in commercial society, any quality can be exchanged for any other, in communism a person's virtues can only be those he actually has:

> If we assume *man* to be *man*, and his relation to the world to be a human one, then love can only be exchanged for love, trust for trust, and so on.

> If you wish to enjoy art you must be an artistically educated person; if you wish to exercise influence on other men you must be the sort of person who has a truly stimulating and encouraging effect on others. Each of your relations to man – and to nature – must be a *particular expression* corresponding to the object of your will, of your *real individual* life. If you love unrequitedly, i.e. if your love as love does not call forth love in return ... then your love is impotent, it is a misfortune.[18]

The argument here is inegalitarian in form. The complaint against a money economy here is, in part, that it disguises real inequalities. The argument for communism is that one's way through life is to be determined by the qualities of character one actually possesses with all the misfortune and failure this entails, and not by ersatz powers that money is able to buy. There are differences in the emphases in the arguments that Tawney and Marx present. Marx's argument is focused on the issues about identity raised in chapter 6. It concerns the conditions in which recognition is given for the actual as against the imaginary qualities that individuals have. That of Tawney has more to do with the theme of authoritativeness. It concerns the conditions in which it is rational to submit to the influence of others. However, the arguments of Marx and Tawney both rely on the distinction I drew earlier between concepts of standing and those of virtues. Both argue for a community of equal standing, not only in politics but also in wealth and power, as a condition for proper distinctions to be made in worth.

To this egalitarian criticism of Smith needs to be added another Hegelian point. Central to Hegel's account of recognition is awareness of the need for social arenas of recognition which are non-market in form: hence the defence of the corporation as a sphere of recognition.[19] The corporation is an association in which a practice is fostered, its internal standards are defined and developed, education is pursued and the marks of achievement are recognised. Through membership of the corporation a person's capability is 'a *recognized* fact'.[20] A central weakness of Smith's defence of the market, a weakness that more recent defences have inherited, lies in his determined anti-associationalism.[21] For Smith, professional associations, trade associations, guilds and the traditional self-governing university are conspiracies against the public, concerned with the pursuit of sectional interests at the expense of those of consumers. In particular, they represent barriers to the free movement of labour, particularly through the practice of the extended apprenticeship. 'It is to prevent [the] reduction of price, and consequently of wages and profit, by restraining free competition which would most certainly occasion it, that all corporations ... have been established'.[22] Smith tends to be blind to the variety of excellences for which recognition is deserved. That blindness has its theoretical basis in his Stoicism. When Smith talks of 'the respect and admiration which are due only to wisdom and virtue', both wisdom and virtue are in the singular. The particular excellences exhibited by those in particular theoretical and practical arts are themselves of no great import, belonging to those events of human life to which the 'Stoical wise man' must display 'a great measure of indifference': for the wise, happiness consists only in the contemplation of the perfection of the universe and the discharge of the duties of whatever place in it to which one is allotted.[23] The skills of the producer are treated purely instrumentally as merely means to the achievement of the goods, not as in Hegel as a means through which individuals can gain a sense of self-worth. Here, Hegel's focus on the very specific and concrete spheres in which excellence is achieved and recognition is due is to be preferred to what he properly characterises as the Stoic's 'lifeless indifference which steadfastly withdraws from the bustle of existence'.[24]

Smith's anti-associationalism has continued to be a central component of the economic liberal's defence of the market. It is at best a partial story. It treats associations simply as interest groups, where the concept of interest is defined in a particularly narrow fashion, and it treats education within a practice as a restriction on the mobility of labour. Recognition then becomes the competitive market good divorced from any skills and the associational arenas in which they are recognised. That anti-associationalism has unfortunately gone uncriticised in much of the Marxian tradition of socialism. A fault in Marx is that, in his criticism of Hegel, he accepts Smith's empirical claim that modern market societies would be premised on the disappearance of associations and shares something of his normative case against them. Thus the story of the transition to modern society is one in which associations disappear:

> The political revolution that overthrew this rule [feudalism] ... inevitably destroyed all the estates, corporations, guilds and privileges which expressed the separation of people from its community. The political revolution thereby abolished the political character of civil society. It shattered civil society into its simple components – on the one hand individuals and on the other the material and spiritual elements which constitute the vital content and civil situation of these individuals.[25]

Marx rather too quickly accepts the story of the development of modern society as one in which the market succeeds in disassociating individuals into isolated individuals. One consequence is that in his normative account of the future world community he tends to speak in universalistic terms of individuals thus disassociated. Marx shares Smith's failure to recognise the normative significance of particular association and the modes of individual recognition they can embody. Hegel's discussion of the significance of that associational dimension of recognition in the economic sphere deserves to be rescued from both latter day liberal followers like Fukuyama and from older Marxian criticism.

9

COMMENSURABILITY AND THE SOCIALIST CALCULATION DEBATES

9.1 The socialist calculation debates

In the next three chapters of the book I will switch the focus of the argument by examining the defences of the market economy offered by Austrian economists in the 1920s and 1930s in what has been called 'the socialist calculation debate'. What was 'the socialist calculation debate'? There is a standard story that goes something like this. In the first two decades of the century an argument was developed by a number of theorists – Barone, Pierson, and Weber[1] – which questioned the possibility of rational economic planning in certain forms of a socialist economy. These objections to socialism were crystallised by Mises in a paper published in 1920,[2] and incorporated into a book in 1922,[3] which purported to show that rational economic calculation would not be possible within socialism. The core of Mises' argument was refined by Hayek in the 1930s.[4] The socialist response to this position was articulated by Lange and Taylor.[5] The socialist calculation debate is presented primarily as a conflict between Mises and Hayek on the one hand, and Lange and Taylor on the other, different sides being accorded the laurels of victory.[6] Who won matters in virtue of the debate's contemporary significance. On the one side, the collapse of the East European economic and political regimes in the 1980s in particular is often taken to confirm the case against the economic rationality of socialism: 'It turns out, of course, that Mises was right'.[7] On the other, the arguments of Lange and Taylor are sometimes taken to support the case for market socialism as the feasible alternative to state socialism.[8]

Thus goes the standard story. The story is false. The belief that there was something called the socialist calculation debate and the story told of it are myths. There was not one debate, but many. In particular, the nature and the extent of the discontinuities between the early and later phases of the debates are missed in the received accounts. They are missed in the main because the received history has come through two of the main protagonists in the debate, Hayek and Lange.[9] Both protagonists accept that there is a shift in the debate, although they offer different characterisations of what that is. For Lange it is a move from the claim of Mises that rational planning is theoretically impossible, to the weaker claim of

Hayek and Robbins that it is not a practical possibility.[10] In Hayek the move is specified rather in terms of a shift in the debate to epistemic ground which he takes to be implicit in Mises' earlier objections. Later commentators follow in talking of a switch from a logical to an epistemological interpretation of Mises argument.[11] While both sides are right to claim that the debate does have different phases neither characterisation will do.

Both Hayek and Lange read Mises argument through the lens of their later debate, and have been largely followed by others in this respect. The immediate intellectual context of Mises' argument is lost. In particular there is a tendency, more evident in Lange than Hayek, to gloss over the work of the Austrian socialist, Otto Neurath, which formed the main object of criticism in Mises' opening paper in the debate, as it had done to Weber's contribution to the debate.[12] The consequence is a distorted reading of Mises' position and a misreading of the history of the calculation debates. Mises' objection to socialism turns not on questions of logic or epistemology, but on assumptions about the nature of practical rationality, in particular, the claim that rational choice between options requires their commensurability in terms of a single unit of value. The subsequent debate involved the different sides taking the opposite party's positions on those assumptions. On the one hand, Taylor and Lange both took for granted the truth of Mises' assumptions about rationality and commensurability. On the other hand, Hayek never shared Mises' assumptions, and, indeed, in his later writing he is much closer to the position that Neurath had assumed than he is to that of Mises. Neurath's criticism of 'pseudorationalism' is echoed in Hayek's later criticism of rationalism. Hayek did not reinterpret Mises in epistemological terms: the references to knowledge in Mises are not central to his arguments. He rather shifted the debate on to different ground which shares more with Neurath than with Mises.

The socialist calculation debates, plural, in fact raised two quite distinct questions about the market economy and the possibility of a non-market economy. The first concerned the nature of practical reason and the possibility of rational action in the absence of commensurability. The second concerned the division of knowledge in society and the possibility of coordinated activity given that division. This chapter examines the first argument. I argue that while Mises may have 'won' the debate, in the sense that subsequent socialist protagonists like Lange largely accepted his position, he lost the argument. As far as the issues in the early phase of the debate are concerned, the laurels of intellectual victory belong not with the socialist or anti-socialist sides but with Neurath and Hayek. I show that the fact that Mises and Lange 'won' the argument has been an unfortunate legacy for subsequent economic theory.

9.2 Who won the socialist calculation debate?

Mises' argument in 'Economic Calculation in the Socialist Commonwealth' is aimed against the possibility of a socialist economy, understood as an economy without a market in production goods. The argument is targeted against two principal opponents. The first were those socialist theorists who advocated replacing money as a unit of economic calculation with another unit: the two most popular candidates were units of labour-time advocated in some of the Marxian literature and energy units advocated by ecological economists such as Popper-Lynkeus and Ballod-Atlanticus. The second target was Neurath who denied that rational economic choice required the existence of a single unit of calculation and advocated a 'natural economy' founded on calculation in kind.[13] Neurath had argued that a socialist economy, since it was to consider the use-value of goods only, would have to be a non-market 'economy in kind', in which there would exist no role for monetary units to compare options:

> We must at last free ourselves from outmoded prejudices and regard a large-scale economy in kind as a fully valid form of economy which is the more important today in that any completely planned economy amounts to an economy in kind. To socialize therefore means to further an economy in kind. To hold on to the split and uncontrollable monetary order and at the same time to want to socialize is an inner contradiction.[14]

In such an economy, while physical statistics about energy use, material use and so on would be required, there would be no need for a single unit of comparison.

> There are no units that can be used as the basis of a decision, neither units of money nor hours of work. One must directly judge the desirability of the two possibilities.[15]

In the absence of a single unit of measurement for decision making, choice requires direct comparisons of alternatives. The consequence is that there is no possibility of excluding political and ethical judgements from even 'technical' decisions. In making this claim, Neurath is criticising not only the market, but also socialist alternatives to the market that employ single units in making decisions, be these labour hours or energy units.

Mises' arguments against both Neurath's position and that of socialists who advocate alternative units of calculation turn on assumptions about the nature of practical rationality and its dependence on commensurability: rational economic decision making, beyond the most simple individual decisions, requires a single measure on the basis of which the worth of alternative states of affairs could be calculated and compared. Thus, for example, given the choice 'whether we shall use a waterfall to produce electricity or extend coal and better utilize the energy contained in coal',[16] we need some way of calculating the advantages and benefits of alternatives, and this in turn required a common unit of measurement. The 'subjective use-values of commodities' provide no units for computation – 'judgements of value do not measure: they arrange, they grade'.[17] Hence such values cannot enter directly into comparisons between options. Nor would labour time provide an adequate basis. Different forms of labour are themselves qualitatively distinct and cannot be subsumed under a common unit: the kinds of reduction of 'complex' to 'simple' labour that are attempted in Marxian econom- ics cannot be sustained. In contrast a common unit of measurement is provided by monetary prices in the market: 'calculations based upon exchange values enable us to reduce values to a common unit'.[18] Monetary values form the only adequate unit of comparison.

While Mises praises Neurath for accepting that socialism entails the absence of a single unit of calculation, his position is taken to have 'insurmountable difficulties'[19] precisely in virtue of its failure to accept the need for such a unit. For Mises rational comparison of options requires monetary prices that measure exchange values such that, by rules of calculation, one is able to have a determi- nate answer to the advantages of alternatives.

The debate between Mises and Neurath turns on differences concerning the nature of practical rationality. For Mises any rational decision, beyond the most simple, requires the commensurability of different values. There needs to be a single common unit which reduces the choice between different options to a matter of calculation. Mises assumes an algorithmic conception of practical rea- son. Rational decision making requires the application of mechanical procedures of calculation to arrive at a determinate answer to any question. That position Mises maintains into his later writings. In *Human Action* it is taken to be a gen- eral feature even of individual rational economic activity:

> The practical man ... must know whether what he wants to achieve will be an improvement when compared with the present state of affairs and with the advantages to be expected from the execution of other techni- cally realisable projects which cannot be put into execution if the project he has in mind absorbs the available means. Such comparisons can only be made by the use of money prices.[20]

Neurath's position is founded upon a rejection of just this account of rational choice. It exhibits what he calls 'pseudorationalism'.

The bases of Neurath's objections to this view are to be found in two earlier papers, 'The lost wanderers of Descartes and the auxiliary motive' (published in 1913) and 'The problem of the pleasure maximum' (published in 1912).[21] In 'The lost wanderers of Descartes and the auxiliary motive', Neurath criticises the algorithmic view of reason, that one can give a set of rules that determine un- equivocally a particular decision: 'in many cases, by considering different possi- bilities of action, a man cannot reach a result'.[22] Our knowledge that informs decision making is uncertain and the rules of rationality rarely determine a unique answer given what is known. A rationalist who believes in reason must recognise the boundaries to the power of reason in arriving at decisions: 'Rationalism sees its chief triumph in the clear recognition of the limits of actual insight.'[23] It is a mark of the pseudorationalist to believe that there do exist rules of insight that determine answers to all decisions. Pseudorationalism exists both in the domain of action and also of thought, for example in the belief that there exist rules for the scientific method which if followed eliminate falsehood and lead to ever nearer approximations to the truth.[24]

In his paper 'The problem of the pleasure maximum', Neurath criticises a second assumption that Mises was to make in his opening salvo against socialism, that values are commensurable, i.e. that there is a measure of values according to which options can be uniquely ordered. Neurath rejects that assumption, somewhat surprisingly, from within a hedonist perspective. Neurath defends a utilitarian and Epicurean position which takes the good of social policy to be the maximisation of happiness understood as pleasure. However, he rightly rejected the possibility of units of pleasure on which calculations could be made.[25] Even given the aim of pleasure maximisation, there is no possibility of a purely technical ordering of states of affairs: pleasures are themselves incommensurable. In his work on planning, this point has a more general significance. It follows that even on the simplifying assumption of a single evaluative category, no planner could ignore substantial value questions and treat a decision in ethically neutral technical terms.

The rejection of the pseudorationalism of algorithmic rules and of the assumption of value commensurability informs Neurath's conception of non-market socialism as an economy of kind, and lies at the basis of his arguments in the socialist calculation debate. Mises' attack on the possibility of socialism exhibits precisely the kind of pseudorationalism in the domain of practical reason that Neurath had attacked in his earlier writings. Neurath reaffirms the ineliminability of non-technical ethical judgements in his later contributions to the socialist calculation debate. Thus Neurath takes up Mises examples of choosing between alternative sources of energy and responds thus:

> The question might arise, should one protect coal mines or put greater strain on men? The answer depends for example on whether one thinks that hydraulic power may be sufficiently developed or that solar heat might come to be better used, etc. If one believes the latter, one may 'spend' coal more freely and will hardly waste human effort where coal can be used. If however one is afraid that when one generation uses too much coal thousands will freeze to death in the future, one might use more human power and save coal. Such and many other non-technical matters determine the choice of a technically calculable plan ... we can see no possibility of reducing the production plan to some kind of unit and then to compare the various plans in terms of such units.[26]

Rational practical thinking need not involve any single unit that reduces decision making to a purely technical procedure. It requires ethical and political judgement.[27]

Neurath's position has real strengths here that subsequent discussion has ignored. The strengths are apparent in a problem that Mises raises with his own position. Mises recognises that, even in a market economy, there exist 'non-economic goods', those 'which are not the subject of exchange value'.[28] Environmental goods provide the exemplar of these:

> If, for example, we are considering whether a hydraulic power-works would be profitable we cannot include in the computation the damage which will be done to the beauty of the waterfalls unless the fall in values due to a fall in tourist traffic is taken into account. Yet we must certainly take such considerations into account when deciding whether the undertaking shall be carried out.[29]

Mises' response to that problem is one that has become standard in the later literature. We cannot avoid making hard choices between 'non-economic' goods and economic goods, and in doing so, whether we like it or not, we are implicitly making economic evaluations of the non-economic:

> If we know precisely how much we have to pay for beauty, health, honour, pride, and the like, nothing need hinder us from giving them due consideration. Sensitive people may be pained to have to choose between the ideal and the material. But that is not the fault of a money economy. It is in the nature of things.[30]

In making that claim Mises is assuming that every choice is implicitly an exercise in economic evaluation. In such hard choices, whether or not we like to admit it to ourselves, we are implicit accountants, putting a price on unpriced goods. The agent in a choice of this kind knows not only the value of everything, but also its price. Rational decision making requires monetary units and, whether we like it or not, in making choices we are making monetary comparisons. The economist is merely making this explicit.

Mises' response to the problem of non-economic goods is implausible. He accepts that in a market economy there are economic decisions that involve non-economic goods that can be and are made without recourse to the use of monetary units. His response to that problem begs the question. Mises simply offers us a redescription of the decisions, which has plausibility only if it assumes what it is supposed to prove – that all rational choices involve units of comparison to which rules of calculation can be applied. It is only if one is already in the grip of an algorithmic picture of practical reason that this has any plausibility. Neurath's account of what is going on here is the stronger. He rightly allowed that comparability need not assume commensurability, that there was not any rule that can be mechanically applied to produce a determinate decision as to which plan to adopt, and that there was an ineliminable role for non-technical judgement in the most technical of decisions.[31]

What is true, however, is that one could not run an economy on the basis of the continuous use of non-technical judgement of the kind that Neurath outlines.

There is a necessary role for rules of thumb, standard procedures, the default procedures and institutional arrangements that can be followed unreflectively and which reduce the scope for explicit judgements comparing different states of affairs. We cannot be exercising ethical and political judgements in a reflective way all the time. There are limits on time, efficient use of resources and the dispersal of knowledge which require rules and institutions. Such rules and institutions can free us space and time for reflective judgements where they matter most. Hence Whitehead's dictum: 'civilization advances by extending the number of important operations we can perform without thinking about them.'[32] Some of the apparent implausibility of Neurath's position to which Mises' and Weber's criticisms appeal lies in the way it appears to assume that direct appraisal of alternatives is always possible.

Three points can be made in response. First, while Neurath never refers to the need for such background rules and institutions, nothing he says is inconsistent with an advocacy of them. Second, the arguments for such institutions and rules do not rely on claims about commensurability. They rely rather on the epistemic points about the coordination of action given dispersal of knowledge; about the embodiment of knowledge in procedures and institutions; and about problems of acting under constraints of time and ignorance. These points raise issues that belong to the second stage of the socialist calculation debates, not the first: I will discuss them further in the next chapter. Third, rules and institutions need themselves to be open to critical and reflective appraisal that itself is non-algorithmic. Institutional practices may embody a practical knowledge; they may also simply serve powerful groups, have socially or environmentally damaging consequences, and so on. Likewise the market may be one way in which dispersed knowledge can be put to good effect. It is not, *pace* early Hayek, the only way – and if its consequences are, for example, ecologically damaging there is a case for putting constraints on markets or, more radically, with Neurath, replacing them with a quite different set of institutions. That we require some rules and institutions to free us for making judgements about what matters does not entail that we require any institution, still less current institutions. Nor does it disallow the possibility of radical institutional changes.

Given a proper account of the first stage of the socialist calculation debate, what becomes notable about the second stage is just how far the central protagonists, Hayek and Lange, take up the positions of what are supposed to be their opponents. On the central issues about practical reason and commensurability, it is Lange who is closest to Mises and Hayek who shares most with Neurath.

Lange simply accepts the central conclusion of Mises' opening salvo in the debate. He presents the problem of socialist calculation and the conditions for its solution thus:

> The economic problem is a problem of *choice* between alternatives. To solve the problem three data are needed: (1) a preference scale which guides the acts of choice; (2) knowledge of the 'terms on which the alternatives

118

are offered'; and (3) knowledge of the amount of resources available. Those three data being given, the problem of choice is soluble.[33]

Lange is setting up here the conditions for the possibility of employing purely technical and calculable procedures for social choices. The assumption that all the goods involved in the choice are commensurable appears in both the first assumption about the data – to invoke a scale is to invoke at least an ordinal measure – and in the second assumption which assumes a single unit of measure in a stronger cardinal sense. Lange shares Mises' positions on commensurability and the nature of practical reason. His central move against Mises is to employ Wicksteed's distinction between price in the sense of the exchange ratio of two commodities in the market, and price in the general sense of the unit through which all commodities can be compared, such that an 'index of alternatives' can be constructed for choices. Price in this second general sense, referred to as 'terms on which alternatives are offered', can be employed for rational calculation within socialism. Price in this sense allows 'the technical possibilities of transformation of one commodity into another'.[34] The central thrust of Lange's argument is to show that there is a technical solution to the problem of choice possible within a form of socialism which has a market in consumption goods but not in production goods. He assumes that the data under 1 and 3 are given. His contribution is to attempt to show that administrators in a planned economy can have accessible to them the data about prices under 2.

Lange simply accepts the technical account of reason that Mises assumes and that Neurath had rejected. Indeed the debate between Mises and Neurath never figures in Lange's account. This is true also of later market socialists. Typical is Roemer who presents the initial phase of the debate thus:

> The first stage was marked by the realization by socialists that prices must be used for economic calculation under socialism; accounting in some kind of 'natural unit,' such as the amount of energy or labor commodities embodied, simply would not work.[35]

Roemer accepts, with Lange, Mises' main conclusion and the only opponents to Mises mentioned are those who advocated an alternative unit of accounting. Neurath's objections to Mises' assumptions about rational social choice go without comment. This simple acceptance of Mises' assumptions by Roemer is unsurprising: they are givens in the neo-classical tradition to which he belongs. It is in the work of Hayek that those assumptions are questioned from within the Austrian tradition.

Hayek's contribution to the socialist calculation debates was to transform the problem of rational economic action in socialism from one of commensurability to one of epistemology. He responds to Lange by criticising the epistemic presuppositions of Lange's solution. He rejects the claim that the data which Lange assumes to be given to the socialist administrators could be given. The central argument against planning and for the market is epistemic. Given the dispersal of local knowledge often embodied in the skills of individuals, no planning agency could have within its orbit all the information required to formulate a rational plan. The price mechanism in contrast does communicate between individuals that information that is required for the coordination of their economic activities, while allowing them to employ their particular knowledge.[36] Hayek presents this argument as an interpretation of Mises' contribution. However, while there do exist passing references to issues of knowledge – Mises contrasts, for example, those individual choices in which costs and benefits can 'easily be perceived as a whole'[37] and social choices in which they cannot – the issues of knowledge are not central to Mises' argument. His problem is one of conditions of commensurability. It is only in the work of Hayek that epistemic issues come to the fore.

In making epistemic concerns central Hayek transforms the problem: his contribution is not to a socialist *calculation* debate at all. When Hayek complains of Lange that 'the claim that in a socialist order economic *calculation* is possible is replaced by the assertion that economic *accounting* is possible without market prices',[38] he is more highlighting his own distance from Mises than from Lange. Mises' objections to the possibility of rational calculation in non-market socialism, like those of Weber, can be understood as accounting problems. Given the choice, for example, between different sources of energy, we must have units for calculation to make a comparison between alternatives: 'To decide whether an undertaking is sound we must calculate carefully. But computation demands units.'[39] It is not Lange that departs from Mises here, but Hayek. In Hayek's work the issue of calculation is largely absent. His main contribution to the debate is to attempt to show how, given a market, one can have rational decisions without a calculation procedure for comparing different social options. In making this move Hayek's position is closer to Neurath's than it is to Mises. This is particularly evident in his later criticisms of 'rationalism' which have much in common with Neurath's attack on 'pseudo-rationalism'.[40] Neither Hayek nor Neurath accept a Cartesian model of rational choice as the application of technical rules to perfect data. For both, our choices are underdetermined by rules and data. For both, the triumph of reason is 'the clear recognition of the limits of actual insight.'[41]

The socialist calculation debate between Lange and Mises is about *calculation*, specifically the conditions in which rational calculation between options in social choices is possible. While both Neurath and Hayek use the term 'calculation' neither is involved in a socialist calculation debate in this sense. Both Hayek and Neurath deny that *calculation* between social options is possible. Neurath's arguments for 'calculation in kind' are effectively arguments for denying that technical calculation is possible in social choices. Such choices have an ineliminable ethical and political dimension that no algorithmic procedures for calculation could capture. Hayek also denies that calculation is possible, on the grounds that the knowledge required for a calculable plan is absent. Unlike Neurath, however, his solution is to deny any role for such social choices. The market is catallaxy ungoverned by any social ends: hence, the kind of ethical judgement that Neurath demands is rejected.[42]

The difference here between Neurath and Hayek on this issue is based in part on differences in the role that the concept of incommensurability plays in their criticism of rationalism. For Neurath incommensurability exists between the values themselves. Since there is no common measure to choose between values, we need to employ practical judgement in making choices. For Hayek, the locus of incommensurability is one level up, between different beliefs about what is of value. There is no common measure or standard of comparison between different beliefs: the norms of reason, in particular, cannot resolve disputes between competing sets of value. Thus the problem for Hayek is how one can allow different individuals with competing values to exist together and coordinate their activities. The 'Great Society' with its rule of law and market institutions solves that problem. In contrast, for Neurath the problem is this: given plurality of incommensurable values (a substantive value position), how are social choices between alternatives possible? The answer demands non-technical judgement.

These differences are founded, however, on a common criticism of the assumptions about rational choice shared by Mises and Lange. The received stories told of a single socialist calculation debate with continuity on both sides throughout are myths. So also are the stories of who the victor was. As far as the socialist *calculation* debate is concerned the laurels of victory belong not the critic or defender of socialism, but the Neurath-Hayek position against that of Mises and Lange. For this reason, the continued dominance within economics of the Lange-Mises assumptions about practical reason is one of economics' enduring foundational problems.

9.3 Incommensurability and economics: the long footnote

The issue of commensurability remains at the heart of disputes about the scope and nature of economics that extend beyond Austrian economics and the socialist calculation debate. It is central to arguments about the nature of rational decision making in environmental and health economics and more generally about the defensibility of decision making procedures such as cost-benefit analysis that depend upon the assumption that all values can be captured by a single monetary measure: the whole debate since is a long footnote to the calculation debates. That this is the case is not surprising: the problem emerges with one standard account of the nature of economics itself. Thus consider Robbins' influential characterisation of the economic problem:

> From the point of view of the economist, the conditions of human existence exhibit ... fundamental characteristics. The ends are various. The time and the means for achieving these ends are limited and capable of alternative application. At the same time the ends have different importance.[43]

An economic problem is one of multiple ends given limited time and means, whereas a technical problem, in contrast, is one of a given end and limited but multiple means.[44] On this account economics is about practical conflict. It concerns those practical conflicts that have their source in limits in time and resources. That is we have a series of goods: healing the sick, educating the young, maintaining economic well-being, promoting the arts, preserving ancient buildings, protecting a landscape, conserving a habitat or species. These goods do not conflict as such. However, they do conflict when conjoined with an empirical fact about the world that rules their common realisation: one major empirical fact that does rule out such common realisation are resource limits. Given limitations on our resources it is not possible to realise all goods. Had we world enough and time, all the goods could be realised. However, we do not. Material and time are limited. Hence, valued ends are in conflict.

On this account the problem of economics is a problem of lost possibilities. There are many goods, but not all are possible. It follows immediately that, for any option chosen, there are other options and associated goods that are forgone. All choices involve lost possibilities. In economists' terms they have opportunity costs: opportunities for other actions forgone in the choice of some option.[45] Correspondingly the efficient use of scarce resources matters because inefficient use of resources decreases the possibilities for realising other goods.[46] Given a conflict between options, the argument runs that we have to compare for each not just the goods that each issues in, but the lost possibilities their pursuit entails.

The major source of the assumption of commensurability in economics lies in the supposition that the rational resolution of practical conflicts requires a common measure though which different options can be compared, such that the loss of one option is compensated by the gains in another. Commensurability is required to resolve the practical conflicts that define our economic predicament. This claim lies at the basis of the utilitarian foundations of both Austrian and neo-classical economics. There has to be a single standard of value to compare options if there is to be rational decision making at all. A classic statement of the position is that of J. S. Mill:

> There must be some standard to determine the goodness and badness, absolute and comparative, of ends, or objects of desires. And whatever that standard is, there can be but one; for if there were several ultimate principles of conduct, the same conduct might be approved of by one of those principles and condemned by another; and there would be needed some more general principle, as umpire between them.[47]

This claim that there must be some single standard or measure if we are to avoid inconsistency is one is one that is echoed in recent arguments in defence of decision making procedures, like cost-benefit analysis, that assume commensurability.

However, even on Mill's argument this conclusion is not quite right. Mill's claim that there must be a general umpiring principle is not the same as the claim that there must be one standard to determine the goodness or badness of different ends and objects. It is possible to have many standards of value, $v_1, v_2 \ldots v_n$ and some ordering principle for determining which takes precedence over others, an umpiring rule. Typical are Rawlsian rules introducing a lexical ordering amongst values $v_1, v_2 \ldots v_n$, such that v_2 comes into play only after v_1 is satisfied, and in general any further standard of value enters consideration only after the previous value has been satisfied.[48] The notion of rights as trumps in moral argument introduces a lexical ordering of this kind.[49] Rights win against any other values. However, they resolve disputes only where trumps plays another suit of values. The appeal to rights as trumps does not resolve conflict within the trumping value suit. The lexical ordering approach still shares the Millian position that the rational resolution of conflicts requires a single umpiring principle: the disagreement concerns whether it be a single supervalue to which all others can be reduced or a priority rule amongst plural values not so reducible.

There is, however, a flaw in the Millian argument for the claim that there must be a general umpiring principle of either kind.[50] The argument involves an implicit shift in the scope of a quantifier. It is possible to grant to Mill that the following is true:

UE. For any putative practical conflict rationality requires that there be a way of resolving the conflict.

It does not follow as Mill claims that a single general umpiring rule is required. That is to make a distinct claim:

EU. Rationality requires there be a method such that for any practical conflict the method resolves the conflict.

The inference of **EU** from **UE** involves a shift in the scope of the quantifiers from:

UE. $\forall c \exists m \ Rmc$

to

EU. $\exists m \forall c \ Rmc$.

The point is made thus by Wiggins in a discussion of a passage from Aristotle's *De Anima*[51] which might appear to be inconsistent with his rejection of value commensurability in other of his writing:

There is no question here of supposing that there is just one evaluative dimension, Φ, and one quantitative measure, m, such that Φ-ness is all that matters, and all courses of action can be compared by the measure m in respect of Φ-ness. What is assumed is only the weaker proposition, which is of the $\forall \exists$ not the $\exists \forall$ form, that for an n-tuple of course of action actually available at time t to an agent x there is some way or other of establishing which of the n-tuple is the better course of action in respect of eudaemonia, and (consequently upon that) the greater good. There is no obvious inconsistency between holding this *De anima* doctrine and maintaining the thesis of value pluralism or incommensurability in the form of the denial of the $\exists \forall$ sentence.[52]

This distinction between resolutions of the UE-type and EU-type is essentially that made by Neurath in distinguishing between rationalism and pseudorationalism. It is the mark of the pseudorationalist to assume that, for rational choice, we need to find a method that can resolve any conflict, that reason requires not standards, measures or methods (plural) but a standard, a measure or a method (singular). The claim that reason makes no such requirement on us – and the corresponding advocacy of both value pluralism and methodological pluralism – lies at the heart of Neurath's contribution to the socialist calculation debate. Practical rationality does not require the existence of a single measure. The point is also made about theoretical rationality and it is in the course of his criticism of the pseudorationalism of Popper's account of the scientific method that the point is perhaps made with greatest clarity.

> We believe we are doing the most justice to scientific work if, in our model construction, we set out from the assumption that always the whole mass of statements and all methods can come under discussion ... Various factors determine the methodical scientist in his choice of a model. We deny that the encyclopedia preferred by the scientist can be logically selected by using a method that can only be generally outlined.
>
> Together with this we not only deny that there could be general methods of 'induction' for the factual sciences, but also that there could be general methods of 'testing' – however, Popper advocates just such general methods of 'testing'.[53]

The possibility of rational resolution of the UE-type rather than the EU-type defines what I have called elsewhere the weak comparability of goods:[54] at any time t in context c given a putative practical conflict of goods there is a way of comparing the different goods to arrive at an outcome that resolves the conflict. The position is compatible with the acceptance of a plurality of incommensurable values and the absence of any lexical ordering or trumping principle. We exercise practical judgement in a particular context to resolve conflicts between different values which present different standards and measures of value. One central reason for being sceptical about the possibility of EU resolution lies in the non-separability of goods and the consequent context dependence of appraisal. The value of many goods depends upon the company they keep. Good puns for example may have negative value in a passage of tragic prose. Courage is no virtue in a Nazi. The property 'giving pleasure' is often positive, but is negative if it is the pleasure in the suffering of innocent others. It is only in a context that we can compare goods. Any general methodological principle that specifies a general value-conferring property can fail when applied to a particular context.

None of this is to deny the reality of practical conflicts nor the importance of representing the lost possibilities that any choice entails. What it does give reason to do is to ask how this can be addressed if the assumption of commensurability is given up. One response is the development of those decision making aids that do not rely on the existence of a single measure, such as non-compensatory multi-criteria decision analysis (MCDA) which is premised on the claim that the resource requirements and effects of alternative course of action may be comparable on a number of different dimensions that cannot be brought into a single unit of measure.[55] These can be more transparent in their statement of lost possibilities than the mere statement of monetary figures. Moreover, and this is I think a strength and not a weakness, it does not pursue what is ultimately a will of the wisp of a complete statement of lost possibilities. But even given these, one needs some account of how resolution is possible in given contexts when notions of maximisation on some single scale of value are given up.

What kinds of resolutions are possible given irreducible value plurality? In the end the answer to that question is simply 'use your judgement after the best possible deliberation'. Practical conflicts issue in conflicts in judgements about how they should be resolved in a particular context. We both agree that this habitat should be protected, but we also both agree that resources need to be given to a local school. The ends conflict, and we differ in our judgements about how this is to be resolved in this context. To resolve this we need to adduce reasons why here one rather than the other should have priority and hence be resourced. We aim at a normative judgement in a particular circumstance. The issue is not about recording given preferences on the issue, but of attempting to alter preferences. 'Use your judgement after the best possible deliberation' is not, however, the only thing that can be said about the resolution of value conflict given incommensurability. Some additional observations are worth adding here.

First, there are weak concepts of maximisation that are compatible with the failure of commensurability. The concept of dominance can still apply: 'For all alternatives x and y, if all criteria rank x above y, then x ranks above y, all things considered'.[56] So also does maximisation in the sense which Aristotle introduces it in discussing the self-sufficiency and completeness of happiness.[57] A good life is something like a maximally consistent set of goods: if we have a set of goods and we can add another without conflict then we should. Given an existing bundle of goods, say friends and a good urban and natural environment and I can add another without loss, say more fulfilling work, then I should do so. The same is also true of social choices. Indeed, as I noted in chapter 2 for Aristotle life in the polis is more choiceworthy since in it we as a community can pursue goods that as individuals we must forgo.[58] However, maximisation in these senses can be given only a very minimal role. It does not tell us what to do given choices that involve the loss of some goods for gains in others or how to appraise different bundles of goods: what to do individually when faced with the loss of friends and environment for more satisfying work, or less satisfying work for the sake of friends; or socially when faced with the distribution of resources across different educational, productive, environmental and health projects which cannot all be realised.

Second, one can clearly make better or worse judgements here. One can say that Joe has lost sight of the importance of friends and family in his obsessive pursuit of his career or that Mary has lost sight of her own projects in her devotion to her family and friends. It is possible to compare across different kinds of goods to make sense of the shape of lives. Some lives just give too much or too little significance to certain goods. Likewise with social orders. Of different social orders one can say that they give too much or too little attention to certain goods, for example that attention to the pursuit of the undoubted advantages that some material goods bring has involved blindness to the loss of decent patterns of work. We can make such comparisons without appeal to a single cardinal or ordinal scale of ranking. Incommensurability need not entail incomparability.

Third, non-substantive models of rationality which do not define rational choice in terms of some best outcome are compatible with incommensurability. I refer here to procedural, expressive and narrative accounts of rational choice.

Procedural accounts of practical reason take an action to be rational if it is an outcome of rational procedures: 'Behaviour is procedurally rational when it is the outcome of appropriate deliberation'.[59] Raz's account of rational action under conditions of incommensurability can be understood as procedural in this general sense: 'Rational action is action for (what the agent takes to be) an undefeated reason. It is not necessarily action for a reason which defeats all others'.[60] A procedural theory is implicit in my response to the problem of choice in conditions of incommensurability: 'use your judgement after the best possible deliberation'. It is implicit in the work of deliberative critics of market based approaches to politics. Rational behaviour is that which emerges from deliberation that meets the norms of rational discussion. Given a procedural account of rationality, what matters is the development of deliberative institutions that allow citizens to form preferences through reasoned dialogue, not institutions for aggregating given preferences to arrive at an 'optimal' outcome.[61]

Expressive accounts characterise actions as rational where they satisfactorily express rational evaluations of objects and persons: 'Practical reasons demands that one's actions adequately express one's rational attitudes towards the people and things one cares about.'[62] Actions are not just instrumental means to an end, but a way of expressing attitudes to people and things. Consider gift-giving: I give a gift to my relatives not as an implicit instrumental exchange which will get something back – I know that what I'll get from my aunt is a pair of socks that will go straight to the Oxfam shop – but as a way of expressing my relationship to them. The point underlies one significant source of boundaries to markets. If I care about something, then one way of expressing that care is by refusing to put a price on it. Thus the following from Herodotus' histories:

> When Darius was king of the Persian empire, he summoned the Greeks who were at his court and asked them how much money it would take for them to eat the corpses of their fathers. They responded they would not do it for any price. Afterwards, Darius summoned some Indians called Kallatiai who do eat their parents and asked in the presence of the Greeks … for what price they would agree to cremate their dead fathers. They cried out loudly and told him to keep still.[63]

Narrative accounts of rational choice of the kind outlined in chapter 3 are likewise compatible with incommensurability. Narrative theories of rational choice argue that choice in human lives, both individual and social, are a matter of deciding not simply some maximisation of valued items, but of how the story of a life of a person or community should continue. This is also true of narrative theories of rational choice of the kind I outlined in chapter 3 that argue that choice in human lives, both individual and social, is a matter of deciding not simply some maximisation of valued items, but of how the story of a life should continue.[64]

However, at the end of comparisons constrained by non-substantive features of rational choice, it is possible that one might simply have a variety of options, each with their own bundle of goods, each coherent and making sense, and with no ordering between them. Say, for example, someone has a version of the old choice between a life of contemplation and a life of action. They are deciding say between going to university and realising their not insignificant mathematical abilities or signing with a major club and developing their considerable football talents. Now there are a series of comparisons that might be made here, but in the end there may simply be no 'best' choice. They are simply different realisations of a good life. Each sacrifices goods and one may regret, with good reason, the losses one makes. One is not indifferent between them in the sense that it matters a lot which is chosen and a person is likely to agonise. But in the end one cannot order them.

A distinction needs to be drawn between the possibility of complete and partial resolution. By complete resolution I mean situations in which, through judgement in a particular context, we can arrive at a unique best choice. By a partial resolution I mean a resolution that arrives not at a unique answer, but a set of admissible solutions which themselves are not ordered. Often admissibility is all that is possible and this is one source of the possibility of plurality in good lives that can be chosen. This is true also of social goods. This plurality of admissible solutions can be constrained but not eliminated by procedural expressive and narrative accounts of rational choice. There are different lives that adequately express different bundles of goods, that have narrative coherence and that have survived full deliberative reflection.

None of this need be a source of worry about practical reason. It rather reiterates Neurath's point: 'Rationalism sees its chief triumph in the clear recognition of the limits of actual insight.'[65] It points to a reasonableness about its limits in determining a specific outcome. Outcomes are underdetermined by reasons. This is true of theoretical reason and there is no reason that we should be more stringent in the case of practical reason.[66] Moreover it gives the basis for a defence of cultural pluralism from within a perfectionist ethical and political theory. Given a plurality of intrinsic goods, it is possible (as I noted in chapter 2) to have different life plans, ways of life and cultures that arrive at quite different bundles of goods which are still coherent, admissible and admirable.

All this said, in virtue of the grip of the assumption that practical rationality requires commensurability, insufficient attention has been given to the issue of rational choice in the absence of commensurability. The recognition of value-incommensurability entails a need to rethink the ways we make decisions without a single measure.[67]

10

EPISTEMOLOGICAL ARGUMENTS
FOR THE MARKET

10.1 The epistemic argument

In the last chapter I noted that there was not one socialist calculation debate but many, and as far as the opening part of the debate on commensurability is concerned, parties to the dispute crossed political boundaries. Mises and Lange stand opposed to Neurath and Hayek. Hayek's criticism of the possibility of socialism turns not on issues of commensurability but rather of epistemology. The epistemological argument against socialism and in defence of market economies concern problems of human ignorance. The argument runs that there are necessary limitations to the knowledge that any particular individual or subset of individuals in society can possess. Hence, there are limitations to the knowledge at the disposal of any central planning board in a planned economy. In contrast to these limitations of centralised planned economies, the market overcomes the problems of human ignorance. The market is presented as a self-regulating economic homeostat, providing the informational feedback between economic actors necessary for the mutual adjustment of their activities. The market may not be perfect, but it is the most efficient communicative device we could have to enable production and consumption to grow and contract in the appropriate places.

What are the sources of human ignorance to which this argument appeals? The first is what Hayek calls 'the division of knowledge' in society – that is, the dispersal of knowledge and skills throughout different individuals in society.[1] Now this division as such places only contingent barriers on the communication of knowledge which could in principle be overcome. Thus, for example, the project of unifying the sciences which was central to Neurath's later work had as its defensible kernel the aim of orchestrating the knowledge contained in different sciences.[2] The intent of the project was the realisation of the coordination of different disciplines. The objective was an encyclopedia in which all the different sciences would be coordinated and incompatibilities addressed, a project that represents a modern form of the enlightenment's encyclopedic ambitions. The problem that it addresses is the way that questions and decisions about particular states of affairs draw on different sciences. This problem is central to any possibility of social planning which calls on a variety of forms of knowledge.

Hayek's point about the division of knowledge does not rely, however, simply on contingent limits that might be overcome by a complete orchestration of science. Rather it concerns the nature of knowledge that is dispersed. Not all knowledge can be articulated in encyclopedic form; even given a unified body of articulated knowledge, there is no reason to suppose that it can deliver 'authoritative' judgements on any particular case. Some knowledge is practical knowledge embodied in skills and know-how that cannot be articulated in propositional form. Some knowledge is knowledge of particulars, local to time and place and cannot as such be stated in universal statements. Even given articulated scientific knowledge the gap between the universal principles of science and the particular context in which they have to be implemented remains to be bridged.

The claims that not all knowledge can be articulated in propositional form and that much of it is about particulars localised to a specific time and place form the central assumptions in Hayek's epistemic case against central planning. While Hayek frames the argument in terms of the division of knowledge in society, the key to his argument is the dispersal through society of that local knowledge that cannot be articulated or vocalised and hence necessarily could not form an item that could be passed on to a central planning body. There will be knowledge dispersed throughout society of which any particular individual or subset of individuals will be ignorant.

A second source of radical ignorance is the unpredictability of human needs and wants. This is in part a consequence of the fact that an individual's needs and wants often cannot be articulated. However, it also has another basis. Needs and wants change with the invention and production of new objects for consumption. To quote a version of this point from a writer who is not an economic liberal:

> Production not only provides the material to satisfy a need, but it also provides the need for the material ... The need felt for the object is induced by the perception of the object. An objet d'art creates a public that has artistic tastes and is able to enjoy beauty – and the same can be said of any other product.[3]

If one also accepts Popper's claim that the progress of human knowledge is in principle unpredictable – if we could predict future knowledge, we would already have it – then it follows that since human invention relies on the progress of knowledge, and wants and needs are created by human invention, then human wants and needs are also in principle unpredictable. Hence at any point in time, we are ignorant about the full range of future human needs and wants. The market it is claimed is a discovery procedure in which different hypotheses about the future are embodied in entrepreneurial acts and tested in the market place.[4]

More recently some Austrians have given a 'radical subjectivist' twist to this latter claim. The argument goes that it is not just that the future is unknowable, but that the future itself depends upon current choices. The market is thus not a discovery procedure but a creative process through which the future is made.[5]

Since the future depends on current choice, there is now strictly speaking nothing to know. Thus Wiseman writes: 'The essence of the radical subjectivist position is that the future is not simply "unknown", but is "nonexistent" or "indeterminate" at the point of decision'.[6] The point is in fact a variant of a position in an old argument that goes back to Aristotle[7] about the relation of future states to current choices reapplied to the market context. Aristotle's general, contemplating the possible sea battle the following day, is replaced by an economic entrepreneur contemplating the possible success of a business project. Thus to restate the radical subjectivist position in traditional logical terms, suppose an entrepreneur E is considering whether to launch a new product P. E judges that if over n consumers buy P at £m then the product will be worth launching. E has to judge now at t_0 the truth or falsity of the claim 'over n consumers buy P at £m at t_1'. Now on the older epistemic version of the Austrian position this is just a matter of the limits of foreknowledge. At this point in time t_0, the claim 'over n consumers buy P at £m at t_1' is either true or false – it has a definite truth value. In logical terms, the principle of bivalence, that every statement has a determinate truth value, i.e. for any assertion, P, it is either true that P or false that P, holds for assertions about future states of affairs. Our problem is that in principle we cannot know what that truth value is. The radical subjectivist basically denies this. The problem is not just one of limits to foreknowledge, but the dependence of future states on current choices. In logical terms, the principle of bivalence does not hold for assertions about future states of affairs. Currently at t_0 the statement, prior to the choices of the entrepreneur, E, and his competitors and the choices of consumers which will together determine whether it becomes true, the statement 'over n consumers buy P at £m at t_1' has no determinate truth value. It is not the case that it is either true or false. To say this is to deny bivalence not the law of the excluded middle, 'P or not P': 'either over n consumers buy P at £m at t_1 or it is not the case that over n consumers buy P at £m at t_1'. Now at point t_0, one might say the claim 'over n consumers buy P at £m at t_1' is either-true-or-false, but not yet either true or false.[8] A few brief comments on this position. First, to call it a radical subjectivist position is historically an oddity, and is due to the somewhat inflated status the notion of 'subjectivity' has in Austrian circles. It is not 'radical', it has been around for two millennia, and it need not be 'subjectivist' – the point is about the relation of current choices to future states and the status of the principle of bivalence and can be stated without reference to the notion of subjectivity at all. It was thus stated in the traditional discussions from Aristotle through to the scholastics. Second, the point is ultimately a metaphysical one. This is not to denigrate it. I think there is good metaphysics and I am open to being persuaded that one should reject bivalence for claims about future states.[9] However, it does not have, as far as I can see, any implications for economic theory that could not be stated by someone who accepted the principle of bivalence together with the Popperian claim that future states are in principle unknowable. In so far as specific claims in economics goes it is an argument about preferred modes of speech. None of the argument that follows is affected one way or another by it.

131

The epistemic arguments developed by Hayek and later Austrians issue in two conclusions that need to be kept distinct: a negative conclusion that a centrally planned economy is unable to solve the problems of ignorance; and a positive conclusion that the free market does. I will not dispute here the negative conclusion.[10] However, the negative conclusion does not entail that the positive argument for the market is sound. It is this positive conclusion that I will criticise in this and the next chapter. The positive conclusion depends upon two claims. The first is that the market does distribute that information necessary for the coordination of actors' plans while allowing them to exploit their local and practical knowledge. This claim fails to acknowledge the ways in which the market itself is a source of ignorance and discoordination. These I outline in this chapter.

That criticism still leaves open, however, the weaker claim that the market is the only feasible alternative to centralised planning. This claim depends upon the second of the two claims underpinning the epistemic argument, namely that there exist only two ways of distributing information in society – either through a decentralised market mechanism or through a centralised planning agency. The strength of the epistemological argument for the market depends in part on the implausibility of assuming that all knowledge could be centralised upon some particular planning agency. The argument ignores, however, the existence of the decentralised but predominantly non-market institutions for the distribution of knowledge. This I criticise in the last section of this chapter and in the next. The implicit assumption that only the market can coordinate dispersed non-vocalisable knowledge is false. Even the centralised firm of existing society must make use of local knowledge that is distributed within the institution. Indeed Hayek's positive argument against centralised planning is one that has been articulated within the history of socialist planning as an argument for democratic and decentralised decision making and for a proper appreciation of the limits of scientific expertise. Hayek himself was not blind to the existence of a variety of non-market institutions that embodied and distributed knowledge. Their existence is recognised, especially in the work of the later Hayek,[11] where the more conservative components of his thought come to the fore and stress is placed on the ways in which knowledge is embodied in traditions and institutional arrangements that are not entirely transparent to rational reflection. However, as I show in the last section of this chapter, there is an unresolved conflict between this conservative component of his thought and the liberalism that pervades his defence of the market and is apparent more specifically in the tension between the account of the market as a mode of coordination and the kinds of practical knowledge it is taken to coordinate.

10.2 Information, price and the division of knowledge

Hayek's epistemic defence of the market starts from the observation that economic problems in part stem from the division of knowledge in society: 'There is

... a problem of the division of knowledge which is quite analogous to, and as least as important as, the problem of the division of labour.'[12] The problem is that of communicating between independent economic actors information dispersed amongst them that is relevant to the coordination of their actions. One needs a mechanism which will 'convey to each agent the information he must possess in order to effectively adjust his decisions to those of others.'[13]

The price mechanism is presented by Hayek as a solution to this problem of the division of knowledge in society. By serving as a numerical index of changes in the relation between the supply and demand for goods, it communicates between independent actors the information that is relevant to the coordination of their economic activities. And, Hayek claims, information of such changes is all that is relevant to actors for them to be able to adjust their activities appropriately.

His claim is illustrated nicely by the following example. Assume a new use of tin is discovered or a source of tin is eliminated: tin becomes more scarce, supply falls relative to existing demand, and the price of tin rises. Hayek argues that this change in price provides all the information about the change in the supply of tin that is relevant to enable actors to suitably adjust their plans. Consumers do not, for example, need to know why the tin has become more scarce. All they need to know is that

> some of the tin they used to consume is now more profitably employed elsewhere and that, in consequence, they must economise tin. There is no need for the great majority of them to even know where the more urgent need has arisen, or in favour of what other needs they ought to husband supply. If only some of them know directly of the new demand, and switch resources over to it, and if the people that are aware of the new gap thus created in turn fill it from still other sources, the effect will rapidly spread throughout the whole economic system and influence not only all the uses of tin but also its substitutes and the substitute of these substitutes, the supply of all things made of tin, and their substitutes and so on; and all this without the great majority of those instrumental in bringing about these substitutions knowing anything about the original causes of these changes. The whole acts as one market, not because any of its members survey the whole field, but because their limited individual fields overlap so that through many intermediaries the relevant information is communicated to all.[14]

The price system in communicating all relevant information acts 'to coordinate the separate actions of different people.'[15] The effect of the mechanism is that the whole of society acts in the way it would have acted, had it been consciously directed by a single mind possessing all the information dispersed throughout the economy. A planned economy is less efficient because no actual mind could possess such information: it effectively reduces the amount of information available in society. However, the market already acts in the way that defenders of a consciously planned economy believe it would act, if it could be directed by a single suitably informed body.

It must be granted that Hayek's account of the market is not without foundation. The market clearly does communicate information to independent economic actors about changes in the relative scarcity of different resources, and consumers and producers do respond to these changes by altering planned production and consumption.[16] The question to be asked is: does the information so communicated in fact lead to the coordination of the activities of independent actors? There are two aspects to this question:

1   Does the price mechanism communicate all the information that is relevant for the coordination of actions?
2   Is the communication of relevant information all that is necessary for the coordination of actions?

I will argue that the answer to both of these questions is no. Hayek is mistaken in his assertion that the price mechanism provides all the information that is relevant to the coordination of the actions of economic actors.[17] And the assumption in his arguments that the communication of relevant information is all that is required to achieve coordination is likewise false.

10.3 Markets, socialism and information

In any competitive market system there is a disincentive to communicate information between actors who are in competition. Put simply, if producers A and B are in competition, and A informs B of his or her activities and B does not reciprocate, then B is in a position to adjust his or her behaviour in order to compete more effectively than A. In this situation, standard game theory applies. While cooperation through mutual communication might be beneficial to both parties, if one cooperates and the other does not, the non-cooperating party benefits. Given that both parties are self-interested, the rational strategy is to act noncooperatively. Non-communication is a competitively stable strategy.[18]

However, the existence of this general disincentive to communicate information does not itself imply a problem of coordination. One must show that the information that the market fails to communicate is information that is relevant to the coordination of actions. The question is more specific: does the market fail to communicate information that is relevant to the coordination of the plans and activities of independent actors? There are at least two kinds of information that competitors will attempt to keep from being communicated: (1) technical and scientific information, and (2) information of their plans. It is the second of these that is most clearly relevant to the problems of coordination. It is information that actors need to coordinate their actions. I discuss the problems of failure of the first kind in the next chapter.

When actors at some point in time make plans concerning future production, they are planning not with respect of demand at the present moment t_0, but with respect to expected demand at some future moment t_1 when their products reach the market. The information the price mechanism provides is that of the relation of supply and demand at t_0.[19] While this information is relevant to the actors' plans, it is not all the information that is relevant in order that actors' plans are coordinated with those of other actors. The information that is relevant is that which will enable the actor to predict demand at t_1. A major component of the information required for such a prediction is that of the plans of other producers which respond to that demand. This is information that the market, as a competitive system, fails to distribute.

This informational restriction is a source of economic failure in the market and is at the basis of Marx's analysis of why the market is subject to booms and slumps.[20] The argument runs roughly as follows: where there is an increase in demand against supply for some good at t_0, producers and consumers respond by increasing production and decreasing consumption. Each responds to the same signal the change in price. However, each agent acts independently of the response of other producers and consumers. The result is that, at t_1, when the plans of different actors are realised, there is an overproduction of goods in relation to effective demand for them. Goods cannot be sold. There is a realisation crisis: producers cannot realise the value of their products. Given this overproduction, demand falls against supply. There is a slump. This eventually leads to a rise in demand against supply, production expands leading to another boom, and so on. It should be noted here that the problem is not one of economic agents making a number of unrelated mistakes in the prediction of future demand. Rather, it is that the market imparts the same information to affected agents, and this information is such that the rational strategy for each agent is to expand production or contract consumption, while it is not rational for all agents to act in this manner collectively.[21] In a competitive economy, the simultaneous distribution of information about supply and demand at t_0 and the suppression of the mutual exchange of information concerning planned responses leads to over production.

Hayek is aware of this problem, and his response lies at the heart of his own account of the business cycle. Hayek argues that information about the planned responses of producers in competition is indirectly distributed by changes in interest rates: the planned increase in production by separate producers is reflected in an increased demand for credit, and hence a rise in interest rates this lowers anticipated profits and dampens the expansion.[22] The credit system, if it is working satisfactorily, will communicate the relevant information. This is one of the reasons why Hayek holds that the explanation of the business cycle must lie in features of the credit system which result in its failure to perform this function. However, this argument is flawed. It is not clear that the relevant information is communicated by changes in interest rates. The problem with Hayek's analysis is this. The information about which a producer needs to be informed if over-expansion in the production of some good is to be avoided is not the general level of demand for credit, but the level of demand amongst competitors. However, interest rates reflect the general aggregate demand for credit in an economy, not the relative demands in different industries. An increase in the planned production of some good by a group of competitors will be reflected in a proportional change in interest rates only if the change in demand for credit by that group is identical with that found in the whole economy, i.e. if rates of change in the demand for credit are even throughout an economy. However, there is no reason to suppose such an assumption is true, given the different production cycles of different industries. Assuming uneven changes in the demand for credit, it is quite possible for overproduction to occur even if the credit system is working 'satisfactorily'. The credit system does not communicate the relevant information. For this reason, it is not the case that we must look to a departure from an ideal credit system to explain the business cycle.

These local booms and slumps in production of the kind outlined are then amplified into general crises precisely through the interconnections in the market that Hayek highlights in his example of the production and consumption of tin. The demand by industrial producers for goods such as machinery or raw materials such as tin are at any point in time based on their expectations concerning demand for their products at some future point in time t_1. To the extent that these are mistaken (for reasons concerning constraints on information flow noted) the price mechanism succeeds in communicating, not information to the producers of primary goods for industrial production, but misinformation. The effects of the failure in coordination in one area are thereby distributed throughout the system. A localised slump becomes a generalised crisis, paradoxically just because the market does connect producers in the way that Hayek highlights. Indeed, Hayek exploits this feature of his model of the market in his own account of the business cycle, according to which manufacturers over-expand in response to misinformation distributed by the price mechanism where this results in over-investment in capital goods.[23]

This analysis of the problems that follow from the competitive nature of the market is also of relevance to the second question concerning Hayek's position raised at the end of the last section. In Hayek's defence of the market, there is an assumption that the communication of relevant information in the market is all that is necessary for the achievement of coordination. He treats the solution of the problem of information distribution as *ipso facto* a solution to the problem of coordination. The two are, however, distinct. The possession of information about the plans and actions of others does not of itself enable one to act so that one's actions are coordinated with those of others. For example, producers possessing information that the demand for the goods they produce is falling relative to supply are not in a position thereby to ensure that their actions are coordinated with those of consumers and other producers. The problem is not simply that of the lack of relevant information noted above. Even given this information, the problem of coordination is not thereby solved. Where plans are inappropriately coordinated, a mechanism is required to adjust those plans. For example, knowledge that (given planned consumption and production of some good) production will exceed demand is of no use to a producer who aims to achieve coordination. Even given mutual knowledge of projected discoordination, no adjustment by any particular actor of his or her own actions will necessarily lead to coordination. There must be some mechanism whereby producers can mutually adjust plans in order that activities be coordinated.

The market, as a competitive order, has no such mechanism for mutual adjustment, for the same reason that it blocks the movement of information. While mutual adjustment might benefit all parties, if one or more cooperates while another does not, *ceteris paribus*, the non-cooperating party will benefit. Given that all parties are self-interested, the competitively stable strategy is non-cooperation: the market inhibits the mutual adjustment of plans. Eventual adjustments of actions are achieved in the market rather via sudden dislocations in economic life, in which overproduction of certain goods leads to the disappearance of certain competing producers, underproduction to an uncontrolled and excessive movement of productive resources to supply demand.

A broadly Marxian analysis of the problems of the market can, then, be reformulated in terms of a criticism of Hayek's defence of the market. The reformulation has the virtue of moving the argument away from the traditional misconceived and sterile version of the critique that focuses on the distinction between *ex post* and *ex ante* economic coordination. On this traditional story the market is taken to be subject to crises because it always blindly responds to demand, allocating resources *ex post*. Within socialism, the problem of economic crises is solved by replacing *ex post* regulation with planned regulation of resources *ex ante*; production is able to anticipate demand rather than anarchically respond to it.[24] Thus presented, the analysis is clearly untenable. On the one hand, the idea that one could rely completely on *ex ante* economic regulation, that one could plan production in such a way that future demand is always anticipated, has plausibility only in the context of a static and simple economy. In the context of a complex, changing economy, there exists necessary uncertainty about future demands and resources which I outlined at the start of this chapter. Hence one needs some *ex post* economic regulator, some feedback mechanism, which will allow the adjustment of plans in the light of unforeseen economic changes.[25] On the other hand, it is a myth that in a market economy actors merely respond, *ex post*, to economic changes. Within a free market, a firm will constantly plan its production to anticipate and shape future demand. The market economy is not an economy without plans.[26] The problems outlined in this section are quite independent of the *ex post* against *ex ante* distinction. It is rather that information that is relevant to economic actors, in order that they be able to coordinate their activities, is not communicated, and that no mechanism exists to achieve the mutual adjustment of plans.

The market in virtue of its competitive nature blocks the communication of information and fails to coordinate plans for economic action. That feature of the market is specific to the market as a system of independent producers in competition with one another for the sale of goods. It is not a consequence of complexity or change. If the problems we have outlined are to be avoided, economic life must be organised in such a way that separate producers are able to inform each other of their plans and act in order that their activities be coordinated. The solution lies in a cooperative economy with some mechanism for distributing information that is relevant in order to coordinate plans, and a mechanism for mutual adjustment of plans given this information. It requires a mechanism that does the job that Hayek falsely claims the price mechanism performs. To say this is not, however, an argument for a market economy of cooperatives. These problems of cooperation that arise in market economies are not solved by transforming privately owned enterprises into workers' cooperatives. Cooperation within enterprises does not entail and, in the context of a market economy, would not result in cooperation between enterprises. The coordination problems of the market are neither properly acknowledged nor solved by recent theories of market socialism.

10.4 Markets, calculation and local knowledge

In the last two sections of this chapter I have argued that the market fails to distribute that knowledge which is necessary for the coordination of plans of different actors. In this final section I turn to another and in many ways deeper conflict within Hayek's own epistemic defence of the market between the market as a mode of coordination and the kinds of knowledge it is taken to coordinate. At the heart of Hayek's argument is the significance of knowledge that is particular and practical in form as against that which is universal and codifiable. In later Austrian writing this part of Hayek's analysis has focused upon the entrepreneur. When recent Austrian economics refers to the local and particular knowledge that is dispersed throughout the economy this has tended to be identified with that of the entrepreneur. To some extent this focus is to be expected given the relationship between coordination and knowledge in Hayek's argument. Thus consider again the tin example that Hayek employs. There is a new demand for tin and the information spreads thus:

> If only some of them know directly of the new demand, and switch re-
> sources over to it, and *if the people that are aware of the new gap* thus
> created in turn fill it from still other sources, the effect will rapidly spread
> throughout the whole economic system ... The whole acts as one mar-
> ket, not because any of its members survey the whole field, but because
> their limited individual fields overlap so that through many intermediar-
> ies the relevant information is communicated to all.[27]

The emphasis is added to bring out the role in Hayek's argument of agents who are aware of new gaps that emerge. Without such agents, no communication. Later Austrian economics has to a considerable degree been concerned to elaborate more explicitly the role of these agents identified as entrepreneurs who are alert to opportunities that emerge. In particular, the work of Kirzner has attempted to develop the account of the entrepreneur that was pioneered within Austrian economics by Mises.[28] The knowledge of the entrepreneur is local. The entrepreneur on this account is an agent who is aware of particular changes, of changes that occur here at this place and time at which new opportunities emerge. Such knowledge necessarily cannot be universal, abstracted from particular locations and times. However, this emphasis on the entrepreneur has meant that a whole dimension of Hayek's position has been lost to view.

When Hayek claimed that the market allowed actors to coordinate their different plans, a central part of the argument was that it does so in a way that allows individuals to use their local and practical knowledge to the full. In contrast, centralised planning cannot realise coordination without the loss of such knowledge. Defenders of a planned economy are taken to exhibit a commitment to a Cartesian rationalism that is blind to the existence of practical and local knowledge: all knowledge is treated by the rationalist as abstract technical knowledge, that can be articulated in propositional form that could in principle be employed by a single planning agency. The market it is claimed avoids that failure. Now to say this is to include not just the coordinating function of the entrepreneur looking for the particular market gaps, but also the local and practical knowledge of producers, of conditions specific to a place and time, of its soils and resources, knowledge that is contained not in the minds of individuals, but in habits and procedures and in institutional arrangements in which they engage. When one looks, for example, at the great agricultural failures of centrally planned economies it is the failure to accommodate such knowledge that is clearly exhibited.

However, thus stated there should be something unsettling for the Austrians about the ways in which markets operate in practice, for far from fostering the existence of practical and local knowledge, they often appear to do the opposite. The growth of global markets is associated with the disappearance of knowledge that is local and practical, and the growth of abstract codifiable information. Hence, there is then something at the least paradoxical about Hayek's epistemic defence of the market, for the market as a mode of coordination appears to foster forms of abstract codifiable knowledge at the expense of knowledge that is local and practical. The claim that the market allows the full use of particular knowledge is not empirically confirmed.

Some of the reasons for this that have to do with features of market economies that tend to be missed in the abstract models of catallaxy that Hayek presents. There is the significance of the power of different actors in the market. The knowledge of weak and marginal actors in markets, such as peasant and indigenous populations, tends to be lost to those who hold market power. The epistemic value of knowledge claims bears no direct relation to their market value. As Martinez-Alier notes:

> Indigenous groups have accumulated an enormous body of knowledge about biological biodiversity and peasant farmers have been selecting and improving seeds for a long time. This knowledge of natural biological

diversity and the conservation of agricultural diversity *in situ* has almost never been valued in economic terms.[29]

Local and often unarticulated knowledge of soil conditions and crop varieties that have considerable value for the long-term sustainability of agriculture has no value in markets and hence is always liable to loss when it comes into contact with oil-based agricultural technologies of those who do have market power. The tendency away from practical knowledge in markets also has a basis in the global nature of both markets and large corporate actors who require knowledge that is transferable across different cultures and contexts and hence abstract and codifiable: 'quantification is well suited for communication that goes beyond the boundaries of locality and community'.[30]

However, there are also reasons for this tendency towards abstraction and codifiability that point to conflicts within the work of both Hayek and the Austrian tradition more generally. Two are of particular significance. First is the conflict between the extreme mutability of market economies and the nature of practical knowledge. As Oakeshott notes, it is the characteristic of such knowledge that it is embodied not in propositions but 'in a customary or traditional way of doing things, or, simply, in practice'.[31] This is not to say that it is unchanging, and not open to improvement. However, it is of the nature of such knowledge that it is difficult to sustain in those conditions of constant change that the market produces and Hayek celebrates under the slogan of 'change for change's sake'. The point is an expression in Hayek's economics of the same conflict that Kukathas has found in his ethical and political theory between the conservative anti-rationalist and liberal rationalist components of his thought.[32] Hayek's defence of practical knowledge belongs to the conservative component of his thought that has much in common with the work of Oakeshott. It runs through his scepticism about the scope of reason, and his accounts of the ways in which values and knowledge are embodied within institutional arrangements which are not entirely transparent to rational reflection. That thread in his thought runs counter to the explicit anti-conservative and liberal component of his thought which, against the conservative disposition which is concerned to preserve the conditions for knowledge embodied in practice, is 'prepared to let change to take its course',[33] and which indeed celebrates the existence of purposeless change as such.[34] The second liberal component of Hayek's argument is strongly rationalist and is inconsistent with the first. It exalts conditions of existence which are not compatible with the sustenance of practical knowledge, and it is not surprising that where markets meet traditional societies, the local indigenous knowledge they carry is undermined.[35]

The second and related conflict is one that runs through Austrian economics and which has been touched upon in the last chapter. The demand for commensurability and calculability that lies at the basis of the first chapter of the socialist calculation debate runs against the defence of local and practical knowledge that is the premise of the second. This is not just a theoretical problem but one with real institutional embodiments. The market encourages a spirit of calculability – of rationalisation in Weber's sense. That spirit is the starting point for Mises' account of practical reason which requires explicit common measures for rational choice and fails to acknowledge the existence of choice founded upon practical judgement. More generally it is not amicable to forms of knowledge that are practical, local and uncodifiable. The point is stated with clarity by Schumpeter:

> [C]apitalism develops rationality and adds a new edge to it ... [I]t exalts the monetary unit – not itself a creation of capitalism – into a unit of account. That is to say, capitalist practice turns the unit of money into a tool of rational cost-profit calculations, of which the towering monument is the double-entry bookkeeping ... And thus defined and quantified for the economic sector, this type of logic or attitude or method then starts upon its conqueror's career subjugating – rationalizing – man's tools and philosophies, his medical practice, his picture of the cosmos, his outlook on life, everything in fact including his concepts of beauty and justice and his spiritual ambitions.[36]

A conception of practical rationality that requires commensurability and hence forms of knowledge that can be treated in a quantifiable fashion is incompatible with the forms of practical knowledge and judgement that Hayek claims the market allows individuals to employ. The realm of technical knowledge is identified with knowledge. The Cartesian rationalism that Hayek criticises has its roots in the market institutions he defends. Here as Weber and Schumpeter note, the differences between modern centralised bureaucratic economies and free-market economies are less notable than the similarities. A spirit of technical rationalism pervades both. Both demand a kind of explicit codifiable knowledge that is open to quantification and can reduce choices to choices employing a single unit of comparison. Again the 'conservative' premises of Hayek's argument are in deep tension with his defence of a market order. The forms of uncodified practical knowledge he believes to be so significant are not fostered as he suggests by a market order. Hence the paradoxical but in the end unsurprising fact that where markets enter into associational spheres there is a tendency to an audit culture that is similar to that of centralised planned economies.[37]

It is notable in this regard the extent to which the shift towards the rationalisation of the firm within capitalist economies is left largely without comment by Austrians. For within the firm the move towards scientific management of the workplace represented by Taylorism earlier in the twentieth century is precisely an attempt to eliminate practical knowledge:

> the development of a science ... involves the establishment of many rules, laws and formulae which replace the judgement of the individual workman ... The workman is told minutely what he is to do and how he is to

do it; any improvement which he makes upon the orders given to him is fatal to success.

The task of scientific management is that of 'gathering together all the traditional knowledge which in the past had been possessed by the workman and then classifying, tabulating and reducing the knowledge to rules, laws and formulae'.[38] The task is clearly impossible and open to the same objection as that which Hayek raises against the possibility of a planned economy. Indeed, the epistemological problems that Hayek raised against centralised planned economies have been echoed within the socialist tradition as a problem within the capitalist firm. Within non-Fabian and non-Bolshevik traditions of socialist thought it often becomes the central point of criticism. Thus, for example, for Cardan it defines the central conflict within modern capitalism:

> The capitalist system can only maintain itself by trying to reduce workers into mere order-takers ... into executants of decisions taken elsewhere. At the same time the system can only function as long as this reduction is never achieved.[39]

While this may not be the 'fundamental contradiction of capitalism' as Cardan claims, it does point to a real conflict within the firm that parallels that which Hayek makes about any centralised economy.

Cardan's comments also point to the ways in which the arguments that are taken to define the socialist calculation debate cross the traditional boundaries. Hayek's epistemic criticism of centrally planned economies have long had their counterpart within the history of debates about socialist planning as an argument for democratic and decentralised decision making and for a proper appreciation of the limits of abstract technical expertise. Cardan represents the end of a long tradition of associational socialism that had argued against the possibility of an economy centralised on Fabian or Bolshevik lines.[40] And just as Hayek's epistemic arguments represents a conservative component in his thought so also this tradition as far as political epistemology is concerned shares much with conservative thought, although neither may be happy to acknowledge the connection. At the level of political epistemology Oakeshottian conservatism properly points to the existence of practically and institutionally embodied knowledge: the technical rationalism embodied in both the market economy and the centralised planned economy entail that neither fosters such forms of knowledge, although both rely on their existence. The problems of political epistemology that Hayek raises from conservative premises are general ones of combining general coordination in the use of resources with the scope for the employment of dispersed knowledge. The mistake in Hayek's argument lies in his failure to note the existence of associations and institutions intermediate between state and market that themselves contribute to coordination. In the next chapter I pursue this point in more detail.

11

PROPERTY IN SCIENCE AND THE MARKET

11.1 Epistemology, science and commerce

In the last chapter I outlined the central epistemological argument for the free-market: the free-market solves and a centrally planned economy fails to solve problems of ignorance. The price system resolves problems arising from the social division of knowledge by communicating between different actors that knowledge which is relevant to the coordination of their actions while allowing them to use their own local knowledge. At the same time it acts as a discovery procedure for uncovering what such future needs and wants will be. Just as conjectures about the physical world are tested and falsified by experiments, so conjectures about future human needs and wants are tested and falsified by competition in the market place. Businesses are the practical embodiment of economic conjectures and competition between businesses in the market parallels competition between conjectures in the sciences.

In the last chapter I began to develop two critical points one might make of this defence of the market. The first concerns the assumption at the base of the argument that there exist only two ways of distributing information in society – either through a decentralised market mechanism or through a centralised planning agency. The strength of the epistemological argument for the market depends in part on the implausibility of assuming that all knowledge could be centralised upon some particular planning agency. The argument ignores, however, the existence of the decentralised but predominantly non-market institutions for the distribution of knowledge and information. This chapter focuses in detail on one such non-market domain: the institutions of the scientific community.

The second critical point which is particularly relevant in this regard is that the epistemological defence of the market tends to ignore the way in which the market itself is a source of the problem of ignorance rather than a solution to it. In a competitive market system, there is a disincentive to communicate information between actors who are in competition. If producers A and B are in competition, and A informs B of his or her activities and B does not reciprocate, then B is in a position to adjust his or her behaviour in order to compete more effectively than A. In this situation, standard game theory applies. While cooperation through mutual communication might be beneficial to both parties, if one cooperates and the other does not, the non-cooperating party benefits. Given that both parties are self-interested, the rational strategy is to act non-cooperatively. Non-communication is a competitively stable strategy. In the last chapter I examined the ways this can lead to a failure of coordination between actors. However, it can also lead to the failure to circulate other information that is relevant to general human welfare. One sphere in which such non-communication between competitors is prevalent in the market is that of scientific and technical knowledge. Competitors in the market, as rational actors, keep novel scientific and technical work non-public. A feature of the market is the existence of an incentive to secrecy and confidentiality in technical information.

This feature of the market leads to major conflicts where the market meets other systems of information distribution – notably, that associated with the scientific and academic communities. The increasing encroachment of market relations into the scientific community has led to a conflict between the 'proprietary secrecy' of the market and the 'open communication' of traditional science. Thus as Nelkin notes:

> Conflicts of interest are ... bound to arise in situations in which university faculty are directly involved in commercial ventures. The academic responsibility of open communication inevitably conflicts with the commercial responsibility to maintain proprietary secrecy.[1]

While the possible conflicts between the norms of science and those of the market are not new,[2] they have become increasingly significant with the increased commercialisation of scientific activity, for example in the spheres of bio-technology and pharmacy. Hence the current political and ethical controversies concerning the attempts to extend patents to new life forms. The details about how such conflicts are being fought out are to be found elsewhere, and I will not discuss them here.[3] I focus rather on the following normative questions: what is wrong, if anything, with the employment of market mechanisms in the scientific sphere? To what extent, if at all, should the market play a role in the activities of scientific research and the distribution of the results of such research? I will approach these questions by focusing on the differences and possible conflicts between the kind of property system presupposed by the market and that found in science.

In section 11.2, I undertake some necessary preliminary clarification of different senses in which one can talk of 'intellectual property' – the sense in which this is presupposed in the context of the market, and the sense in which it is presupposed in modern professional science. In doing so, I point out some of the confusions in the literature on science studies that arise from mixing these different senses of 'intellectual property'. I will take as my starting point not current incursions of markets into science, but a dispute in the sixteenth century between Tartaglia and Cardano which highlights the differences and conflicts between these distinct systems of intellectual property in a particularly vivid way. This example, rather than an example chosen from modern conflicts, has the added advantages that it enables us to concentrate on the question of the appropriateness of market relations to science, and to avoid an added complexity that arises in the modern context, i.e. that scientists in commercial science are often employees, such that the property rights to the results of their research belong not to themselves but to the corporation that employs them. This feature of the modern situation adds a further dimension to the normative problems of the involvement of markets in science concerning an individual's alienation of rights to the fruits of his or her labour. This issue is an important one, but is not one I shall pursue here.[4] My sixteenth-century example lacks this added complication and allows us to focus on the issue of what, if anything, is inappropriate in the market as an institutional framework for science.[5] In sections 11.3 and 11.4, I turn to this central issue of the chapter – whether market mechanisms are appropriate in the scientific domain. In doing so I point to some problems in the analogies drawn by those influenced by Austrian economics between science and markets as 'discovery procedures'.

11.2 Two concepts of intellectual property

An understanding of the dispute between Tartaglia and Cardano requires an examination of the social and economic context of their work. Both mathematicians belonged to the tradition of cossist algebra predominant in Italy and Germany in the sixteenth century. This algebraic tradition was closely linked with the rise of mercantile capitalism and the new needs for improved techniques of computation this engendered. Thus textbooks produced in the cossist tradition employed predominantly mercantile examples and often also included detailed economic information alongside the mathematics. Moreover, mathematicians, like Tartaglia, earned an income from the employment of mathematical skills on behalf of merchants. In this context, publication of mathematical results often served as a form of advertisement for mathematical skills. Another important form of publicity came from competitions in which mathematicians would set each other problems, often with a side bet on the winner. Success in such competitions required novelty in algorithms for the solution of mathematical problems. The origins of the dispute between Tartaglia and Cardano lay in one such competition. Tartaglia had developed an algorithm for solving cubic equations, an algorithm which had been developed earlier by Ferro, who had kept the solution a secret to himself and a few students. One of these students, Fior, who had used the algorithm to win a series of mathematical competitions, challenged Tartaglia to a contest, and lost. On hearing of the contest, Cardano sought out Tartaglia and succeeded in getting the solution from him, although, according to Tartaglia at least, he was sworn to secrecy. However, on finding that the solution had been discovered by Ferro, Cardano published Tartaglia's solution in *Ars Magna*, citing Ferro and Tartaglia as independent inventors of the algorithm. Despite this citation, Cardano's publication produced a heated response from Tartaglia and a major dispute between Cardano and Tartaglia.[6]

This dispute is significant in that it reveals a contrast in the notions of 'intellectual property' between that predominant within the cossist tradition and that which has developed in science in the succeeding centuries. A comment by Mahoney on the dispute is to the point here:

> To the modern scholar imbued with the notion that, as R. K. Merton has put it, 'an idea is not really yours until you give it away' (i.e., through publication), Tartaglia's attitude seems strange. Yet, in sixteenth-century Italy, where mathematics was a competitive business among the cossists, the attitude is more than reasonable.[7]

Implicit in the dispute between Tartaglia and Cardano is a conflict between two different views of intellectual property.

The first view, illustrated by Tartaglia, Ferro, and others in the cossist tradition, is one associated with the market. Property here involves, as Macpherson puts it, 'an individual ... right to exclude others from the use or benefit of something',[8] and relatedly the rights of individuals to transfer some or all of these rights to other individuals. While these rights were not legally enforceable, there was clearly an assumption on the part of cossists like Tartaglia that they did involve ethical claims on others. Tartaglia's attitude to his algorithm was that it was, in a real sense, his and that he had a right to circumscribe the uses which Cardano made of it. More generally, it lay at the base of the secrecy that was prevalent in cossist algebra. Mathematics was, as Mahoney puts it, 'a competitive business'.

The second view of 'intellectual property' is the paradoxical Mertonian concept mentioned by Mahoney – 'an idea is not yours until you give it away'. Ravetz presents a similar characterisation of intellectual property in science: 'As a piece of property, the research report is a rather unusual object. The property comes into existence only by being made available for use by others'.[9]

On this Mertonian view, then, one makes a claim to intellectual property by making public an independently developed original result. A result that is unpublished is not recognised as 'yours'. Given this view of 'intellectual property,' what counts as 'publication' becomes of central importance – and significant for this is the growth of the scientific journal as a primary vehicle for publication, particularly in the early nineteenth century, and the kinds of editorial and peer-reviewing processes associated with it.[10] It is through publication in journal or book form that one lays a claim to property rights over a theory or result.

It might be objected here that there is something problematic in talk of property rights at all. When one talks of property, it normally implies rights to use, benefit from or alienate a thing – rights that have a legal, social, or ethical force. Given this conception of property, the publication of scientific results makes them public or common property: the benefit and use of the theory become the right of anyone within the limits of plagiarism and copyright. Einstein's theory

146

of relativity is not the property of any particular individual. It is common property.[11] Indeed, Merton also refers in this regard to the 'communism' of science:

> The substantive findings of science are a product of social collaboration and are assigned to the community. They constitute a common heritage in which the equity of the individual producer is severely limited. An eponymous law or theory does not enter into the exclusive possession of the discoverer and his heir, nor do the muses bestow upon him special rights of use and disposition.[12]

What sense, then, is there in talk of an individual claiming intellectual property through the act of publication? In a minimal sense, it might be noted that we use the possessive in referring to theories – Einstein's theory of relativity, Boyle's law of gases, and so on. However, this in itself cannot be said to be a basis for talk of property. We can also talk, for example, of Einstein's haircut, without thereby indicating any property relation. If talk of 'property' is to make sense, there must be some sense in which the producer of the theory gains certain rights or powers in virtue of the act of publication.

The rights which Merton and Ravetz are concerned with in their discussion of intellectual property are rights of recognition, most notably through citation and in some cases eponymy, and rights to the benefits that accrue from such recognition. Thus Merton continues the quotation above as follows:

> Property rights in science are whittled down to a bare minimum by the rationale of the scientific ethic. The scientist's claim to 'his' intellectual 'property' is limited to the recognition and esteem which, if the institution functions with a modicum of efficiency, is roughly commensurate with the significance of the increments brought to the common fund of knowledge.[13]

Ravetz stresses the benefits that accrue from such recognition:

> Yet this [intellectual] property is none the less real and important to those who possess it. As a verification of the scientist's accomplishment, it can bring immediate rewards. And as an implicit guarantee of the quality of his future work it brings in interest for some time after its publication.[14]

However, I remain unpersuaded that such talk of the rights to recognition and benefits which a producer attains through publication of a theory should be cashed out in terms of 'property rights' over the theory. It would seem more appropriate here to talk simply of publication making a theory common property, and refer merely to rights to recognition on the side of the producer.

The metaphor of the producer's 'intellectual property' is not in itself a problem, as long as it is clear what is being said. However, problems do arise when the reference to such property rights is developed in ways appropriate to its more normal use as 'private property.' Thus, for example, Ravetz appears to confuse the different senses in his later discussion of the nature of intellectual property in science. Thus he goes on to argue that citation in addition to other functions 'represents a payment for use of the material'.[15] The picture here is that of property in the sense in which it is involved within the market – in which an individual with exclusive rights to something alienates these property rights in exchange for certain payments from those to whom use of the theory is granted. Indeed, Ravetz even goes on to talk of imagining 'an ideal social contract' between producers and users of theories. The metaphor, however, is inappropriate. If one accepts the Mertonian model of intellectual property as resulting from the publication of a theory, an individual does not thereby alienate property rights to the theory; on the contrary, it is only through the act of publication that it is recognised as that individual's. Moreover, as a functional explanation of citation, Ravetz's 'payment model' is implausible: there is after all nothing to motivate the payments.

Similar problems arise for Hagstrom's view that academic publication is an instance of 'gift-giving'.[16] The concept of 'gift-giving', like that of market exchange, assumes a model of property as implying exclusive use of an object. The difference between market exchange and gift-giving is that property rights are alienated to others in the absence of any contractual expectations of repayment by others. There will, of course, be other kinds of expectation of reciprocal action, but failure of such repayment in the case of gifts represents not failure of contract but rather indicates that the social bond between giver and receiver is not in order – hence, concepts such as 'slight' become appropriate where reciprocal action is absent, which would not be at issue in a merely contractual relation. The problem with the property metaphor, then, is that it can result in importing into the sphere of public science concepts of property which are inappropriate. (At its worst the property metaphor lends spurious plausibility to market models of recognition in science that I criticised in chapter 8. As Ravetz properly notes 'intellectual property' in the form of recognition is usually desired as verification of accomplishment. The property metaphor when married with the market models of science can suggest the reverse, that the appearance of doing well is a mere means to property. I discuss this error further later in this and the next chapter.)

We have, then, two distinct possible concepts of property in science. First, a concept of property appropriate to the market – which indeed was found in cossist mathematics in early mercantile capitalism. Second, that which is found in professional science – in which theories are common property, but where the publication of theories by the producer issues in rights of recognition and the benefits of recognition. These two conceptions of property are incompatible in ways illustrated by the Tartaglia–Cardano dispute. As Merton again puts it: 'the communism of the scientific ethos is incompatible with definitions of technology as "private property" in a capitalist economy.'[17]

The problems discussed in this section concerning the use in the study of science of concepts of property appropriate to the market are theoretical: they lead to inadequate descriptive and explanatory models of scientific activity. In the next section, I turn to the normative question which is central to this chapter: what, if anything, is wrong with the employment of market mechanisms in science? Is there any reason to suppose that the kind of professional public science that has developed since the sixteenth century should be preferred to the kind of market mechanism that we find for example in the cossist tradition or, more recently, in research undertaken within private firms?

11.3 Knowledge as commodity

There are two kinds of objections that might be raised against the employment of market mechanisms in the 'knowledge industry'. First, there are those which claim that there are conditions an item must meet to be the sort of thing that can or ought to be a commodity, and that scientific theories and information do not meet these necessary conditions. Second, there are those which claim that the kind of property relations appropriate to the market necessarily conflict with good scientific practice. In this section, I critically examine the first set of objections and show that they fail. In section 11.4 I develop and defend some versions of the second.

The first group of objections, which are to be found in the economics literature, highlight features of theories and information that appear to entail that they cannot be commodities.[18] An initial difficulty that is sometimes claimed for information as a commodity is that one cannot know its value until one has access to it. Thus, for example, Arrow writes:

> There is a fundamental paradox in the determination of demand for information: its value for the producer is not known until he has the information, but then he has in effect acquired it without cost.[19]

The point Arrow makes is a variation on an ancient theme. Aristotle reports of Protagoras that he received payment only after an education: 'he used to tell the pupil to estimate how much the knowledge was worth, and that amount would be his payment'. This attitude he contrasts with the sophists who demand money first: 'for no one would pay them for the knowledge they really have'.[20] However, as stated by Arrow, the problem is overdrawn. Aristotle indeed is using knowledge to illustrate a general problem. After all, it is true of many ordinary commodities that their quality can only be fully appreciated in the processes of use. Fine packaging often disguises a disappointing content. Moreover, it is in any case not necessary to know the content of a theory or item of information in order to be able to assess its probable market value. Its potential market value to a purchaser can be measured in terms of behavioural capacities, i.e. in what it enables an individual to do. Indeed, it was precisely this point that was part of the rationale for competitions in the cossist tradition.

A second possible objection to the possibility of commodification of information and theories is that they cannot be alienated. One cannot, it might be argued, sell a theory, a proof, a piece of information and the like in the way one might sell a bag of fruit or a car; after the transaction, the seller retains the capacity to use and benefit from the good in question. This objection, however, is premised on a misunderstanding of what it is to alienate property: it presupposes a mistaken view of property as a thing and not as a set of rights.[21] Clearly it is not possible literally to transfer a theory in an act of exchange in the same way one can if one sells a car or a bag of apples. However, to alienate property is not to alienate an object as such, but to alienate a set of rights and capacities to use and benefit from an object: this is as possible in the case of information and knowledge as it is in the case of commodities such as cars and apples, as long as suitable use and benefit rights can be defined.

The last point is, however, related to a more substantive argument from within economic theory for the claim that knowledge is inappropriate as an object for exchange on markets. Knowledge is often offered as an example of a public good. Public goods are those that are (1) 'non-rival' in consumption – the consumption of the good by one person does not decrease that of others and (2) 'non-excludable' – individuals cannot be excluded from the benefit of using the good. The claim goes that such goods cannot be adequately provided by the market for each individual has a reason to be a free-rider, to benefit from the consumption of the good without contributing towards its costs. While there may be no pure public goods, many goods like scientific knowledge approximate to public goods. The argument goes that it is non-rival: 'it can be possessed and used jointly by as many as care to make use of it',[22] and the use comes without cost – 'once discovered the law of the deviation of the magnetic needle in the field of an electric current, or the law of the magnetization of iron, around which an electric circulates, costs never a penny'.[23]

David and Dasgupta, in developing the case for treating knowledge as a public good, note that it is codified knowledge that approximate to the status of a public good, that is knowledge that is statable in explicit propositional form and which can be transmitted globally.[24] 'Tacit knowledge' looks a less likely candidate for a public good: practical knowledge embodied in the skills and capacities of scientists is not a non-rival good accessible to all who care to have it. Knowledge thus embodied is open to sale in the market as 'expertise'. Correspondingly, one major source of the commercialisation of science has been the growth of consultancy science, in which specific scientific skills are bought by private and state actors.[25] Likewise, the transference of such skills through the sale of education and training facilities by firms and governments provides a good example of how practical knowledge is already partially realised as a commodity.

However, once this point is admitted, the extent to which 'codified knowledge' has the features of a public good is less clear than might at first appear: any explicit statement of a science is accessible only to those who have had a suitable training within a discipline and have the requisite skills to understand it. A result from some laboratory is likely to be, for most of us, a mere squiggle on paper.

Hence it is not strictly true that 'it can be possessed and used jointly by as many as care to make use of it'. It can be used only by those competent to do so. If it is a public good it is only such within that community of competence. For others to make use of it may require considerable costs in hiring requisite expertise. Hence, the extent to which knowledge approximates to a public good that cannot be an appropriate item for exchange on the market is less clear cut than is often assumed. The degree to which commerce is giving rise to the commercial procurement of scientific expertise both through professional consultancy and in-house commercial research gives one reason to assume that the commodification of much of the 'knowledge industry' is possible.

Finally, the non-excludability attribute of public goods need not apply in the case of knowledge, for it is possible to enforce exclusive use rights by way of intellectual property rights which give agents rights to control its use.[26] Hence knowledge can be brought within the commercial domain through patent, copyright and trade secrecy which define rights of exclusion on behalf of the knowledge holder. Patents grant the producer of an invention that passes tests of originality, novelty and non-obviousness rights to exclude others from using, producing or selling an invention; copyrights protect the particular expression of an idea; trade secrets protect in, common law, rights to keep information from spreading to competitors in the face of reasonable attempts to maintain secrecy, and in particular, give legal enforcement to confidential relationships. The older Tartaglia–Cardano dispute approximates to a dispute about a trade secret.[27] The extension of patent and legally enforceable confidentiality arrangements to a larger number of products of scientifically based research defines the current conflicts between science and commerce. The controversies about intellectual property rights in areas such as bio-technology concern the extension of these and the extent to which they are appropriate. Are the confidentiality agreements forced on scientists or patents on scientific results defensible? These are questions ultimately not of whether information can be commercialised, but whether it should be. They raise general problems about the compatibility of secrecy and democracy, and ethical objection to the monopoly ownership of organisms and genetic resources. They also raise particular problems about the nature of the practice of science, and it is these I develop further in the next section. It is not clear that there are peculiar properties of theories and information that makes them as such inappropriate items for the market.[28] If there is a problem with the use of market mechanisms in science, it is not that scientific theories and information are inappropriate for the market, but that the market is inappropriate for the practice of science.

11.4 Property, commerce and the practice of science

Do the property relations appropriate to the market undermine good scientific practices? In the following I develop three arguments for thinking that they do: (1) that market mechanisms are incompatible with the open communication in science which is a necessary condition for the growth of knowledge; (2) that the market as an institutional framework for science disassociates the external rewards assigned to a contributor to science from the value of his or her contribution to the development of science; (3) that private property in science undermines a commitment to the practice of science.

I begin, however, by considering a case for the defender of the opposing view – that, far from being inappropriate as an institutional framework for science, the market has all the features that will make for the best development of science. A good starting point for such a case is the parallel which the economic liberal makes between competition in science and competition in the market, which I outlined at the start of this chapter. Market mechanisms are appropriate to science since they encourage competition between different research groups. Science, like business, is a competitive enterprise. The virtue of competition in both spheres is that it encourages innovation:

> The proper argument for competition, in science as in business, as a means of improving knowledge is that it promotes alternative conjectures – and their critical examination.[29]

Indeed, it might be noted that my earlier example supports this point. Cossist algebra was important in the development of mathematics. Where mathematics in the universities of the period was moribund, the competitive pressures of commerce encouraged a novelty in algorithms of which Tartaglia's work was a notable example. A similar kind of argument might be made for commercial science. For example, research work in the pharmaceutical, electronic and bio-technology industries hardly suggests that market competition is a brake on the growth of knowledge. One might argue, then, that given the competitive nature of the scientific enterprise, the market is ideally suited to it as an institutional framework.

An initial point that must be made about this argument is that the references to recent examples of market-based research just noted are unsatisfactory. Innovative research in the market sector has taken place against the background of a domain of public knowledge. The sciences have operated within a mixed economy: basic scientific research has been carried out within the public, professional domain; commercial research has been parasitic on this public domain. The problem, which is increasingly a practical as well as a theoretical one, is whether public science is a necessary condition for scientific development or whether it is possible for all science to take place within a market economy. As Nelkin notes of new liaisons between professional science and commercial enterprise:

> Academic science has been a public resource, a repository for ideas and a source of relatively unbiased information. Industrial connections blur the distinctions between corporations and the university, establishing private control over a public resource. Problems of secrecy and proprietary rights are inherent in these new relationships and hold serious implications for both academic science and the public interest.[30]

Nelkin's point here in part reiterates claims made in chapter 7 concerning the institutional conditions for trust. Democracy requires conditions in which there exist sources of public knowledge that are credible and trustworthy. The commercialisation of science undermines those conditions by associating the production and dissemination of knowledge with wealth and power. It renders more intractable the practical epistemological problem that citizens face – who do we trust? At the same time it raises the first and central objection to the market as an institutional framework for science itself.

There is, in a competitive market economy, a disincentive to communicate information. The market encourages secrecy, which is inimical to openness in science. It presupposes a view of property in which the owner has rights to exclude others. In the sphere of science, such rights of exclusion place limits on the communication of information and theories which are incompatible with the growth of knowledge. Thus, for example, the most obvious defect of the competitive nature of cossist algebra is the kind of secrecy exhibited by Tartaglia and Ferro which inhibited the spread of the results to other scholars in a position to contribute to their development. It is partially for this reason that Tartaglia's response to Cardano appears unreasonable to moderns who are sympathetic to a norm in which theories are published and thereby become public property.

The development of scientific knowledge depends upon the publication of results. This is not just an empirical point – that science tends to grow when communication is open. Rather, there is a necessary connection between publication and the growth of knowledge. A necessary condition for the acceptability of a theory or experimental result is that it pass the public, critical scrutiny of competent scientific judges.[31] A private theory or result is one that is shielded from the criteria of scientific acceptability. Since the judgement of competent peers is a necessary condition for the acceptability of a scientific result, the publication of scientific work for the judgement of the scientific community is a necessary condition for its being a contribution to the growth of knowledge at all. Open communication for this reason is an essential condition for the scientific enterprise. This is not to say that secrecy or non-disclosure of results are absent from the scientific community. Individuals and research teams do not keep rivals informed at each stage of their progress. Science is a competitive enterprise. However, the pressure for non-disclosure in science is for non-disclosure of premature work. It remains an essential condition for the final acceptability of the result that it be placed in the public domain. Competition in science is competition between individuals and groups to be first to place before the community a result which will be able to withstand the critical scrutiny of competent judges. Where such an appraisal is successful, one can claim rights to appropriate recognition.

A possible response here is this: that while the market encourages non-disclosure, it is not a necessary feature of the rights of exclusion that come under the rubric of intellectual property rights. Non-disclosure defines those rights that come under common law principles of trade secrecy. Intellectual property rights that are defined under patent on the other hand are intended precisely to enable disclosure within market conditions: monopoly rights over benefits are granted for a limited period in return for disclosure. However, the solution is limited. First, patents still interfere with open communication in science. Thus even where patents act as an alternative to trade secrecy, secrecy is still required during the period in which the patent is being sought. Moreover 'patent before you publish' becomes the rational strategy. The following guidelines from a British university provide a nice example of the way in which property rights in the sense presupposed by the market conflict with the norms of open communication in science:

UNIVERSITY OF _____

Guidelines on Intellectual Property Rights (IPR)

Have you thought that the research you are doing might have commercial potential ...?

Intellectual property may be simply defined as rights relating to new scientific or technological processes. The term refers also to copyright, trade marks, commercial names, etc., but this is of less importance from the University's point of view.

These notes are intended to assist members of staff or research students who think they may possess intellectual property, that is that they have developed or invented a creative product, which may be capable of exploitation.

As a first step please DON'T

  (i) Publish a paper concerning the invention.
 (ii) Deliver a lecture at a conference on it.
(iii) Talk about the invention to industrialists.

If you do any of these things the intellectual property will be in the public domain and anyone can exploit it without reference to the University or to you. An attempt to protect rights after such public exposure would be like slamming the stable door after the horse had bolted.

But DO

Telephone Mr. — —on extension— —

He will tell you about possible means of patenting your intellectual property and the exploitation of it.

The extent to which you and the University can benefit from your intellectual property depends on the nature of your work and who is paying for it. You can almost be sure, however, that you will benefit in material terms from the intellectual property you have produced.[32]

Such circulars are increasingly common: indeed, when I gave an earlier version of this chapter to a university in Australia, using just this British circular, I was asked how I had managed to come by an internal document of their university. The pressure to gain the financial returns on one's product is moving academic institutions to inhibit traditional norms of disclosure. Second, patents are also tending to narrow the community of competence investigating some particular problem. The free use of scientific results by others in the scientific community is restricted.[33] Finally, while patents provide an incentive to publish, within the framework of the market there are inherent, countervailing pressures to avoid patents and keep scientific work a trade secret. There are costs to acquiring patents and limitations to the period over which they operate. Moreover, where scientific work promises to be particularly fruitful of further results, non-disclosure becomes advantageous.

The defender of the market as an institution appropriate for science might respond at this point that my argument fails to note a way in which the market itself can provide a public test for conjectures which is quite akin to that in science. Consider the following parallel between the scientific community and the market place drawn by Loasby. After noting the point that I have just made, that in science 'we have to rely on intersubjective criteria' for appraising theories, he writes:

> That should not be a disturbing proposition to economists used to invoking intersubjective judgements of value in the market, resulting from the appraisals and decisions of competent, well-informed economic agents. The parallel goes further. Scientists seek to advance knowledge, but can do so only by exposing their own ideas to the testing of their fellows and to comparison with other new ideas from other scientists – just as entrepreneurs, seeking to better existing offerings, must expose themselves to the appraisal of customer and suppliers, and to the risk of being surpassed by competitors' offers.[34]

Loasby here is only pointing to parallels between scientific and market competition – he is not suggesting that the market is an appropriate institutional framework for science. But it is open to the defender of the market in science to exploit the parallels. What would be wrong with using the market itself as a public test of the acceptability of theories? Theories and results that failed to pass 'the appraisals and decisions of well-informed, competent economic agents' would fail as they do when subject to the scrutiny of the scientific community. In a free market in knowledge, good ideas force out bad.

This defence of the appropriateness of a market framework for science cannot be sustained. The market provides the wrong kind of public test of scientific knowledge. It does so in at least two ways. In the first place, the market provides the wrong kind of community of evaluators for theories. By this I mean something more than that the community of evaluators would include others apart from scientists. It is rather that there is something wrong with the very parallels that Loasby draws between science and the market: for Loasby, as the value of a scientific theory is determined by judgements of 'competent well-informed scientists',[35] so value in the market place is determined by the judgements of 'competent, well-informed economic agents'. However, the appeal to 'competent, well-informed economic agents' is disingenuous. The market is, in one sense, an egalitarian institution: any individual's preference counts in determining the market value of a good, provided it is backed with cash. Any particular properties of an individual's personal skills, capacities, and competences are irrelevant to whether his or her judgement counts. The only property that counts is their capacity to pay. Informed and uninformed judgements all count equally. Market value is not determined by the 'appraisals and decisions of competent, well-informed economic agents', but by the appraisals and decisions of economic agents *per se*, incompetent as well as competent, uninformed as well as informed. Science, in contrast, is inegalitarian in this sense. Only certain judgements count. The appraisal of the value of scientific work does require competent and informed judges. The judgements of those without the requisite competence are irrelevant. The market does not provide the right kind of community of evaluators for scientific work.

Neither does the market provide the right kind of criteria for evaluation of scientific work. The value a theory has to the development of scientific knowledge is not appropriately related to its market value. The market value of information and theories is instrumental: it is a measure of their immediate usefulness in the service of commerce, technology, or even (as is the case in the cossist tradition) in gaining publicity for one's marketable skills through victory in competitions. Such usefulness is only contingently related to the significance of a theory to the internal development of the sciences for which qualities such as fruitfulness for further research, explanatory power, simplicity, and the like are the appropriate criteria of judgement. Relatedly, markets will value theories that have immediate to near-future implications; theories and information of more significance to the internal development of science have implications over a longer time-scale. It is such reasons that are at the basis of the observation that markets favour research with immediate application and disfavour research of a more fundamental kind.

This last point raises the second objection to the market as an institution appropriate to science: given the employment of market mechanisms, the value of a contribution to the development of science is dissociated from the external rewards that the institutions that support science assign to the contributor. Because the market value of information and theories is instrumental, and is at best only indirectly related to the significance a theory has to the internal development of science, its rewards to the contributor to science are not properly related to the significance of the contribution. In contrast, the processes of assigning recognition developed by professional science such as peer review, citation, and the like, even if they are not perfect, are at least of the right kind to ensure that the contribution to the internal development of science is matched by external rewards – appropriate recognition and its related benefits. This problem can be stated usefully in terms of MacIntyre's Aristotelian distinction between practices and institutions.[36] The practice of science is characterised in terms of its internal goods – i.e. those goods which cannot be identified without reference to the kind of activity it is. The institutions of science are concerned with the distribution of external goods – i.e. goods such as material wealth, power, and status which can be identified independently of any particular activity. In the system of property in science that has emerged over the past three centuries, the institutions of science are of the right kind to support the practice of science, whereas the system of property distribution associated with the market is not.

MacIntyre's Aristotelian distinction between internal and external goods points to a third possible objection to the introduction of market mechanisms and more specifically its related property system into science: namely, that private property in science is incompatible as such with a commitment to the internal goods of science. The exclusivity of property rights in market goods is incompatible with a commitment to such internal goods; to exclude other individuals from the use of or development of a theory who are committed and able to contribute to the further development of a practice is thereby to indicate a failure of commitment to the development of the practice itself. Thus Ferro and Tartaglia, in keeping secret their algorithm, reveal by their behaviour that the goals of the development of algebra are subordinate to goals of an exclusively competitive kind. The 'communism' of science highlighted by Merton is a particular case of a communism implicit in all well-ordered human practices.[37] The use of property relations of the market place in science is incompatible with a commitment to the internal goods of science. Theories and information are not the kinds of items to which exclusive property rights are appropriate, given a view of science as an autonomous practice with its own internal goods.

However, this objection as it stands is open to the following rejoinder. The argument above confuses an individual having the right to exclude others from a theory with an individual's exercise of that right. While it is the case that an individual's excluding others from a contribution to science does show a failure in his or her commitment to that practice, the use of the system of private property involved in the market is, in itself, neutral. It is open to the individual to exhibit his or her commitment to the practice of science by waiving the exercise of the rights of exclusion.[38] This response is, I believe, a strong one, although within a market economy each individual is forced to exercise at least some of his or her rights of exclusion. Let us concede that the third objection fails as stated. However, its central point can be restated thus: given an introduction of market property relations into science, the act of publishing without some form of payment will count as a supererogatory act of gift-giving. The individual who so acts becomes the self-sacrificing gift-giving altruist found in Hagstrom's idealised model of the scientific community. What the market will have effected is an institutional redefinition of an individual's self-interest which narrows its range.

Whereas in existing scientific institutions to publish one's results is to act in a self-interested way, the market redefines this as an act against one's own interests.

Consider, for example, the import of the circular on intellectual property rights quoted earlier in the chapter. I am a scientist who hitherto has taken it as a matter of course that I publish my findings in public scientific journals and give accounts of my work to others at scientific conferences. By doing so I contribute to the development of my discipline and I may count this as one of my most important interests: it forms part of my identity as scientist. I gain recognition of the significance of my contribution from others whom I recognise as competent of such judgements. Recognition comes through the very act of publication in a peer-reviewed journal, through citation, eponymy and so on. Through the act of publication I pursue my own central projects in a way that is not at all incompatible with my pursuing ends which are also other-regarding. Consider now the effect of the circular quoted above. It places the act of publication in a new institutional setting, the market, with its distinct concept of intellectual property, and a different definition of what one's own interests are taken to be. To publish now is to waive one's property rights and to consequently forgo the satisfaction of one's interests. To publish or to deliver a lecture prior to 'intellectual property rights' being legally defined is now to act against one's interests, now defined in terms of the 'benefit in material terms' from work with 'commercial potential'. Institutionally an act of publication is defined as an act of self-sacrifice. It is of course open for scientists to so act, but to do so is now a strong supererogatory act that works against the expectations given in the revised institutional setting. Hence, given that the scientific community is not a community of rationalist saints, the market undermines a commitment to the internal goals of science.

The main point here is again an Aristotelian one.[39] For Aristotle, the correct response to the egoist who asks questions such as 'Why have friends?' or 'Why act virtuously?' is that the egoist has a narrow conception of what his or her goods are. The egoist assumes a narrow range of goods – 'the biggest share of money, honours, and bodily pleasures' – and asks how friends or virtues bring these goods. One should respond not by trying to show how the egoist can realise these goods through acts of friendship and virtue, but by pointing out that the egoist has misidentified what the goods of life are.[40] This basic Aristotelian point, however, needs a sociological dimension, for it is the institutions themselves that define what counts as one's interests. In particular, the market encourages egoism not primarily because it encourages an individual to be 'self-interested' – it would be unrealistic not to expect individuals to act for the greater part in a 'self-interested' manner – but rather because it defines an individual's interests in a particularly narrow fashion, most notably in terms of the possession of certain material goods. In consequence, where market mechanisms enter a particular sphere of life, the pursuit of goods outside this narrow range of market goods is institutionally defined as an act of altruism. For this reason, the market undermines the pursuit of the internal goods of practices like those of science. Human practices require an associational background that foster the commitment to the internal goods of the practice.[41]

11.5 Epistemology, egoism and association

I finish by noting some of the implications the argument has for the Austrian epistemological arguments with which we began the chapter. Those arguments suffer from a kind of institutional blindness which has plagued much political argument in the late twentieth century. A bureaucratic state apparatus and the free-market are offered as the two possible institutional settings for the pursuit of the various practices that are required for a good human life: the latter wins by default once the undoubted epistemic failings of the former are made clear. The great variety of intermediate social institutions and associations which are required to foster the internal goods of practices disappear from view. Yet it is here (as was noted at the end of the last chapter) that much of the practical knowledge to which Hayek appeals is sustained. As will be apparent from this chapter, such associations have their own means of quality control and distribution of information that can be radically disrupted by market institutions. These associational spheres typified by the scientific community are threatened both by state and by commercial society. The tendency to picture social and economic life in terms of either an all embracing centralised planning board or the governance of market norms underplays the way both can disrupt other important institutions in which knowledge is embodied and distributed and through which individuals' activities are coordinated. The classical notion of politics as an association of associations deserves to be revived if for no other reason than to stand as a corrective to this picture.

The arguments of this chapter raise problems however not only for the epistemological case that is offered for the market, but also for what might be called the motivational case, that defends markets as the best way of harnessing the self-interested pursuit of individuals. The arguments of the last section give some reasons for doubting the force of this line of reasoning. These critical arguments are developed further in the following chapter.

12

PUBLIC CHOICE THEORY: SELF-INTEREST AND UNIVERSAL ECONOMICS

A general consideration that is often offered in defence of the market economy is that it runs with the grain of human nature. It is an order that is able to work successfully given individuals who are 'self-interested', 'egoistic', or at least who are of 'limited altruism'. Social institutions should be ideally designed on the assumption that this is so, either because it is so – that is what humans are like – or because, even if it is not, it is best we assume the worst. Alternative arrangements of the kind that socialists have traditionally defended make unrealistic demands on the altruism of agents. They require self-sacrificial behaviour on the part of individuals that cannot be realistically met. The consequence is that they fail to meet the needs and aspirations of individuals. In contrast while markets proceed on the assumption of egoistic agents, they produce outcomes that can be defended from the standpoint of the impartial altruist.

The arguments of the last chapter have already given reasons for doubt about the terms in which this argument is stated.[1] The concept of 'acting from self-interest', as such, is without content: it all depends upon what individuals take their interests to be and this changes with different institutional settings. In this chapter I develop this argument in response to the most influential defence of markets on the basis of universal self-interest, and in many ways most sophisticated – that offered by public choice theory.

12.1 The challenge of public choice theory

The starting point of public choice theory is the claim that the assumptions made by economists about the nature of the economic agent in the market place are universal in the scope of their application. There is no reason to assume that what is true of actors in the market ceases to be true when they enter non-market situations. If it is true that individuals act as rational self-interested agents in the market place, 'the inference should be that they will also act similarly in other and nonmarket behavioral settings'.[2] The scope of the economic theory thus understood is quite general. In principle the theory applies in any social setting be it politics, the family, scientific community, or any other association.

While it promises to be universal in scope, to explain everything from families to voluntary associations, the central application of public choice theory has been to the political realm. It is indeed sometimes characterised thus: ' "Public Choice" ... is really the application and extension of economic theory to the realm of political and governmental choices.'[3] Applied to the political domain the theory is aimed against attempts to rectify market failure by state action. Thus a standard story in neo-classical economics runs that state action is justified to resolve problems of 'market failures' that arise when real markets depart from 'ideal markets' which, according to the fundamental theorem of neo-classical economics, yield Pareto-optimal outcomes. 'Market failures' due to externalities or the existence of public goods are typically invoked as the rationale for the use of state administered decision making procedures such as cost-benefit analysis to realise optimal outcomes by other, normally bureaucratic, means.

The public choice theorist objects to this line of argument on the grounds that it assumes that both bureaucrats and politicians are benevolent actors concerned to realise the common good or welfare of all.[4] That assumption presupposes that the axioms that define the rational actor in neo-classical theory cease to apply behind the office doors of the bureaucrat or politician. The actors are no longer taken to make rational choices that maximise their own utility. They rather become altruistic channels through which the maximisation of the general utility is achieved. The axioms of neo-classical theory are assumed not to apply in the non-market setting of politics: 'the conventional wisdom holds that the market is made up of private citizens trying to benefit themselves, but that government is concerned with something called the public interest.'[5] The assumption made in neo-classical defences of state rectification of market failures, that state actors are benign and impartial, represents a failure of theoretical rigour and nerve to apply consistently the axioms defining the rational actor. There is no reason to assume that state actors suddenly become different and more benign when they enter the arena of government. The axioms that characterise the rational agent in economic life should be taken to apply also to the explanation of the behaviour of bureaucrat and politician in their political activities.

For public choice theories state action does not and could not produce the optimal outcomes of 'ideal markets' by other means. State actors act to maximise their own interests not the 'public interest'. Bureaucrats are taken to aim at maximising the size of their bureau budget, since that is correlated with their utility:

> Among the several variables that may enter the bureaucrat's motives are: salary, perquisites of the office, public reputation, power, patronage, output of the bureau, ease of making changes, and ease of managing the bureau. All except the last two are a positive function of the total budget of the bureau during the bureaucrat's tenure ... A bureaucrat's utility need not be strongly dependent on every one of the variables which increase with budget, but it must be positively and continuously associated with its size.[6]

Likewise, in public choice explanation of the behaviour of voters and politicians, it is assumed that voters act like consumers and political candidates like firms. Candidates aim to maximise votes and hence gain political office, voters to maximise the satisfaction of preferences for those goods the state can deliver.[7]

Once economic theory is applied to politics, the state no longer appears as a beneficent representative of the public good. Rather, it is argued that the self-interested behaviour of bureaucrat, politician and voter lead, if unchecked by institutional reform, to the constant expansion of government expenditure and provision, producing outcomes that are irrational and inefficient. 'Market failure' gives way to 'government failure'.[8] The public choice theorist typically appeals to a free-market economic policy, which attempts to rectify market failure, not by using the state to realise efficient outcomes by bureaucratic means, but by institutional changes within the market.[9] 'Government failure' is thereby avoided.

For example, the public choice response to environmental problems that arise from 'market failure' – externalities, public goods and the absence of a market price on many environmental goods – has been to find solution within the market sphere itself. Direct government intervention is not required to solve problems of market failure. Rather, they can be resolved by a redefinition of property rights within the market. Thus, Coase's theorem is invoked to resolve the problem of externalities:[10] given perfect competition and the absence of transaction costs,[11] solutions to negative externalities, for example pollution, are possible through a process of bargaining, if property rights are properly assigned either to the 'damaging' agent or the 'affected' agent. If the damaging agent has the rights, then the affected agent can compensate him not to continue the damaging activity; if the affected agent has property rights, the damaging agent can compensate her to bear the damage. Thus, in the former case a pollution sufferer might compensate the polluter, in the latter the polluter might compensate the sufferer. Similarly, where unpriced public goods such as clean air and water exist, the optimal solution is not to place a shadow price on the goods, but to define property rights, if not directly over them, then over their use, for example through pollution permits. Tradable pollution permits which allow markets in pollution are defended on the grounds that they address the interests of the actors directly, and hence do not make unrealistic demands on conscience or law; that they encourage pollution to diminish where it is cheapest for it do so; and that they even allow those with preferences for non-pollution to express those preferences directly within the market.[12] The problems of environmental damage consequent on 'market failure' can be resolved by directly bringing environmental goods and bads within the realm of market contract. The problems have a solution within the sphere of voluntary market exchange and without recourse to government intervention that leads simply to 'government failure' worse than the failures it is supposed to cure.

The public choice approach to politics is not without its virtues. While, as will become evident, I have deep misgivings about the basic assumptions of public choice theory, it is difficult not to have sympathy with public choice scepticism about any theory that simply assumes that political actors are benign. Indeed, such scepticism need not be associated with free-market economics. Thus, for example, the same scepticism is expressed in a very different political idiom in Marx's early critique of Hegel's benign view of bureaucracy: the bureaucracy does not stand above the egoistic domain of civil society, representing a universal interest; rather it is itself of civil society, the appeal to a universal interest disguising the pursuit of its own interests.[13] While it may be false that actors are necessarily and always motivated by narrow concerns with self-advancement, one cannot simply assume in advance that they are not.

However, while there is something right about the public choice critique of state benevolence, the general claim it makes about the universality of the self-interested economic agent should be rejected. While public choice theory gets its political clout, plausibility and sense of realism from its application to the state, it claims a much wider scope. At its most imperialistic, it aspires to provide a new foundation for the social sciences, aiming to bring the whole of social life within its ambit: not just politics, but the family, non-state associations, the norms that govern social behaviour in different societies are all brought within its domain.[14]

This expansionary project is abetted by those who have independently used economic models of human activities often with a similar deflationary purpose. Thus to return to the subject matter of the last chapter, a great deal that goes under the title of the sociology of scientific knowledge is merely an application of economic models to science and has quite appropriately been characterised as a public choice analysis of science. Scientists are depicted as utility maximising actors who act in competition with each other in the pursuit of their self-interest. What counts as 'true' is determined by the outcome of processes not different in kind to standard market forces.[15] The model of science offered by Latour and Woolgar (discussed in chapter 8) is typical in this regard: science is characterised in terms of a market in credibility, with scientists as investors and the eventual value of the theory being determined by supply and demand.[16] The deflationary purpose of the model parallels that of the public choice approach to politics. Hence as Hands notes:

> [T]he economics of science is an inquiry that *should* come easy for economists ... For years economists have undermined and delegitimized the self-righteousness of politicians – 'you are not acting in the societal or national interest, but your own self-interest' – now the argument can be applied to scientists.[17]

For this very reason, however, the move may be uncongenial to mainstream public choice theory, for it is self-undermining. If applied to science it entails that public choice theory itself has to be understood as an act of self-interested actors. My question should not be, 'Is the theory true?', but 'What interests does it serve?' Thus, the first question one should ask on picking up a volume by a public choice theorist is 'What is the author's interest in writing this book?', where interest is to be understood, for reasons to be explored, in a peculiarly narrow fashion. Thoughts about a possible interest in arriving at truths about the social world should be put aside just as they are for 'altruistic' politicians. The text is an exercise in rhetorical persuasion that has some other end. Wider commitments expressed in the texts, to individual freedom, free-markets and so on should also be treated as so many guises through which self-interest is pursued. If economic theory is to apply 'non-market settings' it has to apply to the production of academic texts in economics. This highlights a deep problem in the public choice perspective. There is a performative contradiction in operation in the authors' utterances in public choice texts. If one took seriously what they are saying in their theories, one could not take seriously their acts of saying them. However, whatever motives they might be pursuing in terms of career, status, power and money, I will in the following take the acts of writing in good faith. I do so because I believe that the theory is false.

In the following I will question two central assumptions that underpin the public choice argument:

1   the assumption that individual preferences are prior to and explanatory of institutional arrangements
2   the assumption that 'egoism' or 'self-interested' behaviour is universal.

I will argue that the first assumption is false and is implicitly assumed to be so in actual public choice arguments. The second assumption is not so much false as empty: the very concepts of 'egoist' and the 'self-interested agent' and those of the 'altruist' are contentless in themselves. Once content is added, it is either uncontentious and uninteresting that agents are self-interested, or it is contentious but false that they are so.

12.2 Institutional economics: the old and the new

Public choice theory is often presented as a part of a revival of institutional economics. It represents a response, from within the neo-classical tradition, to the neglect of institutional questions in that tradition. Thus, problems concerning the institutional conditions in which markets operate, for example concerning the definition of property rights against which market transactions take place; problems concerning the consequences of certain institutional forms, such as the unrestrained operation of existing political and bureaucratic institutions; and finally normative problems concerning the specification of optimal institutional arrangements, all become central from the public choice perspective. While this renewed focus on institutions is to be welcomed, for those of us educated outside of this perspective, the neo-classical approach to institutions is still liable to strike one as oddly skewed. There is a clear difference between this new institutional economics and the older institutional economics that traditionally opposed the neo-classicals' institutional myopia.[18] I include within the category of old institutional economics not only the American tradition of institutionalism which included Veblen and Commons,[19] but also that economics that took place within a broadly Aristotelian tradition, including the work of both Marx and Polanyi,[20] as well as much of the classical economic tradition.[21]

A central difference between the old institutionalism and the new neo-classical variant concerns the relation of institutions and preferences. The new institutionalism represents the extension of neo-classical theory into new domains and hence begins with the conventional axioms that define the rational agent within neo-classical theory. In doing so it starts with the assumption that preferences are given. Preferences are taken to be prior to and explanatory of institutions. Individuals both in market and non-market settings act as rational self-interested agents. The question which, on the public choice account, needs to be answered is this: what institutions should we construct given that individuals are rational self-interested agents, who pursue their own ends both in the market place, and in 'nonmarket behavioral settings'.[22] The explanatory problem is to explain the emergence and nature of institutions given that assumption. Reference to institutions appears only in the explanandum, not in the explanans. The central normative problem becomes that of how to fashion institutions given that individuals are egoists. More generally it shares the assumption of both modern neo-classical and Austrian economics that any principle of 'optimal' outcomes must itself be purely want-regarding: it takes as given the wants people happen to have and concerns itself with the satisfaction of those wants.[23]

Old institutionalism differs from the new in that it allows individuals' preferences to be explained by reference to the institutional context in which they operate: references to institutions appear in the explanans, not just in explanandum. Given those assumptions the normative problem becomes that of determining which institutions should be sustained in order that individuals develop desirable preferences: it tends to be ideal-regarding. That assumption underlies the classical political thought of Aristotle. The end of the polis is the good life,[24] where the good life is characterised in terms of the virtues: hence, the best political association is that which enables every person to act virtuously and live happily.[25] Hence also his influential criticism of the market in terms of its encouragement of the desire for the unlimited acquisition of goods and thus the vice of *pleonexia*, the desire to have more than is proper.[26] The old institutional economics in the wide sense outlined above is the inheritor of this classical tradition.

Old and new institutionalism start from very different explanatory assumptions, and generate distinct normative questions. Which version of institutionalism is to be preferred? The question, in so far as it concerns explanation, is in the end one that has to be answered by reference to the canons of rational enquiry – adequacy to empirical evidence, explanatory power, consistency and so on. However, at present a strong presumption must be made for the old institutionalism. I say this, not only because of the absence of empirical support for many of the standard public choice positions,[27] but because the new institutionalism has failed in any case to carry out its eliminative project of deleting references to institutions within its explanans. Reference to institutional contexts is smuggled in at the level of its assumptions about individuals' conceptions of their interests. Thus while public choice theorists claim to start from preferences that exist prior to institutions, their accounts of the nature of the self-interested preferences of individuals, of their 'utility function', changes according to the institutions they are describing. Within the market it is typically assumed to consist in the acquisition of consumer goods; within the political domain power through the acquisition of votes; within bureaucracy, promotion and advancement in status within the bureaucratic order.

Two points need to be made about these shifting assumptions about the actors' conceptions of self-interest. The first and more basic is that a simple and now familiar observation about the characterisation of action entails that certain interests cannot even be specified outside of a particular institutional context. Consider the politician's interest in the acquisition of votes. Individuals can perform the actions of voting or acquiring a vote only when they are embedded in a particular position in an institutional context: it is *qua* citizen that an individual can felicitously vote, and only *qua* candidate that an individual can be elected. Moreover, the action of voting itself depends on a complex set of institutions that embody and are constituted by particular shared understandings. Only within certain institutional settings can the behaviours of marking crosses on papers, the raising of hands and so on be understood as 'voting'. In others, say the raising of the hand in the auction room or the lecture hall, or the marking of crosses against names in a classroom, they have different meanings. Hence, an interest in 'acquiring votes' or 'winning an election' is an interest that is possible only within a specific institutional setting. Similar points apply to the interest in 'promotion' and that of 'buying' or 'selling' 'consumer goods': such interests themselves presuppose an institutional context.[28] It is worth adding here, that not only do assumptions about institutional context enter into the descriptions of interests, but also they arrive in the more substantive assumptions about the boundaries between different institutions in the modern world. It is, for example, simply assumed that votes and political office are not the sort of things that, in modern society, can be bought or sold.[29]

The second point about public choice assumptions goes beyond the mere possibility of specifying interests to substantive explanatory problems: that is, in defining individual preferences differently in different contexts, public choice theory implicitly assumes, quite correctly, that different institutional settings foster different conceptions of self-interest. Within the market setting, interests are defined in terms of the acquisition of property rights over objects; within the political domain, power is assumed to be the object of a person's interest; in the realm of bureaucracy, it is identified as the acquisition of status through promotion. The explanatory claims of the older institutionalism enter as unannounced, unnoticed and unwelcome guests into the new institutionalist's assumptions about the 'utility function' of the agent in different contexts. At the explanatory level existing public choice theories have not eliminated reference to institutions from their explanans. Substantive explanatory work has already been done at the level of claims about individuals' conceptions of their interests.

The implicit acknowledgment of the way that different institutions foster different conceptions of an individual's interests has important implications for the public choice theorists' claim that they are simply extending the axioms of neo-classical theory concerning the rational self-interested agent into new domains. Two points need to be made here. First, given a full specification of the conceptions of individual self-interest, it is simply not true that one can transfer assumptions about self-interested behaviour in the market to other domains. In other institutional contexts, quite different conceptions of interests are apparent, which can and do conflict with that fostered by the market.

Consider the old conflict between aristocratic and market institutions which concerned the classical economics of Hume and Smith. Typical is Hume's remarks about the incompatibility of absolute monarchy and commerce:

> Commerce, therefore, in my opinion, is apt to decay in absolute governments, not because it is there less *secure*, but because it is less *honourable*. A subordination of ranks is absolutely necessary to the support of monarchy. Birth, titles, and place, must be honoured above industry and riches. And while these notions prevail, all the considerable traders will be tempted to throw up their commerce, in order to purchase some of those employments, to which privileges and honours are annexed.[30]

The comment has some power. In traditional aristocratic societies, honour is institutionally defined as the object of one's interest: to sacrifice one's honour for money would be a sign of vulgarity. That conflict between the bourgeois world of markets and the aristocratic world of honour played an important part in the cultural shifts in eighteenth- and nineteenth-century Britain.

Again, consider the topic of the last chapter – the commercialisation of science. It would be a mistake to see this either, in the fashion of public choice theory, as simply a way of taming 'professionals' who, under the guise of 'scientific values' conspire against the public in the pursuit of the same set of interests they have as 'market actors'; or, as opponents of public choice might have it, as an invasion of a purely 'altruistic' practice (science) by a sphere of egoistic behaviour (markets). It rather involves a shift in individuals' conceptions of their interests. In traditional scientific institutions one's interests were characterised in terms of recognition by peers of a significant contribution to one's discipline, recognition achieved through publication in a peer-reviewed journal. Commercialised science brings changes in the nature of intellectual property rights such that publication is redefined as an act in conflict with one's interests. Hence the spread of university instructions *not* to publish results, since to do so will be to miss the 'benefit in material terms from the intellectual property you have produced'. The assumptions about self-interested behaviour in the market cannot be transferred to other institutional contexts. In different roles in different institutions agents have quite distinct conceptions of their interests.

167

12.3 Self-interest, egoism and avarice

The points made in the last section highlight a second difficulty in the public choice position. It is far from clear just what assumptions about the economic agent in the market that a public choice theorist is supposed to be taking over into non-market domains. The axioms that define the rational agent in neo-classical theory are a quite minimal attempt to characterise consistency in preferences. The rational economic agent is assumed to have preferences that are complete, i.e. agents can express preferences over any and all goods; reflexive, i.e. every good is as good as itself; and transitive, i.e. such that if x is preferred to y and y to z then x is preferred to z. The rational economic agent, thus defined, is then assumed to be concerned to maximise the satisfaction of a set of preferences, the 'utility function' in neo-classical jargon, under the constraint of a finite budget. Now, while I believe some of the neo-classical assumptions should be rejected, for example that concerning transitivity,[31] I do not believe that they should be rejected because they assume an 'egoistic' individual. That individuals are 'self-interested' in the sense that they are concerned to satisfy a consistent set of preferences under budget constraints does not imply that agents are egoists in any strong sense of the term. It all depends what preferences they have: 'The postulate that an agent is characterised by preferences rules out neither the saint nor Genghis Kahn.'[32]

The rhetorical power of public choice theory depends on its smuggling in through the 'utility function' a particular egoistic characterisation of individuals' preferences. Egoism, in the sense in which it is usually employed, either as a term of derogation, or as a term of political and ethical 'realism', depends on a particular account of the preferences individuals are taken to have. The egoist in the normal sense is an individual who desires only the possession of a narrow set of goods that can be possessed to the exclusion of others: 'the biggest share of money, honours and bodily pleasures',[33] to take Aristotle's list, to which one might add 'political power'. Public choice theory does assume such an egoist with preferences for this narrow range of goods. In doing so it inherits the late eighteenth-century shift in the language to describe the unlimited acquisitiveness, in which the classical terms *pleonexia*, greed, avarice and love of lucre were replaced by the term 'interest', and hence 'self-interest' was redefined in a narrow fashion.[34] However, in taking for granted this concept of self-interest, it goes beyond the basic formal axioms of neo-classical theory, and implicitly introduces substantive claims about the content of agents' preferences. Moreover, in doing so, its 'realism' becomes quite unrealistic.

To an egoist thus conceived the classical response, articulated by Aristotle, forms the proper reply: they have simply misidentified what the goods of life are.[35] Thus, for example, those who are exclusively concerned with the unlimited acquisition of money are improperly called rational economic agents: they are neither 'rational' nor, in the classical sense of the term, 'economic'. The term 'rational economic agent' thus used is a technical euphemism for which the proper description is 'moneygrubber'.[36] Similar points apply to the professional politician driven simply by the desire for political power, the 'politico' or 'hack', or bureaucrat driven by the desire for promotion, the 'careerist'. The derogatory terms employed to describe those individuals express the proper attitude one should have towards them. They are individuals with a hopelessly narrow view of the goods that life has to offer. Moreover, contrary to the 'realism' of public choice, and despite the increasing colonisation of the non-market domains by the market, the recognition that this is so has not entirely disappeared.

It is false to assume that since individuals act as narrowly interested agents in the market place, 'the inference should be that they will also act similarly in other and nonmarket behavioral settings'.[37] Individuals are motivated by a variety of ends outside the market place: the scientist, by the desire to solve some problem; the ornithologist, by the desire to sustain a habitat in which a variety of birds can be found; the climber, by the desire to climb some new line on a rock face; the musician, by the desire to play a new and technically demanding work; the parent, by the desire to see the child happy and fulfilled; and so on down an endless list. None of this is to deny the existence of egoistic individuals. It is to deny that one can reduce individuals' interests to that narrow set of preferences exhibited in the market place and the centres of political power.

The weaknesses of public choice assumptions in this regard are most apparent in their treatment of associations.[38] The term 'association' can refer to a variety of formal and informal societies that are neither direct competitive actors within the market, nor direct competitors for political office, although they can and do have effects on both markets and political outcomes. They include voluntary associations that pursue some particular good – natural history societies, climbing clubs and the like; associations that exist within the economic sphere, but in which actors engage with one another in non-market ways – trade unions, professional associations and so on; organisations that serve some particular interest that is affected by state action – pressure groups, and some charities; and finally public institutions that are often financed by the state, but are not of the state – universities, schools, hospitals, conservation councils and so on. Such associations form a mixed bag and it is problematic to treat all under the same heading – the last group of institutions in particular fits uneasily with others. Public choice is at its most vulnerable to empirical criticism in its treatment of voluntary associations. Their very existence is a problem given the assumption of a rational actor able to free-ride on the benefits they might bring. As Hirschman notes of Olson's influential *The Logic of Collective Action* (1965):

> Olson proclaimed the impossibility of collective action for large groups ... at the precise moment when the Western world was about to be engulfed by an unprecedented wave of public movements, marches, protests, strikes and ideologies.[39]

That empirical weakness is a consequence of its assumptions about the nature of 'self-interest'. In public choice theory all associations are treated as 'interest groups', where the term 'interest' is understood in the narrow sense in which it has come to be defined since the eighteenth century.[40] Given that narrow definition of interests pursued by associations, the problem becomes one of how an individual would incur the costs of joining an association rather than free-ride on others. The attempt to reduce all associations to interest groups in that sense is however a mistake. It fails to make proper distinctions between different kinds of associations. Some do exist simply to pursue some narrowly defined interest. However, others exist to pursue some good or 'interest' in the wider sense of the term: consider the wide variety of natural history, conservation and environmental associations. Still others aim both at particular interests and some good: professional associations, even where they are conspiracies against the public, are not merely conspiracies as the public choice theorist supposes – they also have an interest in the goods the profession serves, be it medicine, education, philosophy, economics, nature conservation or whatever. Finally, other associations might begin in 'self-interest' narrowly defined, but develop other interests while in their pursuit, for example in fellowship itself.

Not only does public choice theory fail to distinguish between different kinds of association, but also it makes a corresponding failure to distinguish between the different goods or interests an individual may have as a member of an association. A member of an association concerned with the pursuit of some practice, say science, can have two kinds of interests: first, in some achievement internal to the practice itself, in some particular empirical discovery or theoretical development; second, in some external good the association offers, in some form of recognition, in some institutional position, in an increased salary or whatever.[41] The public choice theorist, in implicitly defining interests in a narrow manner, has to treat the first kind of interest as 'really' simply instrumental for the second. However, that is quite implausible. Thus, in many settings, it is difficult to get individuals to fill administrative positions, even where it means promotion, because that would involve sacrificing time on the internal goals that really interest them. Moreover, some of the apparently narrower desires for possessing external goods an institution has to offer have their basis in interests internal to the practice it promotes: a scientist, for example, may desire promotion not out of mere careerism, but because it is a form of recognition of her achievements by competent peers.

The weakness of public choice theory when it is applied to associations is that it is precisely in associations that the wide variety of motivations and interests that move individuals is exhibited. In markets individuals do exhibit a preference for the acquisition of consumer goods; in politics, as it exists now, an interest in the achievement of power does predominate; and in bureaucratic organisations, an interest in career advancement is a disposition that is fostered. However, in other associations a preference for a wide variety of goods is apparent. Moreover, as the old institutionalism asserts, such preferences are not given that are brought to the associations. They are interests that are fostered by them. Indeed, just as an interest in amassing votes is not possible outside a particular institutional context, so many of the interests fostered by associations could not exist without some such institutional context. Thus as Raz notes, it is only in the context of particular social forms that an interest in 'bird watching' is possible:

> some comprehensive goals require social institutions for their very possibility. One cannot pursue a legal career except in a society governed by law, one cannot practise medicine except in a society in which such a practice is recognised ... Activities which do not appear to acquire their character from social forms in fact do so. Bird watching seems to be what any sighted person in the vicinity of birds can do. And so he can, except that that would not make him into a bird watcher. He can be that only in a society where this, or at least some other animal tracking activities, are recognized as leisure activities, and which furthermore share certain attitudes to natural life generally.[42]

Not only are such interests in a wider set of goods distinct from those exhibited in institutional contexts such as the market or politics, a commitment to such goods is defined in terms of a refusal to make them commensurable with goods that satisfy the narrow set of interests that define those contexts. Hence, the now well-documented refusals of individuals to respond to willingness to pay surveys on environmental goods. They uncover widespread and proper convictions about the kinds of things that can be bought and sold. There are commitments that are central to the well-being of agents that are partially constituted by a refusal to put a price on goods. The person who could put a price on friendship, simply could not have friends. They simply do not understand the loyalties that are constitutive of friendship. Moreover they are thereby excluded from much of what is best in human life. Likewise, with respect to other goods that individuals value, including significant places, environments and non-human beings.[43] Thus, whatever the truth of Aristotle's comments about 'the many' of the classical Greek world, and one suspects aristocratic prejudices in this regard, the many of the modern world do not exhibit a concern only for that narrow set of goods that is characteristic of the egoist: money, status and power. Individuals engage in a large array of non-market and non-political social associations and practices, and have a correspondingly broader conception of their interests than that ascribed to them by the public choice theorist. The extent to which the behaviour of actors in the market and political world is at all civilised depends on those wider social engagements.

In its saner, more conciliatory, and, in the proper sense of the term, 'realistic' moments, public choice theory grants that individuals are not always egoists in the narrow sense, that they are not solely motivated by the desire for money, power and status. The claim is restated in a normative way: that, while it may in fact be false that all persons are egoists, driven by avarice, we need to assume, in the design of good institutions, that they are. The principle of institutional design thus stated is supported in a variety of ways, and by appeals to a number of authorities. Sometimes it is made in economic terms: that ethical constraints are a scarce resource, the use of which should be minimised.[44] At others principles of justice are invoked: the 'immoral' or 'egoistic' should not be allowed to gain 'unfair' advantage over his or her altruistic fellows.[45] Often it is simply invoked as a principle of institutional design that represents an inherited political wisdom. Buchanan calls upon the authority of Mill's *Consideration on Representative Government* – 'the very principle of constitutional government requires it to be assumed that political power will be abused to promote the particular purposes of the holder'.[46] Reference is also sometimes made to Hume: 'Political writers have established it as a maxim, that, in contriving any system of government, and fixing the several checks and controls of the constitution, every man ought to be supposed to be a *knave*, and to have no other end, in all his actions, than private interest',[47] where Hume explicitly denies that this is in fact true: 'it appears somewhat strange, that a maxim should be true in *politics*, which is false in *fact*'.[48]

This normative claim about institutional design contains a partial truth. The problem of the vulnerability of institutions to the vicious, the egoist, the careerist, and the lover of lucre and power, are problems that any plausible social and political theory has to take seriously. It does not follow, however, that institutions must thereby be designed around the assumption that all persons are thus motivated. The institutions that one would arrive at by that principle are themselves likely to foster the very vices they are designed to check.

One important instance of this point is the familiar case against pure contractarian accounts of good institutions. The contractarian begins from the assumption that institutions be designed around egoists: the only defensible institutions are those which narrowly interested individuals would agree to enter through voluntary contract. The problem with that position is that 'a contract is not sufficient unto itself':[49] contracts themselves are possible only against the background of non-contractual relations which both build and depend on trust, where trust is an attitude that it is irrational to take given the assumption of universal egoism. The point is one familiar to conservative political thought concerning the ethical presuppositions of the market. It is stated thus by Burke:

> If, as I suspect, modern letters owe more than they are always willing to own to ancient manners, so do other interests which we value full as much as they are worth. Even commerce, and trade, and manufacture, the gods of our oeconomical politicians, are themselves perhaps but creatures; are themselves but effects, which, as first causes, we chose to worship. They certainly grew under the same shade in which learning flourished. They too may decay without their natural protecting principles.[50]

Without a background of non-contractual relations, contract itself is impossible.

Moreover, the classical thinkers invoked by public choice theorists are misinterpreted if they are understood as providing arguments for a general principle of institutional design founded upon some narrow egoism. While Hume does believe that 'avarice, or the desire of gain, is a universal passion which operates at all times, in all places, and upon all persons',[51] he does not believe it is the only passion and in different institutional contexts it is either fostered or subject to countervailing passions. His specific point about knavery in politics is simply misread if it is understood as an early statement of the public choice principles. His point is one that applies solely to the political and concerns the behaviour of men when they act in parties, such that the countervailing check of honour is absent. Likewise, J. S. Mill's principle is a very particular principle about political power. To invoke J. S. Mill's *Consideration on Representative Government* in support of the public choice perspective is to ignore the central thesis of that book, which is concerned not with the design of institutions around the assumption of egoism, but rather with both the educative and corrupting effects of institutions on the individual: 'the first question in respect to any political institutions is, how far they tend to foster in members of the community the various desirable qualities moral and intellectual'.[52] It is Mill's question about institutions that animates the normative dimension of classical institutional economics. Universal egoism, in the derogatory sense of the term in which it refers to an interest in the acquisition of possessive goods, is neither a truth about individual behaviour in all institutional settings, nor a sound principle of institutional design. The new institutionalism needs to give way to the old.

Having attempted to bury public choice theory, as part of a proper funeral oration, I return to two earlier points uttered in its praise. First, it is quite right to insist that one cannot simply assume a benign state inhabited by beneficent state actors, politicians and bureaucrats, who answer either to the preferences of consumers or to the judgements of morally upright voters. The specific arguments for scepticism about state actors are ones with which I have little quarrel. Second, the public choice theorist is right to insist that one consider questions about the institutional framework in which decisions take place. However, those questions need to be widened beyond those the public choice theorist allows. The problem is not that of either explaining or designing institutions given universal avarice, but that of examining the ways in which institutions define and foster different conceptions of interests. Individuals' conceptions of their interests needs to be the end point of analysis, not its starting point. Thus explanatory and normative questions posed by new institutionalism should be replaced by those posed by old institutionalism. For reasons outlined, I believe that emphasis on the institutional context will lead analysis away from both market-centred and state-centred approaches to human economic and social welfare towards an association-centred perspective.[53] There is a need for a new focus on the question of what associations best develop the goods of a human life, and what conditions are required in order that such associations flourish.

POSTSCRIPT: MARKETS, ASSOCIATIONS AND SOCIALISM

In a book published in 1915 surveying contemporary political thought of the period Ernest Barker offered the following diagnosis of the political tendencies of the age:

> We seem to be living in days in which we are called upon to revise in every direction our old conception of the State. We see the State invited to retreat before the guild, the national group, the Church.[1]

When it was written this statement was quite a reasonable one to make, at least as far as the socialist side of the debate went. The period just prior to the First World War had been the highpoint of syndicalism in both Europe and the United States. The picture of the state in retreat from a political and economic world founded upon associations of producers was one that was that appeared to have some plausibility.

By the time the reprint of the book I own appeared, in 1951, Barker's comment looks plain odd. The intervening years had seen the triumph of Bolshevism and the decline of any more decentralised associational vision of socialism. After the war those who advocated a form of associational socialism, the guild socialists in Britain and council communists in Europe, belonged to small groups detached from any large movement, and syndicalism was in decline. Socialism meant centralised state planning. That remained true also in the social democratic parties of Europe – 1951 was a highpoint in the Keynesian world order, in which the future of a social democratic consensus appeared assured. Hence, it was a period in which there still seemed some point to Hayek's complaint that 'if it is no longer fashionable to emphasise the "we are all socialists now", this is so merely because the fact is too obvious',[2] where socialism could be taken to be shorthand for any form of centrally planned economy.

By the time I bought the book in a second-hand bookshop in 1990 the statement was still unbelievable, although for very different reasons. In the UK I had just lived through a decade in which I had been ruled by a political party ostensibly dedicated to the retreat of the state. The retreat was not however a retreat before non-state associations, but before the market. Independent associations

174

were seen as bastions of union and professional power themselves to be broken and subjected to the disciplines of markets. This anti-associationalism in part explained the paradox that as the state retreated before the market in economic life, at the same time it advanced in other spheres of civil society. Hence, to take the changes in education for example, the spread of market norms into universities has been paralleled with a management regime that is akin to a centralised state-planned command economy. The idea of a university as a self-governing association itself has gone the way that Adam Smith wished it to go some two centuries ago.[3] At the same time internationally the state is in real retreat from globalised markets. The decline of state socialism is not only a consequence of the appalling example provided by the East European and Asian regimes that unfortunately went under that title, but also because the state as an instrument for realising social goals appears to be in decline. However, one needs to be wary in making such pronouncements. One of the lessons of the fate of Barker's claims is just how bad political theorists can be in ascertaining the tendencies of the age. It may be that Hegel is right that the owl of Minerva flies only at dusk, but so also do bats. It is certainly not my purpose here to make any predictions about the future.

My purpose in drawing attention to the passage by Barker is rather to point to the narrowing of political visions that has occurred in the twentieth century. In the background of much social and political theory of this century has been a fairly bleak alternative of state-run centrally planned economies or free-market economies, or some mix of the two. Given that debate, the market has won by default. The alternative of an economy run from a central planning office in which both political and economic power is concentrated in the hands of a few has failed. Hence the popularity of markets. If it is not fashionable to emphasise the 'we are all believers in capitalism now', this is not just because it is taken to be obvious, but also because it is an embarrassment. My main purpose in this book is to give reason to stop before defaulting to the market. The vicissitudes of political argument in the century should give us at least reason to pause.

My main drift in this book has been negative: to remind us that even on its strongest ground the case for market economies is weaker than is now standardly supposed. Arguments from neutrality, welfarist arguments, arguments from freedom and autonomy, the claim that the market is a sphere of recognition, the suggestion that only the market makes rational social choices possible, the arguments that markets solve the problems of human ignorance, that they run with the grain of human nature, these central arguments in defence of the market economy are weaker and more ambivalent than is often supposed. This is the negative case of the book. However, running through the book has been a defence of associations and the non-market orders within existing society and implicitly through these a case for an associational socialism. These implicit arguments can be taken in a weaker or stronger direction.

The weak form of the argument would be that according to which the main problem is one of boundary maintenance, of protecting non-market associational

175

orders from the incursions of market norms. The position is broadly Hegelian, of sustaining those associational forms, of something like corporations in Hegel's sense, that are required to sustain the internal goods of practices within the framework of civil society understood as a market order. A similar position has been articulated by Walzer,[4] and has been popular within recent political theory. It has been particularly influential on that part of socialist theory which accepts a role for markets, but one that is bounded and does not encroach on other spheres.[5] For Walzer, liberal politics involves an 'art of separation' which creates freedoms by building walls between different institutions – churches, schools, universities, families and markets. The walls serve two purposes. First, they ensure that goods in one setting are not convertible into goods in another. Economic success should not bring political power, political power should not determine religious authority and so on. The aim is 'complex equality' – in which different goods are distributed according to the distinct understanding of different institutions and practices, and not by some other dominant external institution. Second, and this is implicit in the last sentence, the walls protect the integrity of each institution and practice – each institutional setting has its 'particular patterns of rules, customs and cooperative arrangements'[6] – and politics should keep each separate, including itself as a practice. In particular, in the capitalist world the problem is that of 'the confinement of the market to its proper space'. This and not the Marxist goal of 'the abolition of the market',[7] should be the aim of the socialist.

The stronger form that associationalism could take would be to see in associations the possibility of an alternative non-market economic order. While Marx is the source of much non-market socialism (as I noted earlier in chapter 8) the associational position is not one to be found within Marx, who tends to inherit the classical economists' scepticism about associations. It was however defended by a socialist theorist who has already made a number of appearances in this book, Otto Neurath. Neurath was committed (as noted in chapter 9) to a non-market model of socialism. In response to problems about the compatibility of planning with freedom and ecology, and a growing scepticism about the technism implicit in his own earlier work, Neurath, in his later writings, defended an associational socialism. The existence of a variety of associations with power and functions distributed amongst them is defended as an institutional condition for freedom:

> [T]he 'freedom' of a democratic country might be described by the fact that each member is permitted to have more than one loyalty, e.g. to his family, to his local community, to his profession, to his political party, to his church, to his lodge, to an international movement and to his country. One expects, in a democratic country, that a citizen knows how to handle these various loyalties and to assemble them in one way or another.[8]

The basis of dictatorial or totalitarian regimes lies in the 'tendency for one, and only one loyalty to "devour" all the others, and various loyalties are not permitted to grow up side by side'.[9] Recently that familiar account of totalitarianism which lies at the basis of the case for the associational model of socialism is often stated in the language of civil society. What is significant about Neurath's version of the associational model is that it remains strongly anti-market and makes a clear distinction between the flourishing of associations and the flourishing of exchange relations, a distinction that many recent uses of the term 'civil society' have blurred.[10] He avoids the assumption, which has dogged much twentieth-century political thought and action, that we must choose either state planning or the 'internationalism of the "money-order" '.[11]

Neurath develops a modern version of the classical account of political and social life as an association of associations discussed in chapter 2. His picture of a socialist society is of a 'societas societum' in which economic life is not governed by market principles, but in which 'civil society' in the sense of thriving public associations exists. Thus he rejects the centralisation of powers and functions in the state in favour of dispersed overlapping planning authorities. While it is independent of the guild socialist model which forms the intellectual heritage of recent associational socialism, it shares the appeal to the structures, if not the content, of medieval Europe:

> We know from the Middle Ages how 'overlapping' authorities can work. There could be international organization which would be responsible for the administration of the main natural resources, e.g. an organization dealing with iron, others with coffee, rubber, foodstuffs which could act as members of an international planning board – such organizations could be in action before a world commonwealth would be organized.[12]

Similarly 'big rivers with their banks could be "internationalized" '.[13] More local units of self-government with powers of regional planning might exist alongside such larger functional units.[14] A significant feature of the international functional units of planning that Neurath describes here is that they are of the kind required if global resources are to be used in an ecologically rational way, in particular to overcome international 'tragedy of the commons' problems. Neurath's associational model of socialism has a clear ecological dimension. Moreover it is one that manages to avoid the narrow localism of some green thinkers,[15] and the authoritarian statism of others[16]. His account deserves to be better known.

The arguments in this book are inspired by the strong form of associational socialism offered by Neurath. My commitments lie in that direction and elsewhere I have given reasons for preferring it to the weak form.[17] However, my main aim in this book has been more modest – to defend non-market associations in a world increasingly dominated by market norms, and to puncture the intellectual case for a market economy. The arguments of this book are consistent with both weak and strong forms of associationalism. And it has to be admitted that stronger visions of a radically new social order are unlikely to find a wide audience in the late twentieth century. There are some bad reasons for this, most notably the increasing turn away from the enlightenment project of a rationally ordered social life. While there may be a need to recognise both the limits of human reason and the misconceptions about its nature that came with the enlightenment, the rejection of the project is I believe a mistake. If the enlightenment invented the idea that happiness and freedom are a possible aim of society, then the invention was a sound one.

There are, however, different and more understandable sources of scepticism. The vision of a non-market associational order is possibly a utopian vision and the late twentieth century is an unhappy place for utopias. The century is littered with wrecks of dystopias that resulted from utopian visions. Hence, for those sceptical of grand claims for social change, I offer the weaker form of associationalism. I do not do so, however, in the spirit of Walzer's liberal art of separation, but more in the spirit of resistance. Even if a non-market social order of the kind Neurath defends is not possible, there are still good reasons to resist the expansion of market domains in existing society. For even if it turns out that the market economy and modern state are institutions we are stuck with – and I retain my possibly utopian hope that they are not – it is only against the background of a thriving associational life that they can be civilised.

NOTES

1 IN PARTIAL PRAISE OF ADVERSARIES

1 Typical is Rorty's remark: 'logical arguments ... are ... in the end not much more than ways of getting people to change their practices' (Rorty 1989, p. 78).

2 Two books that do seriously engage in argument with the Austrians are Wainwright 1994 and Fleetwood 1995.

3 For clear and well-developed defences of market socialism see Miller 1989 and Roemer 1994. See also Le Grand and Estrin 1989.

4 For an excellent discussion of the various different types and meanings of the concept of the 'market' see Sayer 1995, ch. 4.

5 For useful discussions of these issues see Sayer 1995 and Hodgson 1988.

6 Mauss 1954 is particularly influential. Of special significance for discussion of the possible role of gift as against market in modern society is Titmus 1970 and Hagstrom 1965. On different forms of gift economies see Polanyi's work which is itself heavily influenced by Aristotle (Polanyi 1957a and 1957b).

7 Aristotle *Politics* II. A defence of some form of combination of private ownership and common use is a theme in Christian writing from the *Acts* onwards. I discuss Aristotle's position in a little more detail in O'Neill 1997a.

8 The point would not be worth making if it were not for some bad arguments that do assume that only 'substances' or material things can be commodities. See for example Nelson 1995.

9 See Polanyi 1957c. I discuss the misinterpretation of the phrase further below.

10 My own statement of it owes much to Meikle's perceptive discussion in Meikle 1995.

11 See Sugden 1981, p. 10.

12 Marx 1973, pp. 487–488.

13 For typical examples of such attacks on market essentialism see Hindess 1987 pp. 147–158; Cutler 1988; Tomlinson 1982, ch. 7 and 1990. The anti-essentialism about markets of Hindess and Cutler has its roots in a general anti-essentialism that appears in their earlier work: see for example the criticism of Hilferding for his essentialism in Cutler *et al.* 1977, p. 69. Another influential anti-essentialist 'post-Marxist' text which includes specific criticism of essentialism about the economy is Laclau and Mouffe 1985, pp. 75–85 and *passim*.

14 I criticise this line of argument in O'Neill 1994a.

15 Friedman 1979 has been particularly significant in this regard.

16 'Theoretical economics has the task of presenting not merely the "*laws*" of economic phenomena to us, but also their "*general nature*" ' (Menger 1985, p. 198; original emphasis).

17 On the relation between Austrian economics and Aristotelian essentialism see B. Smith

1986 and 1990. For an essentialist reading of Austrian economics see Mäki 1990a and 1990b.
18 See Mises' unfortunate incursions into 'methodological apriorism' (Mises 1949, ch. 2).
19 Hindess 1987, ch. 9.
20 Gray offers a Kantian reading of Hayek's position which is set against the 'Aristotelian method of seeking essences or natures of things' (Gray 1984, p. 6). For criticism of Gray see Peacock 1993.
21 For critical realist accounts of Hayek's position see Fleetwood 1995 and 1996 and Lawson 1994.
22 Gray himself acknowledges that this is possible (Gray 1984, p. 117).
23 For a further elaboration of Marx's essentialism and its debt to Aristotle, see Meikle 1985; especially ch. 3. See also Wood 1981, part 5, and O'Neill 1994a.
24 Aristotle *Topics* I.
25 In the language of Locke, the atomic structure of copper is its real essence, the explanatorily dependent properties, its nominal essence (Locke, *Essay Concerning Human Understanding* III, 3). See also Aristotle's distinction between 'real' and 'nominal' definitions in *Posterior Analytics* II.
26 Hindess 1987, p. 149.
27 Ibid. p. 159.
28 Ibid. p. 150.
29 Polanyi 1957c, p. 139.
30 Hegel 1967, 163R.
31 Wittgenstein 1960, p. 17 (original emphasis); see also Wittgenstein 1958, paragraphs 66 and 67.
32 Wittgenstein 1958, paragraph 66.
33 Dore 1993, p. 66.

2 POLITICS, ECONOMY, NEUTRALITY

1 Rawls 1972, section 50, pp. 325–332.
2 Aristotle *Politics* 1280b 38f.
3 Ibid. 1324a 22.
4 Raz 1986, ch. 5
5 Dworkin 1978, p. 127.
6 Devlin 1965.
7 Mill 1975, pp. 28–29 (my emphasis).
8 Ackerman 1980, ch. 1 and 1990; Larmore 1987, ch. 3; Habermas 1986, p. 170.
9 Larmore 1987, p. 53 (original emphasis).
10 Hayek 1976, p. 109.
11 Ibid. pp. 109–110.
12 Hirschman 1970.
13 Hayek 1973, 1976 and 1979.
14 See the distinction between want-regarding and ideal-regarding principles in Barry 1990.
15 Hirsch 1977, p. 119.
16 On the contrast between the market and the forum see Elster 1986.
17 Larmore 1987, p. 43 (original emphasis).
18 Aristotle *Politics* II ii.
19 In broad terms I believe that Aristotle's defence of the family, understood as a defence of special relations, is sound, while his defence of private property is not. For a discussion of the latter see Irwin 1987.
20 Aristotle *Politics* 1261b 10ff; cf. Aristotle *Rhetoric* I.7.

21 Aristotle *Politics* 1252b 27ff pp. 5–6 (original emphasis).
22 Aristotle *Nicomachean Ethics* 1097b 14ff; cf. 1172b 31–34.
23 For an influential defence of this inclusivist reading Aristotle's account of *eudaemonia*, see Ackrill 1980.
24 Aristotle *Nicomachean Ethics* 1096b 23ff.
25 Aristotle *Politics* 1253a 26–29; see also 1253a 2–4.
26 Aristotle *Nicomachean Ethics* 1097b 8–11.
27 For a useful discussion see Irwin 1988, §219.
28 Aristotle *Nicomachean Ethics* 1166a 8.
29 Aristotle *Politics* 1252a 1–7 (my emphasis).
30 Aristotle *Nicomachean Ethics* 1160a 8–30.
31 Berlin 1969.
32 See Rawls 1972, ch. VII.
33 Larmore 1987, p. 43.
34 Aristotle *Politics* VII vii.
35 For another Aristotelian route to this conclusion see Nussbaum 1990.
36 Kant 1991a, p. 51 (original emphasis).
37 Hayek 1976, p. 107.
38 Aristotle *Politics* I viii 1256b 27ff p. 26.
39 Aristotle *Politics* 1236b 31.
40 The use of the term 'chrematistic' I outline here is that which Aristotle employs most widely in the *Politics*. Aristotle does however sometimes use it in a more neutral sense: for an account of the different uses see Barker in Aristotle 1948, pp. 226–227.
41 Aristotle *Politics* I viii 1256b 40ff p. 27.
42 Aristotle *Politics* I ix 1257b 28ff p. 31.
43 Aristotle *Politics* I ix 1257b 40f p. 32.
44 See for example Aristotle *Politics* I viii 1256b 26–39 p. 26.
45 Marx 1970, ch. 4. See in particular the reference to Aristotle in footnote 2 pp. 150–151.
46 Polanyi 1957c, p. 54.
47 Polanyi 1957c, pp. 53–54; cf. Polanyi 1957a.
48 Polanyi 1963, cited in Stanfield 1978, p. 6.
49 See for example Hayek 1988, pp. 45–48.
50 Polanyi 1957c, p. 256.
51 For a characteristically vigorous defence of the market in these terms see Gray 1992.
52 Mulgan 1977, p. 17.
53 Ibid. p. 17.
54 Ibid. p. 17 (my emphasis).
55 See Cole 1920 and Neurath 1942.
56 See for example Walzer 1984, p. 318. Marx himself separates these two sense of civil society: see Marx 1974c, pp. 232–233.
57 See, most famously, A. Smith 1981 I.x.c.27. Opposition to associations remains a central component of defences of the free market: see for example Hayek 1979, ch. 15.
58 Cited in Arendt 1986, p. 322.

3 ECONOMIC THEORY AND HUMAN WELL-BEING

1 For the classic statement of the new welfare economics see Hicks 1946, ch. 1. For a good textbook treatment see for example Lancaster 1983, ch. 7.
2 Her preferences are also taken to be complete, i.e. for all alternatives a and b, either a is preferred to b, b is preferred to a, or the agent is indifferent between them. Her preference structure is also taken to have other formal characteristics: preferences are reflexive and separable.
3 Harrod 1938, p. 389.

4 A. Smith 1982a VI.i.15.
5 Jevons 1970, p. 91.
6 Ibid. p. 83.
7 'It is essential to note that the economist does not claim to measure any affection of the mind in itself, or directly; but only indirectly, through its effect' (Marshall 1962, I.II.1, p. 13).
8 See Carter 1968, p. 81.
9 Marshall 1962, III.iii, p. 1.
10 Pigou 1920, p. 24.
11 Ibid. p. 11. Total welfare is defined more widely and while Pigou tends to subjective state account of well-being he sometimes appeals to a broader conception:

> Human beings are ... 'ends in themselves' ... [A] man who is attuned to the beautiful in nature or in art, whose character is simple and sincere, whose passions are controlled and sympathies widespread, is in himself an important element in the ethical value of the world; the way in which he feels and thinks constitutes a part of welfare.
>
> (Ibid. pp. 12–13)

12 See Menger 1950, appendix A.
13 Ibid. pp. 52–53.
14 Ibid. p. 53.
15 Ibid. pp. 54–55 and appendix A.
16 Mises 1960, p. 151.
17 Mises 1949, p. 21.
18 Some recent welfare economics has seen a welcome return from formal to substantive concepts, most notably through the work of Sen. Sen employs a broadly objectivist account of well-being. Well-being is defined in terms of 'functionings' – the 'beings and doings' that are constitutive of a person's life: for example, adequate nourishment, good health, self respect, participation in a community. The measurement of well-being is approached in terms of persons' capacities and freedoms to achieve well-being thus characterised. See Sen 1987a and 1993. Sen's approach is one in which I have broad sympathy, although for critical comments see O'Neill 1993d, pp. 73–75.
19 Samuelson, for example, interprets the shift to a formal definition of utility as 'a steady removal of moral, utilitarian, welfare connotations from the concept' (Samuelson 1938, p. 344). Hence his earlier comment: 'any connection between utility ... and any welfare concept is disavowed. The idea that the result ... could have any influence upon ethical judgements of policy is one which deserves the impatience of modern economists' (Samuelson 1937, p. 161).
20 Broome makes similar claims without the positivism: see Broome 1991a, p. 65 and 1991b.
21 See Hicks 1981a for a response to the positivist position.
22 There are other methodological reasons offered for this move which I do not discuss here, in particular the influence of behaviourism and the claim that economics stay at the level of observables, at 'revealed preference' exhibited in market behaviour.
23 Wood 1990, p. 55.
24 This is a stronger version of the claim than that which Wood discusses according to which subjective determination is a matter of a person's well-being being 'at least to some extent' determined by their beliefs.
25 Aristotle *Nicomachean Ethics* II, ch. 6.
26 Menger 1950, p. 120.
27 The scholastics follow Augustine in defining the utility of objects in these terms.

Hence the distinction between the order of value in nature and that of utility. The first order that run thus: 'living things are ranked above inanimate ... the sentient rank above the insensitive ... the intelligent take precedence over the unthinking ... the immortal beings are higher than mortals'. The order of utility runs differently: 'on this other scale we would put some inanimate things above creatures of sense'. The first order is the order determined by 'rational consideration in its free judgement', the second by 'the constraint of need, or the attraction of desire' (Augustine *City of God* XI, ch. 16). In his discussion of the just price Aquinas follows Augustine: 'the price of commercial commodities is not assessed in accordance with their relative position on some absolute scale in the natural world ... but in accordance with their usefulness to men' (Aquinas *Summa Theologiae* 2a2ae, question 77 article 2). The position survives in Locke, who follows the scholastics in holding to a dispositional account of the 'intrinsic worth' of objects: 'the Intrinsick Natural worth of any Thing consists in its fitness to supply the Necessities or serve the Conveniences of human Life; and the more necessary it is to our Being, or the more it contributes to our Well-being the greater its worth' (Locke 1991, p. 258). The intrinsic worth of an object is in that sense a 'passive power' of the object. See the useful comments of Kelly 1991, pp. 82–83.

28 For example both Parfit and Griffin present hedonist, desire satisfaction and objective list theories of well-being as alternatives to each other, but in the same game. See Parfit 1984, appendix I and Griffin 1986, part one.

29 Mises 1960, p. 151.

30 Aristotle *Metaphysics* 1072a 29.

31 Mises 1960, p. 151.

32 Griffin 1986, p. 14.

33 See Locke 1991, pp. 256–258.

34 A. Smith 1981 I.iv.13.

35 A. Smith 1981 IV.vii.a.19. The move from Smith's paradox to objectivism is more clearly illustrated in the opening pages of Ricardo 1973, ch 1, section I.

36 Menger 1950, p. 146 (original emphasis).

37 Mises 1960, pp. 167–174.

38 Ibid. p. 170.

39 Ibid. p. 168.

40 More recently the term 'radical subjectivism' has been used within the Austrian tradition to state a claim about the nature of the future, that future social states are dependent on current subjective choices by individuals. I discuss this further in chapter 9. It is independent of other claims made here.

41 Hayek 1955b, p. 31. Hayek goes on, however, to make the quite mistaken inference that the social world is fully determined by individuals' conceptions, that 'so far as human actions are concerned, the things *are* what acting people think they are'. For criticism of this move see Fleetwood 1995, ch. 4, Lawson 1994 and O'Neill 1997e.

42 Mises 1960, p. 148. This claim is clearly logically independent of subjectivism as an explanatory or ontological thesis.

43 Hume 1975, p. 219.

44 I discuss the concept of value freedom in detail in O'Neill 1993d ch. 9.

45 Mises 1949, p. 21.

46 See Robbins 1935, chs 1 and 2.

47 Robbins 1938, p. 637 (original emphasis). See also Robbins 1935, ch. 6. For criticism of the argument from within a preference utilitarian perspective see Harsanyi 1982. An excellent recent collection on the issue is Elster and Roemer 1991.

48 This account of pleasure is effectively demolished by Ryle. See Ryle 'Pleasure' in Ryle 1960 and Ryle 1963 pp. 103–106.

49 Thus Robbins makes it clear that he is making a distinction between the normative and positive components of economics, not claiming that the normative should be eschewed:

> All I proposed to do was to make clear that the statement social wealth was increased should run, *if* equal capacity for satisfaction on the part of the economic subjects be assumed, *then* social wealth can be said to be increased ... All that I intended ... was that [economists] might better realise the exact connection between the normative and the positive, and that their practice as political philosophers might be made thereby more self conscious.
>
> (Robbins 1938, pp. 638 and 640)

50 The problems are confounded in the attempt by Hicks to offer the compensation test as a value neutral objective test of efficiency which avoids interpersonal comparisons:

> How are we to say whether a reorganization of production,which makes A better off, but B worse off marks an improvement in efficiency? ... [A] perfectly objective test ... enables us to discriminate between those reorganizations which improve productive efficiency and those which do not. If A is made so much better off by the change that he could compensate B for his loss, and still have something left over, then the reorganization is an unequivocal improvement.
>
> (Hicks 1981b, p. 105)

Two points are worth making. First, the criterion of efficiency is not value neutral (Little 1957, ch. 6). Second, as Sen pithily puts it:

> The compensation principle is either redundant – if the compensation is actually paid then there is a real Pareto improvement and hence no need for the test – or unjustified – it is no consolation to losers, who might include the worst off members of society, to be told that it would be possible to compensate them even though there is no actual intention to do so.
>
> (Sen 1987b, p. 33)

51 Mises 1949, p. 21.

52 A similar combination was attempted in his earlier *Socialism*:

> Philosophers had been arguing about the ultimate Good for a long time before it was settled by modern investigation. At the present day Eudaemonism is no longer open to attack. In the long run all the arguments which philosophers from Kant to Hegel bought against it were unable to dissociate the concept Morality from that of Happiness ... [T]he tenets of intuitionistic ethics ... are irreconcilable with scientific method.
>
> (Mises 1981, pp. 359–360/original p. 400)

53 For recent statements of the theory see Brandt 1979, Griffin 1986, Lewis 1989 and Railton 1986.

54 See O'Neill 1993a.

55 Griffin 1986, p. 17. For this reason I think the subjectivism in Hume's essay 'Of the Standard of Taste' (Hume 1985f) is ultimately unstable. Griffin appears to have moved in the direction of endorsing this objection (Griffin 1991 and 1996).

56 I develop the distinction in more detail in O'Neill 1995b. The distinction parallels that often made about truth. For example, while truth cannot be defined in terms of convergence, convergence is the best criteria of truth we might have.

57 I owe the term to Jonathan Aldred.

58 Harsanyi 1982, p. 55.

59 There is a straightforward inferential error in some recent environmental philosophy through which the capacity to value is extended to nonrational parts of nature. The argument runs that since for any living being x there are objects and states of affairs y_1 ... y_n that are valuable to x, it follows that x values y_1 ... y_n. The inference is plainly mistaken. Water may be good for trees. But trees do not value water. There is a distinction to be made between y being valuable for x and x valuing y. It is of note here that the argument depends on the reduction we have been criticising here of the concept of 'y being valuable to x' to the concept of 'x valuing y'. Valuing requires certain cognitive capacities. Non-rational nature does not display those activities. Hence autonomy in the sense it is used in political and moral philosophy cannot apply to nonrational nature. There may however be a weaker sense of autonomy that can be displayed by nonrational nature: living things have powers and patterns of development and can be said to behave autonomously when they display these.

60 See O'Neill 1994c.

61 Where a thin theory of the good refers to the good 'restricted to the essentials' and is supposed to determine the class of primary goods that rational individuals will necessarily require to pursue whatever ends they might have (Rawls 1972, section 60), a thick theory of the good specifies particular ends.

62 Nussbaum 1990, p. 217.

63 See Simon 1972.

64 See Holland and O'Neill 1997 and O'Neill 1997b.

65 That thought is I think at the heart of Hayek's account of progress as change for change's sake.

66 Marx 1973, p. 488.

67 I develop these points in more detail in O'Neill 1993a and 1994b.

68 Kant 1991b, p. 50.

69 The same is true of some romantic leftism. I remember an argument in China I had with the daughter of a visiting Oxford Maoist who was bitterly disappointed that the peasants had radio cassette players – this from a person who had a state of the art machine at home, who had the luxury of travelling around the globe to visit the exotic and who ignored the openings of horizons a radio can bring.

4 THE MARKET AND HUMAN WELL-BEING

1 Jevons 1970, ch. VIII, p. 254 (original emphasis).

2 Preferences are also assumed to be reflexive and complete.

3 Hahn 1984, pp. 111–134 and 1989 pp. 108ff.

4 A. Smith 1981 I.

5 Ibid. and *passim*.

6 Mises 1960, p. 151.

7 Hayek 1976, pp. 15–30.

8 Ibid. p. 6.

9 Ibid. p. 5.

10 For a useful discussion of the relationships between Austrian plan coordination standards and Pareto-optimality, see Schapiro 1989.

11 Lane 1978, p. 803.

12 For a useful recent survey of the literature see Lane 1991, part VII.

13 Cf. Keynes 1961.

14 Hirsch 1977, p. 26.

15 Pigou 1920, p. 28.

16 Similar problems are evident in the field of environmental economics in which the attempt to extend the 'measuring rod of money' to include environmental goods is indicative of the way in which the growth in economic welfare has entailed a real loss

in the environmental goods. The attempt to solve this by extending the money measure is, for reasons I outline elsewhere (O'Neill 1993d), misconceived.

17 A. Smith 1982a IV.1.8.
18 A. Smith 1981 I.xi.c.7.
19 'We suffer more ... when we fall from a better to a worse situation, than we ever enjoy when we rise from a worse to a better' (A. Smith 1982a VI.i.6).
20 A. Smith 1982a VI.i.15.
21 Ibid. VI.i.11.
22 Ibid. VI.i.13.
23 Ibid. 1982a IV.1.10; cf. Smith 1981 I.xi.c.7.
24 A. Smith 1982a IV.1.10. The theme of this passage reappears in *The Wealth of Nations*: 'A revolution of the greatest importance to the publick happiness [commerce], was ... bought about by two different orders of people, who had not the least intention to serve the publick. To gratify the most childish vanity was the sole motive of the great proprietors. The merchants and artificers ... acted merely form a view to their own interests' (1981 III.iv.17). The use of invisible hand metaphor reappears in IV.ii.9.
25 A. Smith 1981 I.IV.1
26 A. Smith 1982a I.iii.3.5..
27 Ibid. VII.iii.3.16.
28 Marx 1973, pp. 487–488.
29 Ibid. p. 488.
30 This is true also of more recent indirect arguments for markets. A similar paradox is stated by Maritain 1958, pp. 21–22 and discussed by Novak 1982, ch. XI and *passim*. It is a feature of Novak's discussion of Maritain that the conflicts Maritain at least recognises and his earlier work develops in detail are simply wished away.
31 Montesquieu 1989, part one, book V, ch. 6.
32 'The high rate of profit seems everywhere to destroy that parsimony which in other circumstances is natural to the character of the merchant. When profits are high, that sober virtue seems to be superfluous, and expensive luxury to suit better the affluence of his situation' (A. Smith 1981 IV.vii.c.61).
33 The phrase is that of Hirsch 1977, part III. For a useful survey of the literature see Hirschman 1982.
34 See Lane 1991 for a powerful restatement of this point. The point was recognised by A. Smith 1981 V.i.f.50.

5 AUTONOMY, FREEDOM AND MARKET

1 In the sphere of circulation individuals contract as free-agents; in the sphere of production they appear again as capitalist and labourer, superordinate and subordinate (Marx 1970, p. 172.) In buying labour power the buyer gains rights of direction. These arguments have come to the fore again in recent feminist objections to commercial surrogacy. (See in particular Pateman 1988, chs 5–7.) In entering a surrogacy contract a woman loses rights of self-direction over acts central to her identity.

> The worker contracts out right of command over the use of his body, and the prostitute contracts out right of direct sexual use of her body. The selves of the worker and the prostitute are, in different ways, both put out for hire. The self of the 'surrogate' mother is at stake in a more profound sense still. The 'surrogate' mother contracts out the right over the unique physiological, emotional and creative capacity of her body, that is to say, of herself as a woman.
>
> (Pateman 1988, p. 215)

These arguments are ones with which I concur and it is not because of any weakness but rather for reasons of space that I have had to leave them aside.

2 This kind of argument is found in arguments for neutrality in Rawls, Ackerman and Ronald Dworkin. For useful discussions see G. Dworkin 1988, ch. 1 and Mason 1990.

3 There are exceptions to this interpretation. Gray, for example, notes that 'Hayek's conception of freedom has some strong positive connotations' (Gray 1989, p. 63).

4 Hayek 1960, p. 11

5 Ibid. p. 17. The quotations are from Dewey 1935, p. 41 and 1938, p. 74; and R. Perry 1940, p. 269.

6 In outline the debate runs roughly as follows: the negative theorist insists on the distinction between liberty and the conditions for its exercise. The positive theorist responds by arguing that if intended constraints on the actions of others count as a restriction on liberty, as it does on the negative conception, then so also should unintended but foreseeable and alterable consequences of social arrangements that effect individuals' possibility of exercising choice. They should do so since there is no ethically significant distinction to be made between responsibility for the intentional consequences of an action and responsibility for the foreseeable and alterable consequences of an action: hence constraints on the exercise of choices that result from either, including those that arise from poverty or the lack of property in the means of production, should count as restrictions of freedom. To this argument a second is sometimes added, or offered as an alternative response: that, if negative liberty is of value, then so also are the conditions for its exercise, and hence what is called 'positive liberty'. Two comments on the debate. First, it would I believe be a mistake to deny there is an ethically significant difference between being subject to the will of another agent and being constrained by social arrangements, between personal unfreedom and structural unfreedom. That there is such a significant distinction has been central to traditional socialist accounts of wage labour and the transition from pre-capitalist to capitalist societies. To insist that there is a distinction to be made is not to say that personal and structural unfreedom are not both objectionable. It is to resist the conflation of the two and the ethical considerations appropriate to each. Second, the assumption in much of the debate that one could resolve substantive ethical and political differences by coming up with the correct conceptual analysis of 'liberty' is a mistake. The central question ought to be not, 'which analysis of the concept of liberty is to be preferred?', but rather, 'why ought liberty in the senses defined be of ethical significance?'.

7 For an argument of this kind see Nozick 1980, p. 331.

8 Berlin 1969, p. 131.

9 Hayek 1960, p. 17.

10 He himself fails to note the difference between Berlin's and Dewey's use of the term 'positive liberty'. See for example his references to Berlin's essay in Hayek 1960, p. 425 fn.26.

11 Hayek 1960, p. 12.

12 Berlin 1969, p. 131.

13 Hayek 1960, p. 79.

14 Ibid.

15 See for example Buchanan's defence of liberty as a condition for the person who 'can envisage himself as a product of his own making, as embodying prospects for changing himself into one of the imagined possibilities that might be' (Buchanan 1979a, p. 110).

16 Hayek 1960, p. 21.

17 Most significant here is Raz 1986. A useful discussion of perfectionist liberalism and the market is to be found in Hurka 1993, ch. 13.

18 Gray 1992, p. 25.

19 Raz 1986, pp. 373–378.

20 For a development of those arguments Gray 1993a, pp. 306–314 and Keat 1994.

21 C. Taylor 1985, pp. 190–191.
22 My position owes much to John Benson:

> The virtue of autonomy is a mean state of character with regard to reliance on one's own powers in acting, choosing and forming opinions. The deficiency is termed heteronomy, and there are many terms which may be used to describe the heteronomous person, some of which suggest specific forms of the vice: credulous, gullible, compliant, passive, submissive, overdependent, servile. For the vice of excess there is no name in common use, but solipsism might do, or arrogant self-sufficiency.
>
> (Benson 1983, p. 5)

23 Gray 1993b, p. 137.

6 AUTONOMY, IDENTITY AND MARKET

1 Mill 1974, p. 76.
2 Mill 1929, p. 232.
3 Hayek 1960, p. 12.
4 Weil 1952, pp. 142–143 and 158–160.
5 Ibid. p. 142.
6 MacIntyre 1985, p. 220. See also Sandel 1982.
7 MacIntyre 1985, p. 32.
8 Ibid. p. 220.
9 Gilligan 1982. On the parallels with communitarianism see O'Neill 1993b.
10 Baier 1989, p. 46. The last quotation in the passage is from Gilligan 1982, p. 173.
11 Mill 1929, p. 232.
12 In contrast to Baier, Gilligan recognises that as a feature of moral maturity.
13 A. Smith 1981 III.iv.11 and V.i.b.7.
14 Mill 1929, pp. 233–234.
15 For a discussion of Mill's position see G. Smith 1990.
16 Marx 1973, p. 163.
17 Ibid. p. 162.
18 Hegel 1967, part III.
19 Hayek 1960, p. 41.
20 Ibid. p. 41.
21 Marx and Engels 1968, p. 38.
22 Oakeshott 1962a, p. 170.
23 Cf. MacIntyre 1985, ch. 15.
24 Translation in A. Smith 'Letter to the *Edinburgh Review*' in A. Smith 1982b, p. 252. For a more recent translation see Rousseau 1984, p. 119.
25 A. Smith 1982a I.iii.2.1, p. 50.
26 A. Smith 1982a IV.1.10–11 and 1981 I.xi.c.7.
27 A. Smith 1982a I.iii.3.
28 Hume 1975, p. 232.
29 Marx 1974d, p. 377 (original emphasis).
30 Orwell 1968, p. 515.
31 Jameson 1991, p. 18. Jameson properly acknowledges his debt to the situationists description of the society of the spectacle in thus describing the post-modern condition. The situationists themselves retain a much clearer critical stance than do their recent theoretical offspring. However, the picture of the post-capitalist society they draw itself calls upon an indefensible picture of autonomy, on the ideal of life as constant self-creation.

32 Kellner 1992, p. 153.
33 Ibid. pp. 153–154.
34 Some of that ambivalence resides in the invocation of a model of the 'dialectic' which forces good humour upon us: 'As for that reality itself ... the as yet untheorized original space of the new "world system" of multinational or late capitalism (a space whose baleful aspects are only too obvious), the dialectic requires us to hold equally to the positive or "progressive" evaluation' Jameson 1991, p. 50). The claim is remarkable. Nothing about the 'dialectic' ensures that the social world progresses – decline and disintegration are not ruled out by some logic to history. And one might, unlike Hegel, 'look negativity in the face' and simply weep.
35 Kellner 1992, p. 154.

7 AUTONOMY, AUTHORITY AND MARKET

1 Kant 1991a, p. 54 (original emphasis).
2 Ibid. p. 55. For an elaboration and defence of what I believe to be the defensible core of this ideal see O'Neill 1995b.
3 This is sometimes granted by its proponents. Thus Lindley writes of Mill's account of the rational believer the following:

> The person who fails to consider properly alternative opinions to his own is either led by authority, in which case the principles to which he appeals for guidance in choosing a way of life are *external* to him, or they are simply principles given by inclination ... for no reason. In either case ... there is a lack of self-determination. This has the initially surprising consequence that most of us are not autonomous in regard of our scientific beliefs, and indeed that complete autonomy is unattainable for beings with finite minds.
> (Lindley 1986, p. 51; original emphasis)

Nothing Lindley subsequently says resolves the problems he raises, for the trouble lies not in our finitude, but in the value of autonomy to which we are supposed to aspire. The passage to which Lindley refers is that of Mill 1974, p. 55.
4 Wolff 1970, pp. 13–14 (original emphasis).
5 See O'Neill 1993c. The point is developed well in Shapin 1994.
6 Winch 1967, p. 99 (original emphasis).
7 One part of the craft of suspicion that is worth noting here is the recognition of the limits of authority, not just in the familiar cases in which for example scientists make pronouncements on matters of ethics, politics and religion in which they have no competence, but also in those cases in which they do. I refer in particular here to the distinction between abstract and universal principles of science and the concrete and particular contexts in which it is applied. The principles of good agriculture cannot be read off the sciences of bio-chemistry or biology, for all that these are relevant: the local, specific and often unarticulated knowledge of practitioners has a necessary place in action. Hence Aristotle:

> Nor is intelligence about universals only. It must also come to know particulars, since it is concerned with action and action is about particulars. Hence in other areas also some people who lack knowledge but have experience are better in action than others who have knowledge.
> (Aristotle *Nicomachean Ethics* 1141b 15ff)

Hence, for example, the justifiable scepticism of farmers in Cumbria of the reassurances of nuclear scientists following an accident at a nuclear power station: local knowledge of the behaviour of their animals gave them justifiable grounds for scepticism. I discuss these points at greater length in O'Neill 1993, ch. 8.

8 Kant 1991a, p. 55.

9 W. R. Hamilton letter to Robert Graves, 17 October 1843, in Graves 1885, pp. 441–442. Both Hamilton and Robert Graves belonged to the romantic circle around Wordsworth. Wordsworth discouraged his poetic ambitions.

10 Nietzsche 1974, s. 290.

11 Ibid. s. 335.

12 Nietzsche 1967, essay II, s. 2 (original emphasis).

13 Ibid. essay II, s. 2 (original emphasis).

14 Nietzsche 1968, s. 11 (original emphasis).

15 Foucault 1980.

16 Foucault 1986, p. 43.

17 Newman 1884, p. 8.

18 Kenny 1992, pp. 6ff.

19 Kant 1991a, p. 55 and Wolff 1970, p. 15.

20 The point is stated with clarity in the early Hare. Thus Hare writes that

> one of the most important constituents of our freedom, as moral agents, is the freedom to form our own opinions about moral questions, even if it involves changing our language. It might be objected that moral questions are not peculiar in this respect – that we are free also to form our own opinions about such matters as whether the world is round. In a sense this is true; but we are free to form our own moral opinions in a much stronger sense than this. For it we say that the world is flat, we can in principle be shown certain facts such that, once we have admitted them, we cannot go on saying that the world is flat without being guilty of either self-contradiction or the misuse of language … [N]othing of this so can be done in morals.
>
> (Hare 1963, p. 2)

Hare's own development has seen a progressive shift away from that position.

21 Hayek 1960, p. 79.

22 See for example Perry's rejection of objectivism on the grounds that if true 'it would be possible to prove to a person, by moral argument, that his most careful and sincere moral opinion about something was wrong', a view that is characterised as not just incorrect but 'offensive' (T. Perry 1976).

23 To say this is to deny here that there are ethical or political experts in the same sense that there are experts in scientific or other practical spheres. To affirm that claim is in turn to reject the view that there are special theories one must know in order to ethically deliberate and arrive at good decisions. It is thus to deny in particular the assumption, prevalent amongst some proponents of utilitarianism, that applied ethics is like applied physics, a question of getting the right ethical theory and then applying it (for a classical utilitarian defence of the role of moral experts see Austin 1954); and at risk of denying lucrative employment prospects, there is no reason why philosophers should be understood to have special expertise here – they have no expertise beyond the practical skills in appraising arguments which a training in philosophy often brings. It is also to deny that there are special ways in which knowledge in ethical matters can be achieved which are not open to the ordinary person.

24 Mill 1994, V ch. 8, p. 338.

25 See O'Neill and Solomon 1996.

26 For a discussion of this distinction between these two modes of market colonisation of other spheres see Keat 1993.

27 For a discussion of these see chapter 11.

28 On these changes see Fairclough 1993.

29 See for example Warnock 1989, p. 25 and *passim*.

30 Buchanan 1979b, pp. 362–364.

31 Ibid. p. 265.

32 The move is a popular one not just for universities, but also for other spheres. It is echoed in Rupert Murdoch's criticism of notions of 'quality' in the media. Whose criteria are being employed to describe what is a 'quality newspaper' or 'quality television'? For a discussion see O'Neill 1992a.

33 See in particular, the influential market model employed by Woolgar and Latour 1979, pp. 206ff. I return to these in the next chapter. For an overview of the ways in which recent sociology of scientific knowledge have employed market models of science see Wade Hands 1994.

34 For an elaboration of the connections between post-modernism and the defence of consumer culture see Jameson 1991.

35 Mill 1991, p. 82.

36 The theme is central to Paul Lafargue's wonderful book *The Right to Be Lazy* (1917).

37 Tawney 1964, p. 87. Compare the section on money in Marx's *Economic and Philosophical Manuscripts*.

38 For a more detailed discussion of this point see O'Neill 1993d, ch. 8.

39 Paul Lancaster is the source both of this observation and the present formulation of it.

40 'In everything we do, whether we are in hospital, travelling along a motorway or in the underground, we depend on the skill, ability, understanding and intelligence of ... ordinary people' Cooley n.d., p. 94.

41 For a powerful elaboration of the argument the market society fails in privileging the consumer over the producer see Lane 1991.

42 MacIntyre 1985, pp. 188–189.

43 Aristotle *Politics* III xi 14.

44 See Hayek 1949a and 1949b.

45 The distinction is that of Hirschman 1970.

46 See Hayek 1949b, pp. 85ff.

47 I develop that in more detail in O'Neill 1993d, ch. 8 and 'Democracy, Trust and the Public Use of Reason' presented at the seminar, *Beyond Cost-Benefit Analysis: Deliberation, Judgement and Public Policy*, Zurich 1996.

48 They often arise in discussions of multi-culturalism. See C. Taylor 1992, pp. 61–73 for criticisms of the failure to keep different forms of recognition apart.

8 THE POLITICS OF RECOGNITION

1 See for example C. Taylor 1992.

2 See for example Fraser 1995a and 1995b.

3 Fukuyama 1992, p. 314.

4 The distinctions I employ here owe a great deal to Vlastos 1962. I use 'standing' here where he employs the concept of 'worth', and 'virtue' where he uses the concept of 'merit'. The term 'worth' is I think unhelpful here, since it is used in the appraisal of the virtues of persons and their products: for example, 'there is little aesthetic worth in this picture'. The concept of 'merit' also brings with it a certain unwelcome baggage: in political theory it invokes particular theories of justice.

5 Fukuyama 1992, p. 182 (original emphasis).

6 Aristotle *Nicomachean Ethics* I, ch. 5.

7 See A. Smith's distinction in *The Theory of Moral Sentiments* III.2 between 'the love of praiseworthiness' and 'the love of praise': 'To be pleased with groundless applause is a proof of the most superficial levity and weakness. It is what is properly called vanity' (III.2.4).

8 Fukuyama is conscious of the existence of associations as spheres for recognition (Fukuyama 1992, ch. 30). Following Tocqueville he also notes their significance as a foundation for democratic life (Ibid. pp. 322–323). Finally he is aware of the ways in which associational life is undermined by the capitalist marketplace (Ibid. p. 325). His liberalism is not one that holds that the sphere of contractual relations is either self-sufficient or adequate as a source of recognition. However his failure to note the dependency of recognition of other goods weakens his own criticism of the individualistic 'Anglo-Saxon' model of liberalism. He misses the critical resources within Hegel's account. Thus in his defence of an associational form of liberalism he turns to Tocqueville (Ibid. ch. 30): Hegel's discussion of corporations, the associations of skill in civil society that educate and protect their members, gets just a passing mention (Ibid. pp. 322–324) and its full significance is missed.

9 Hegel 1967, 253.

10 Ibid. 253A.

11 MacIntyre 1985, pp. 190–191.

12 See note 7 for Smith's definition of vanity. The most notable instance of the confusions of self-esteem and vanity is to be found in Nozick 1980, ch. 8: for admirable criticism see Skillen 1977.

13 The point is that of Hirsch 1977.

14 Walzer 1983, p. 253.

15 Walzer does not miss this point entirely. See his discussion of the distinction between self-respect and self-esteem. For a discussion of Walzer which has been influential on my thoughts here see Keat 1997.

16 Woolgar and Latour 1979, p. 206 (original emphasis).

17 A. Smith 1982a I.iii.3.1.

18 Marx 1974d, p. 379 (original emphasis).

19 It is not of course the only sphere. The virtues displayed in everyday social relationships are of greater significance than is often granted: we remember people for their 'minor' acts of kindness and generosity more than for their great achievements.

20 Hegel 1967, 253.

21 See A. Smith 1981 I.vii. 28–31 and I.x.c. 1–63 and *passim*; cf. A. Smith 1982c ii.35–37, and letter to William Cullen, 20 Sept. 1774 in A. Smith 1987.

22 A. Smith 1981 I.x.c.17.

23 See Smith's pithy statement of the ideal in 1982a VII.ii.I.21.

24 Hegel 1977, para. 199.

25 Marx 1974c, pp. 232–233.

9 COMMENSURABILITY AND THE SOCIALIST CALCULATION DEBATES

1 Pierson 1935, Barone 1935 and Weber 1978, ch. II, especially sections 12–14. Other figures that belong to the prehistory of the debate are Pareto and Bohm-Bawerk.

2 Mises 1920.

3 Mises 1922.

4 Hayek 1949a and 1949b.

5 Lange and Taylor 1956.

6 See Hayek 1935 and Lange and Taylor 1956. For different appraisals of the outcome of the debate see A. Buchanan 1985, ch. 4; Lavoie 1985; Schapiro 1989; Steele 1992; Blackburn 1991.

7 Heilbroner 1990, p. 92.

8 Roemer 1994.

9 For Hayek's account see his 'The Nature and History of the Problem' in Hayek 1935;

see also Hayek 1949c and 1984. Lange's account is found in the opening section of Lange 1956; see also the introductory essay by Lippincott in Lange and Taylor 1956.

10 Lange 1956, p. 62.

11 See for example A. Buchanan 1985, p. 110.

12 Hayek is the better of the two here, as he is generally on the historical detail. See his brief discussion of Neurath in Hayek 'The Nature and History of the Problem' in Hayek 1935, pp. 30–31. Lange makes no mention at all of the Neurath work.

13 His specific object of criticism was Neurath's 1919 report to the Munich Workers' Council (Neurath 1919). Neurath's work also formed the central target of Weber's contribution to the prehistory of the socialist calculation debate. See the extended discussion of Neurath's work in Weber 1978, ch. II, section 12, pp. 100–107. Weber's argument is more careful than that of Mises. He argues that some 'value indicators' (plural) must take the place of prices for rational planning and he expresses some doubt as to what they might be. The objection is weaker than Mises in the sense that it does not rule out the possibility of such indicators. However, it has more clout in that, unlike Mises, he makes no simple commensurability assumption.

14 Neurath 1919, p. 145.

15 Ibid. p. 146.

16 Mises 1981, p. 98. The part of Mises text from which I quote here is a reproduction of his first essay in the socialist calculation debate 'Economic Calculation in the Socialist Commonwealth' of 1920. A translation of this essay by S. Adler appears in Hayek 1935.

17 Mises 1981, p. 98.

18 Ibid. p. 99.

19 Ibid. p. 104.

20 See Mises 1949, p. 209.

21 Neurath 1912 and 1913.

22 Neurath 1913, p. 4.

23 Ibid. p. 8.

24 What marks the philosophy of Descartes is a realisation of the limits of rules of reason in action, but a failure to recognise similar limits in the rules for the direction of the mind. Just as in action, so in theoretical matters, reason underdetermines our theories. For a development of this point aimed at Popper's philosophy of science, see Neurath 1935.

25 Neurath 1912, p. 119.

26 Neurath 1928, p. 263.

27 This line of argument also undermines Weber's criticism of Neurath which relies on the distinction between 'technical' and 'ethical' matters. See Weber 1978 p. 104.

28 Mises 1981, p. 99.

29 Ibid. p. 99.

30 Ibid. p. 100.

31 I defend the possibility of rational choice without commensurability in more detail in J. O'Neill 1993d, ch. 7 and 1997c. The problems with Mises' position have come to the fore in recent debates in environmental economics in which the issues in the argument between Mises and Neurath have resurfaced. The assumption that Mises makes – that rational choice requires a single unit to compare options – is shared by neo-classical economics. It is made explicit in the attempt to bring unpriced environmental goods into its ambit. See for example Pearce *et al.* 1989, p. 115.

32 Whitehead 1911, p. 42. The passage is invoked by Hayek 1955a, p. 87. The point is also central to institutional economics: for a useful discussion see Hodgson 1988.

33 Lange 1956, p. 60.

34 Ibid. p. 61.

35 Roemer 1994, p. 28.

36 See Hayek 1949a and 1949b. For criticism see O'Neill 1989.

37 Mises 1981, p. 98.

38 Hayek 1984, p. 61 (original emphasis).

39 Mises 1981, p. 98. Weber, in his criticism of Neurath, similarly treats the problem as one of finding 'a suitable accounting method' (Weber 1978 p. 103).

40 See for example Hayek 1973, ch. 1. The parallels between Hayek and Neurath are particularly evident in their common criticisms of Cartesian rationalism.

41 Neurath 1913, p. 8.

42 I discuss Hayek's position in greater detail in O'Neill 1995a.

43 Robbins 1935, p. 12.

44 '[T]he problem of technique arises when there is one end and a multiplicity of means, the problem of economy when both the ends and means are multiple' (Robbins 1935, p. 35). In these terms cost-benefit analysis is a method for making economic decisions, cost-effectiveness analysis is an aid to technical decisions.

45 In both Austrian and much neo-classical economics, cost is understood in purely 'subjective' terms as preferences that go unsatisfied. The opportunity cost of an option is then simply identical to the preferences that might have been satisfied but are foregone by the choice of an option. Given this account since preferences are then such that their intensity can in principle be measured by willingness to pay, then it might look at least plausible to suggest a monetary representation of lost opportunities, at least as they affect current consumers. However, nothing forces us to accept this subjectivist account of costs. If we assume an objectivist account of goods, then there remain major problems with any monetary representation of lost possibilities. The difficulty of incommensurability simply re-emerges. If values cannot be properly expressed in monetary terms, or, indeed, if irreducibly plural values cannot be captured by any single measure, be it monetary or non-monetary, then the attempt to capture opportunity costs in monetary terms will be unsuccessful. Either certain valued options that might be forgone will be misrepresented.

46 See Steele 1992, pp. 6ff.

47 Mill 1884, book 6, ch. 12, section 7. It is notable that Robbins also appears to take it as given that an ordering of ends is possible. Robbins 1935, pp. 12–14 and *passim*.

48 Rawls 1972, pp. 42ff. and 61ff.

49 R. Dworkin 1977, p. xi.

50 It is worth noting here that the structure of Mill's argument is identical to that of Hobbes in *De Cive* VI, 18 (Hobbes 1991) and *Leviathan* (Hobbes 1968) ch. 29 for the existence of a single absolute sovereign authority in any polity who is the ultimate arbiter and enforcer of law. The criticism levelled against Mill here is likewise structurally identical to that of Hart 1961, pp. 33–50. For a discussion see Goldsmith 1980.

51 Aristotle *De Anima* 434a5–10.

52 Wiggins 1980, p. 256.

53 Neurath 1935 pp. 122–123. The criticism deserves to be better known. It captures the rational kernel of Feyerabend's position without the irrationalist rhetoric. Consider Feyerabend's claim: 'there is only *one* principle that can be defended under *all* circumstance and in *all* stages of human development. It is the principle: *anything goes*' (Feyerabend 1978, p. 28; original emphasis). The claim is open to development in two ways. The first is the rationalist reading which denies that rationality requires EU: if you tried to come up with a method that applied at all times and place, the only method would be anything goes, but that only shows the mistake of the EU account of reason. That is Neurath's position. The second is the irrationalist position that accepts that reason requires EU, but claims that science fails to meet the requirement. Feyerabend's rhetorical flourishes suggest that second position. I should also add that he is wrong to say that the only principle that applies always and everywhere is anything goes. It is rather the principle: use your judgement.

54 See O'Neill 1993d, ch. 7.

55 Munda 1995 and Munda *et al*. 1994. On the foundation of non-compensatory MCDA on incommensurability see Martinez-Alier *et al*. 1997.
56 See Hurley 1989, pp. 231ff.
57 Aristotle *Nicomachean Ethics* 1097b 14ff; cf. 1172b 31–34.
58 See O'Neill 1995a.
59 Simon 1979, p. 68.
60 Raz 1986, p. 339.
61 See O'Neill 1996 and 1997c.
62 Anderson 1993, p. 18.
63 Herodotus *Histories* 3.38. I discuss these points at length in O'Neill 1997d.
64 On this see O'Neill 1997b and Holland and O'Neill 1997.
65 Neurath 1913, p. 8.
66 There is a different problem here about the status of the ideal of convergence. On a realist view of science there is an ideal optimimum on which we should converge, i.e. on that which is the true. Truth is the aim of convergence not convergence the definition of truth. Indeed, given the underdetermination of theory by evidence there is no reason to assume that in the long run science will converge. A normative realist will hold similar claims to be true of norms. The irrealist will not. In that sense they differ in their expectations about the possibility of 'optimal' outcomes. This said realism is compatible with the tragic, i.e. that 'it ought to be that A' and 'it ought to be that B' and 'it is not possible that A and B'. The two ought claims can be both true and do not lead without other principles of deontic logic that are open to question to what is inconsistent with realism, the contradiction 'it ought to be that A and it is not the case that it ought to be that A'.
67 Cf. Williams 1972, p. 103.

10 EPISTEMOLOGICAL ARGUMENTS FOR THE MARKET

 1 See Hayek 1949a and 1949b.
 2 The project of a unified science aimed in part at showing that the divisions of knowledge could be overcome for the purposes of rational socialist planning. Subsequent accounts of the project of a unified science have tended to oversimplify the programme. The project took one of four forms: (i) a reductionist project in which all the sciences would be logically derivable via bridge-laws from physics; (ii) a programme for a unified method which would be followed by all sciences; (iii) a project for a unified language of science; and (iv) a project that would integrate the different sciences, such that, on any specific problem, all relevant sciences could be called upon – a project for the 'orchestration of the sciences' (Neurath 1946). All four doctrines were defended by positivists in different states of its history. However, in subsequent critical accounts of the doctrine, the first has tended to be taken to define the project, and the last has tended to be ignored, or at least has been taken as a project of integration through reduction. Neurath rejects the first reductionist project completely: 'would it not be preferable to treat all statements and all sciences as coordinated and to abandon for good the traditional hierarchy: physical sciences, biological sciences, social sciences and similar types of "scientific pyramidism"?' (Neurath 1944, p. 8). Neurath also rejected the second doctrine, the possibility of a unified method for the sciences. As I noted in Chapter 9 it defined what he called pseudorationalism: hence his opposition to both the absolutism of falsificationism and of verificationism. On method Neurath was a pluralist. Neurath defended the third and fourth projects, that of unifying the language of science and that of the coordination of the sciences. In the project of a universal physicalist language or 'jargon' for the sciences Neurath expresses a more familiar positivist commitment to the elimination of 'metaphysical' terms for unified science. The position is I believe indefensible. It is not insignificant that in his papers

Neurath continually uses vocabulary that fails his own physicalist sanitisation programme. To state and defend that project he requires the use of such terms. Moreover, it is not a necessary condition for the project of orchestration. Just as the programme of the orchestration does not require a unified method, neither does it require a sanitised language. I discuss these issues further in O'Neill 1995c.

3 Marx 1974a, pp. 132–133.

4 See Hayek 1978, pp. 179–190 and Kirzner 1985.

5 See Buchanan and Vanberg 1991.

6 Wiseman 1989, p. 230. See Shackle: 'the content of time-to-come is not merely unknown but nonexistent, and the notion of foreknowledge of human affairs is vacuous' (Shackle 1983, p. 33). See also Shackle 1979.

7 See Aristotle *De Interpretatione* ch. 9. For the discussion of Boethius and other scholastics see Davies 1983. Other discussions include R. Taylor 1957 and Cahn 1964. What follows owes much to conversations with Richard Gaskin and his 'Fatalism, Foreknowledge and the Reality of the Future' (Gaskin 1994).

8 See Dummett 1978, p. 338.

9 Anyone who defends what is now called 'radical subjectivism' needs to defend specifically logical claims against possible objections which have their own long history from Cicero (*De Fato* XVI, 37–38: Cicero 1941) to Quine (1953 and 1987). Minimally it requires the rejection of classical two-valued logic, for some version of a three-valued or many-valued logic (Lukasiewicz 1967; Haack 1974, ch. 4; Wright 1984). It requires some account of how an indeterminate future is compatible with the theory of relativity. For an argument that the rejection of bivalence for propositions about the future is incompatible with the theory of relativity see Putnam 1975. It also appears to require a revision of some of our customary ways of speaking. Thus one way of specifying the difference between the epistemic version of the Austrian argument and the 'radical subjectivist' position is in terms of what is the proper thing to say is when predicted events come to pass. Suppose the entrepreneur predicts or guesses 'over n consumers buy P at £m at t_1' and it comes to pass that over n consumers do indeed buy P at £m at t_1. Given the purely epistemic Austrian position which accepts the principle of bivalence, one can say 'the entrepreneur's prediction was true'. On the radical subjectivist position this is strictly speaking false. What one should say is that 'the entrepreneur's prediction became true'. Likewise to say 'he guessed correctly' is strictly speaking false. One has to say 'the guess turned out to be correct'.

10 The epistemic case against the possibility of complete centralised planning is broadly sound. However, it is open to question what a completely centralised economy would look like: actual planned economies, either within the market, firms, or state run, never could or did centralise all decisions. I return to this point below.

11 For useful discussions of the changes in Hayek's work that is relevant to the arguments developed here see Fleetwood 1995, chs. 9–10 and 1996.

12 Hayek 1949a, p. 50

13 Hayek 1944, p. 36.

14 Hayek 1949b, pp. 85–86.

15 Ibid. p. 85.

16 The point is indeed endorsed by Marx 1973, p. 161.

17 Hayek's positive discussion of the notion of relevant information is a major weakness in his defence of the market; cf. Hayek 1949a, pp. 50ff and 1949b, pp. 84ff for Hayek's analysis. Hayek cites as irrelevant information that is concerned with why a particular item has become more or less scarce, and suggests that all that is relevant is how much more or less scarce it has become. However, the relative scarcity of items and the reasons for that scarcity hardly exhaust the full gamut of information that is distributed throughout society which might be relevant to the coordination of economic activities and plans.

18 The use of the indefinite article is intentional. While non-communication is a stable outcome, in game theory it is possible, given indefinitely repeated games, low discount rates and a sufficiently small number of actors for a stable, cooperative, non-communicative outcome to emerge. For a discussion of such supergames see M. Taylor 1976 and Schotter 1981.

19 The price of a commodity does not, of course, simply reflect the relation of supply and demand at t_0. It is also modified by the beliefs of consumers at t_0 concerning future states of the relation of supply and demand. However, what the market necessarily fails to distribute is information concerning producer plans in response to demand, and this information is relevant for coordination. The market's failure to distribute this information leads to overproduction for the reasons outlined.

20 These elements in Marx's analysis are developed at length in his most systematic discussion of crises in Marx 1969, ch. XVII, especially sections 8 to 11; see also Karl Marx 1970, ch. 111, section 1. The points are stated most explicitly in informational terms in *Grundrisse* (Marx 1973, pp. 160–161). The thrust of Marx's argument is as follows: the possibility of crises in the market economy is a consequence of the spatial and temporal gap between the processes of production and sale of commodities; this possibility becomes a reality in the capitalist market in virtue of its additional features of being a competitive social order in which the production and sale of commodities is undertaken with the purpose of increasing the value of capital.

21 In his otherwise fair and generous response to an earlier statement of my argument, Steele rather misses this point. He writes as if the problem was simply one of inaccurate prediction and not one of individually rational responses to a signal resulting in collectively irrational responses (Steele 1992, pp. 248ff.). Hayek in contrast does attempt to show that the credit system will constrain the actions of different actors such that each will be coordinated with others.

22 See Hayek 1931 and 1933.

23 Ibid. There is, at this level, much in common between Marx's and Hayek's analyses. The significant difference lies in the explanation of the original source of the misinformation distributed from manufacturers of consumer goods to manufacturers of capital goods. Hayek assumes that, *ceteris paribus*, the price system does distribute all information that is relevant to the coordination of plans. Misinformation enters through the disturbance of the price system by the expansion of credit or money which artificially alters the relative prices of goods. The Marxian view I present here rejects the assumption that, in the absence of 'disturbances', the price system does distribute all information relevant to coordination. The market, in virtue of its competitive nature, fails to distribute all relevant information. This, for the reasons outlined, leads to over-expansion in some part of the economy. This, in turn, imparts false information to the producers of capital goods via the price mechanism. The extent to which local overproduction will lead to a general slump depends on the degree of interconnectivity between that part of the economy in which initial overproduction occurs and other parts of the economy.

24 See Selucky 1979, pp. 6ff and Nove 1983, pp. 39ff.

25 See Nove 1983, pp. 40ff and Hodgson 1984, pp. 115ff.

26 See Nove 1983, p. 40. Hayek makes this point in a number of places; see for example Hayek 1944, pp. 242–246 and 1949b, pp. 78–79.

27 Hayek 1949b, pp. 85–86 (my emphasis).

28 See in particular Kirzner 1972, 1979; Mises 1949, ch. 14. The work of Schumpeter has also been influential (Schumpeter 1934) although his later work on the decline of the individual entrepreneur points in a very different direction from recent Austrian economics (Schumpeter 1987, ch. 12). See Reekie 1984 for a useful overview of the Austrian position.

29 Martinez-Alier 1996.

30 Porter 1995, p. ix.
31 Oakeshott 1962b, p. 10.
32 The point is the organising argument of Kukathas 1990.
33 Hayek 1960, p. 400.
34 Ibid. chs 2, 3 and postscript.
35 See Martinez-Alier 1996.
36 Schumpeter 1987, pp. 123–124.
37 See Power 1994.
38 F. Taylor 1966.
39 Cardan 1974, p. 45.
40 A good overview of the tradition is to be found in Schecter 1994. Wainwright 1994 examines some of the parallels between radical traditions and Hayek's arguments.

11 PROPERTY IN SCIENCE AND THE MARKET

1 Nelkin 1984, p. 25.
2 See for example Weiner 1989.
3 For a good survey, see Nelkin 1984, Eisenberg 1987 and Mackenzie *et al.* 1990. The politics of patents on life are subject to continuous change. See *GenEthics News* for developments. For a discussion that is particularly consonant with the arguments of this chapter see Martinez-Alier 1996.
4 For discussions of the issue see Hettinger 1989, Goldman 1989 and Kuflik 1989.
5 The example also raises a more theoretical issue. There is a certain view of the development of modern capitalism that is largely shared both by critics of the market like myself and by its liberal defenders of the market: this is the view that the development of capitalism involves the spread of market relations into an ever-increasing number of spheres of life. Now this claim in its crude form needs to be abandoned. The early period of capitalism witnessed major exclusions of the market from certain spheres of life – notably political offices and honours, the means of salvation in the form of indulgence, and certain kinds of information and knowledge. The dispute between Cardano and Tartaglia provides a good example of the latter.
6 Some of the documents from this dispute are collected in Fauvel and Gray 1987; see also Cardano 1968.
7 Mahoney 1989.
8 Macpherson 1973, p. 122.
9 Ravetz 1973, p. 245.
10 This point is exhibited in some of the priority disputes in early nineteenth-century mathematics. Thus, for example, Cayley and Graves independently developed an algebra of octaves – Graves in letters to Hamilton, Cayley in a note to a journal paper. Symptomatic of the growing centrality of the journal as the recognised means of publication, Cayley received the honour of eponymy – the numbers are now called Cayley numbers. I discuss this case in more detail in O'Neill 1993c. In this regard, Wightman's comment on the dispute between Cardano and Tartaglia is not off the point: 'Today his [Cardano's] behaviour would be regarded as normal, Tartaglia's as reprehensible. But the matter is not settled quite so easily, for in the first half of the sixteenth century there was no Mathematical Gazette' (Wightman 1962, p. 32).
11 Macpherson 1978, pp. 4ff.
12 Merton 1968, p. 601.
13 Ibid. p. 601.
14 Ravetz 1973, p. 246.
15 Ibid. p. 247.
16 Hagstrom 1965.
17 Merton 1968, p. 612.

18 For a discussion, see Hodgson 1988, pp. 163ff. and Lamberton 1971.
19 Arrow 1962, p. 616.
20 Aristotle *Nicomachean Ethics* IX, ch. 1.
21 Macpherson 1978, pp. 3ff.
22 David 1992a, p. 11; cf. Dasgupta and David 1991; David 1992b.
23 Marx 1970, p. 365, ch. 15, section 2.
24 Dasgupta and David 1991; David 1992b.
25 See Funtowicz and Ravetz 1993.
26 David 1992b, p. 9.
27 My thanks to Paul David for this observation.
28 There is a related but distinct question that might be raised here – i.e. under what conditions scientific information, theories, and principles can be patented. There is a widespread view that only the applications of scientific theories can be patented, not the theories themselves. See Hettinger 1989, pp. 32–33. Part of the problem here lies in the distinction between 'discovery' and 'invention'. Patent is supposed to be applicable only to invention. However, the distinction between invention and discovery is much less clear cut than is assumed. See Kneale 1955 and O'Neill 1998.
29 Loasby 1986, p. 53.
30 Nelkin 1984, p. 29.
31 This is not to say that 'truth' in science simply means 'passes the scrutiny of competent judges'. One needs to distinguish the definition of truth from criteria for testing truth: passing the appraisal of competent judges is a criterion for testing for truth, not a definition of it.
32 My thanks to Tony Skillen for this example.
33 For detailed discussion of these points see Eisenberg 1987 and Mackenzie *et al.* 1990.
34 Loasby 1986, pp. 42–43.
35 Ziman 1978, p. 6, cited in Loasby 1986, p. 42.
36 Alasdair MacIntyre 1985, pp. 87ff. The arguments that follow have an Aristotelian heritage. In Aristotle's own work it appears specifically in his criticism of chrematistic acquisition which we discussed in chapter 2. A central component of Aristotle's objection to chrematistic acquisition lay in its corrosive effects on practices. MacIntyre's concept of a practice is Aristotelian: practices refer to those human activities that have internal ends which are partially constitutive of the kind of activity and which define the virtues and excellences that are characteristic of the practices (Aristotle *Nicomachean Ethics* 1097b 25–27 and 1098a 8–15; see also Plato *The Republic* 342d 2–7). Chrematistic acquisition is corrosive of practices. Hence Aristotle's comments on the effects of the chrematistic art of acquisition upon the pursuit of practices:

> if they cannot get what they want by the use of that art – i.e. the art of acquisition -they attempt to do so by other means, using each and every capacity in a way not consonant with its nature. The proper function of courage, for example, is not to produce money but to give confidence. The same is true of military and medical ability; neither has the function of producing money; the one has the function of producing victory, and the other of health. But those of whom we are speaking turn all such capacities into forms of the art of acquisition, as though to make money were the one aim and everything else must contribute to that aim.
>
> (Aristotle *Politics* I ix)

The pursuit of the external ends can corrupt a practice: where a practitioner has been so corrupted, he or she takes the pursuit of the external ends to have priority over the internal ends. The point is applied to the intellectual practices, specifically to philosophy. Thus it is not the end of philosophy to make money, but within the market it can be pursued to that end. Hence sophism is a corrupt form of philosophy: 'the art of the sophist is the semblance of wisdom without the reality, and the art of the sophist is one who makes money from apparent but unreal wisdom' (Aristotle *De Sophisticis Elenchis* I). The commitment to the internal goods of the practice is undermined. For an excellent discussion of the issues raised in this paragraph see Meikle 1995, ch. 4.

37 It is something like this point that I assume must underlie the following observation of MacIntyre's on the different forms of property relation appropriate to internal and external goods:

> We are now in a position to notice an important difference between what I have called internal and what I have called external goods. It is characteristic of what I have called external goods that when achieved they are always some individual's property and possession. Moreover characteristically they are such that the more someone has of them, the less there is for other people. This is sometimes necessarily the case, as with power and fame, and sometimes the case by reason of contingent circumstance as with money. External goods are therefore characteristically objects of competition in which there must be losers as well as winners. Internal goods are indeed the outcome of competition to excel, but it is characteristic of them that their achievement is a good for the whole community who participate in the practice.

(MacIntyre 1985, pp. 190–191)

38 Compare Arrow's response to Titmus. Titmus argues against the introduction of markets in blood that it undermines the possibility of individuals acting altruistically: it deprives individuals of the 'their freedom to give or not to give' (Titmus 1970, p. 239.) Arrow asks the telling question: '*Why* should it be that the creation of a market for blood decrease the altruism embodied in giving blood?' (Arrow 1972, p. 351; original emphasis). It is still open for an individual to waive rights to possible payment and give the blood freely. Why should an act of free donation 'be affected by the fact that other individuals receive money for these services' (Ibid. p. 351)? The question is a proper one. The answer I suggest is this, that the mixed system changes the meaning of the act by institutionally redefining individuals conceptions of their interests. Without a market, a donation is an expressive act of solidarity with others. It is not typically seen as an act of self-sacrifice. The introduction of a market redefines the act. The donor is now free to choose between free donation and paid donation and that choice itself alters the nature of the free donation. It redefines the choice of free donation as an act of self-sacrifice. The latter is a scarce resource. One cannot expect individuals to sacrifice what is seen as their self-interest for a significant portion of their lives, and where there is a particular institutional definition of self-interest, only the exceptionally robust can be expected to resist the definition. Hence the mixed system decreases the occasion for acts of solidarity.

39 While this point is an Aristotelian one, the overall position I defend here is not. An economy in which goods are held as private property but given over to common use corresponds to Aristotle's ideal (Aristotle *Politics* 1329b41–1330a2). One of his main arguments for this ideal is precisely that it provides the occasion for the exercise of the virtues of generosity (Ibid. 1263a30–b14). For a discussion see Irwin 1987. The scientific community of gift-giving agents looks like a particularly Aristotelian picture of the good community. However, I find Aristotle's defence of property unconvincing for Aristotelian reasons: it requires too much in the way of self-sacrificial altruism to be realistic. The virtue of the communism of science and the system of recognition associated with it is that it institutionally defines other-regarding action as a part of an individual's self-interest. I discuss this further in O'Neill 1997a.

40 Aristotle *Nicomachean Ethics* 1168b.
41 The arguments in this section are developed in more detail in O'Neill 1992b.

12 PUBLIC CHOICE THEORY: SELF-INTEREST AND UNIVERSAL ECONOMICS

1 This is not to say there are not positions that are not properly criticised for demanding excessive self-sacrifice. A glance at the speeches of Mao or of both deposed dictators of Eastern Europe and their nationalist successors will reveal endless exhortations to self-sacrifice:'At no time and in no circumstances should a Communist place his personal interests first: he should subordinate them to the interests of the nation and the masses' (Mao Tse Tung 1967, p. 198). The result would be at best the paradoxes of altruism, of individuals all unhappily striving for the happiness of each other. Such reliance on self-sacrifice is however not a necessary part of the socialist tradition. It is for example foreign to the work of Marx and Engels: 'The communists by no means want to do away with the "private individual" for the sake of the "general" self-sacrificing man' (Marx 1974a, p. 105). What socialism does require is individuals with sufficiently wide interests to incorporate common activities, causes and concerns with others. This, however, is not an unrealistic demand.
2 Buchanan 1972, p. 22.
3 Buchanan 1978, p. 3. Compare Mueller: 'Public choice can be defined as the economic study of non-market decision making, or simply the application of economics to politics' (Mueller 1979, p. 1).
4 See Olson 1965, p. 98.
5 Tullock 1970, p. v.
6 Niskanen 1973, pp. 22–23; see also Niskanen 1971. Downs 1967 defends a different version of a public choice account of bureaucracy which includes altruistic motivations alongside narrower egoistic ones.
7 The major text defending this position is Downs 1957. An earlier classic attempt to apply economic models of behaviour to political actors, but with a more sceptical view of consumer sovereignty, is Schumpeter 1987.
8 This theme runs through much of the literature on public choice. See for example Brennan and Buchanan 1980, Buchanan 1975, especially ch. 9, Buchanan and Wagner 1977, Niskanen 1971 and Wolf 1987.
9 For a classic statement of this position which involves the standard property rights solution see Buchanan and Tullock 1962, ch. 5.
10 Coase 1960.
11 Buchanan attempts to show that the theorem still has relevance in conditions of imperfect competition (Buchanan 1969) and, under an Austrian reinterpretation, that transaction costs are not relevant to its truth (Buchanan 1986).
12 See Dales 1968. For a useful survey market solutions to environmental problems see Rose-Ackerman 1977.
13 See Marx 1974b.
14 See for example Becker 1978 and 1981, Hirschleifer 1985, Olson 1965, Radnitzky and Bernholz 1987 and Schotter 1981.
15 For a discussion see Wade Hands 1994 and Mäki 1992. For a move in the other direction that explicitly attempts to extend economics to science see Radnitzky 1987a and 1987b.
16 Latour and Woolgar 1979, pp. 205ff.
17 Wade Hands 1994, p. 97 (original emphasis).
18 The following owes much to Hodgson 1993 and 1988.
19 See Commons 1934 and Veblen 1919.

20 Polanyi 1957a, 1957b and 1957c. For a discussion of the influence of Aristotle on Marx and Polanyi see S. Meikle 1979, 1985 and 1995 and O'Neill 1993d, ch. 10.

21 I refer here to the tradition from Hume and Smith through to Mill. Compare, for example, the views about the role habit plays in the formation of dispositions of character in Hume 1985d, 1985e and 1985g, and in A. Smith 1981 V, ch. 1, with those developed by Veblen 1919.

22 Buchanan 1972, p. 22.

23 On the distinction between want-regarding principles and ideal-regarding principles see Barry 1990.

24 Aristotle *Politics* 1280b 38f.

25 Aristotle *Politics* 1324a 22.

26 Aristotle *Politics* I, chs 8–9. For a discussion see Polanyi 1957a and Meikle 1979 and 1995.

27 See Dearlove 1989.

28 For classic discussion of this familiar point which is of particular relevance for the discussion here, see C. Taylor 1971.

29 See for example Buchanan and Tullock 1962, ch. 9.

30 Hume 1985a, p. 93 (original emphasis). See also Aristotle's remarks on the effects of wealth on character in Aristotle *Rhetoric* II, ch. 16.

31 See for example the problems with the assumption concerning transitivity in Anand 1993, chs. 4 and 7; O'Neill 1993d, ch. 7.

32 Hahn and Hollis 1979, p. 4.

33 Aristotle *Nicomachean Ethics* 1168b 16.

34 On this shift of terms see Hirschman 1977, especially pp. 31–42. It is notable just how recent most of the terms for self-interest are. For example, the term egoism was coined only in the mid-eighteenth century, while the concept of altruism appeared only with Comte in the nineteenth century. See Price 1988 for a useful outline of this shift. This is not to say that much of what we now call 'egoistic' behaviour came into existence only in that period. What changed was the terms of description: there has been a shift away from specific vice terms such as avarice, ambition, pride, envy, vanity, vainglory, conceit and the like. The single older term that might be thought to do the work of egoism, 'self-love', does not have the same negative import: hence, the commandment 'love thy neighbour as thyself'. The shift in the debate to the generic terms of egoism and self-interest has made opaque and apparently unproblematic claims that in the older language were clear and obviously contentious. Vice-terms have a content. They describe dispositions of character to have specific desires and feelings towards particular objects. Modern terms like egoism – the disposition to act in what one believes to be in one's own interests – are not like that. One can shift between broad and narrow senses of interests, utility, preference and the like. Hence, questions that can be stated quite clearly in the older vice-terms become difficult to state unambiguously. Consider the following questions: is there a universal tendency to avarice in all persons? If avarice were a universal disposition could a good social order be constructed? Is avarice conducive to individual flourishing? These are questions to which any answer will involve substantive issues. The questions are ones to which different answers are sensible and different answers would need to be argued for. Consider for example answers in the Augustinian tradition: to the third question, 'no', – avarice, the insatiable appetite for worldly things is a source of human unhappiness; to the first question 'yes' for we are fallen creatures; and to the second question also a qualified 'yes', an earthly political order of sinners is possible and indeed has to be constructed on the basis of the assumption that we are fallen beings. I state the Augustinian positions not to endorse them – I reject his answers to the first and second questions – but to note that they are substantive and falsifiable claims. They also had an influence on the prehistory of economics. More generally eighteenth-century economic writing is still largely written in the language

of vice and virtue. In Mandeville's work for example it is the vices of avarice, prodigality, pride, envy, vanity and folly that have unintended beneficial consequences (Mandeville 1988, I pp. 25 and 100ff). However, in the modern idiom of interests and 'utility' maximisation, the questions and answers are robbed of substance. Consider the following parallel questions: is there universal tendency in all persons to maximise their own expected utility? If there is a universal disposition to the maximisation of personal utility could a good social order be constructed? Is the pursuit of the maximisation of personal expected utility conducive to individual flourishing? Modern welfare economics answers yes to all three questions. The first positive answer is an axiom defining the rational economic agent. The second positive answer is the basic theorem of welfare economics: ideal markets issue in Pareto-optimal outcomes. The third is often taken to be true by definition. However, when pressed the answers are vacuous as to the content of desire, for utility maximisation is simply a matters of satisfying whatever wants one has: saint and sinner both satisfy the claims, they just have different wants. However, the answers have a rhetorical power of 'realism' in virtue of their appearing to entail stronger and more contentious Augustinian claims. The self-interested agent looks like the avaricious individual, but when pressed turns out to be nothing but an agent with desires. Public choice theory plays upon that ambiguity.

35 Aristotle *Nicomachean Ethics* IX, ch. 8. Compare the following anecdote about Euclid:

> Someone who had begun to read geometry with Euclid, when he had learnt the first theorem asked Euclid, 'But what advantage shall I get by learning these things?' Euclid called his slave and said, 'Give him threepence, since he must needs make a profit out of what he learns'.
>
> (Stobaeus 1939, p. 437)

36 I owe this last point to Andrew Collier: 'if "rational economic agent" is defined to mean "person who pursues monetary gain in preference to all other aims" its corresponding term in ordinary English is not its homonym, but "moneygrubber" ' (Collier 1990, p. 118).

37 Buchanan 1972, p. 22.

38 The classic text is Olson 1965; see also Olson 1982.

39 Hirschman 1985, p. 79. As Hirschman goes on to say, it is perhaps true that:

> the success of Olson's book *owes* something to its having been contradicted by the subsequently evolving events. Once the latter had run their course, the many people who found them deeply upsetting could go back to *The Logic of Collective Action* and find in it good and reassuring reasons why those collective actions of the sixties should never have happened in the first place.
>
> (Ibid. p. 79)

See also the problems that rational choice Marxism has with the explanation of collective class action.

40 In making *that* assumption they are the inheritors of the views of Smith: Smith was never an anti-socialist thinker – there was when he wrote no significant socialist movement to oppose; he was an anti-associationalist thinker: professional associations, trade associations and guilds are conspiracies against the public, concerned with the pursuit of particular sectional interests. See A. Smith 1981 I.x.3 *passim*. However, the case against associations permeates the entire work. Modern neo-liberal invocations of Smith tend to forget that he wrote in the eighteenth century before any significant socialist movement existed, and that his work was directed as much against professional associations and guilds, as it was against certain kinds of state regulation of trade.

41 I draw again here on the distinction MacIntyre makes between practices and institutions in MacIntyre 1985, ch. 14.
42 Raz 1986, pp. 310–311.
43 I develop this point further in O'Neill 1993d, pp. 118–122. See also Raz 1986, ch. 13.
44 Buchanan and Tullock 1962, pp. 27ff.
45 Ibid. pp. 302–306.
46 Buchanan 1978, pp. 17–18.
47 Hume 1985c, p. 42 (original emphasis).
48 Ibid. pp. 42–43 (original emphasis).
49 Durkheim 1964, ch. 7 part II, p. 215.
50 Burke 1826, p. 155. For a discussion see Pocock 1985.
51 Hume 1985b, p. 113.
52 Mill 1975, p. 29. For a powerful recent defence of perfectionist liberalism see Raz 1986. It needs to be noted here that Mill's perspective on the role of institutions on individuals' preferences sits uneasily with the psychologism he defends in Mill 1884, book 6. However, it is the psychologism that needs to go, not the institutionalism.
53 See also in this regard the welcome rediscovery of associational models of socialism: Hirst 1989, Martell 1992, Yeo 1987.

POSTSCRIPT: MARKETS, ASSOCIATIONS AND SOCIALISM

1 Barker 1928, p. 159.
2 Hayek 1944, p. 3.
3 A. Smith 1981 I.x.c.7 and V.i.f.6.
4 Walzer 1983 and 1984.
5 See for example Miller 1989.
6 Walzer 1983, p. 325.
7 Marx 1974c, p. 220.
8 Neurath 1942, p. 429.
9 Ibid. p. 429.
10 See chapter 2. I develop this point at greater length in O'Neill 1993d, ch. 10.
11 Neurath 1942, p. 434.
12 Ibid. p. 433.
13 Ibid. p. 434.
14 Ibid. p. 435. I discuss Neurath's position in more detail in O'Neill 1995c.
15 Sale 1985.
16 Heilbroner 1975, especially ch. 4, and Ophuls 1977.
17 O'Neill 1993d, ch. 10.

REFERENCES

Ackerman, B. 1980 *Social Justice and the Liberal State* New Haven, CT: Yale University Press.

Ackerman, B. 1990 'Neutralities' in R. Douglas, G. Mara and H. Richardson eds. *Liberalism and the Good* London: Routledge.

Ackrill, J. 1980 'Aristotle on *Eudaemonia*' in A. Rorty ed. *Essays on Aristotle's Ethics* Berkeley: University of California Press.

Anand, P. 1993 *Foundations of Rational Choice under Risk* Oxford: Clarendon.

Anderson, E. 1993 *Value in Ethics and Economics* Cambridge, MA: Harvard University Press.

Aquinas, T. 1975 *Summa Theologiae* London: Eyre and Spottiswoode.

Arendt, H. 1986 *The Origins of Totalitarianism* 2nd edn. London: André Deutsch.

Aristotle 1908 *Metaphysics* Oxford: Clarendon.

Aristotle 1928a *De Interpretatione* E. Edgehill trans. London: Oxford University Press.

Aristotle 1928b *De Sophisticis Elenchis vol. I* W. Pickard-Cambridge trans. London: Oxford University Press.

Aristotle 1928c *Posterior Analytics* G. Mure trans. Oxford: Oxford University Press.

Aristotle 1928d *Topics* W. Pickard-Cambridge trans. Oxford: Oxford University Press.

Aristotle 1946 *Rhetoric* R. Robert trans. Oxford: Clarendon.

Aristotle 1948 *Politics* E. Barker trans. Oxford: Clarendon.

Aristotle 1972 *De Anima* Oxford: Clarendon.

Aristotle 1985 *Nicomachean Ethics* T. Irwin trans. Indianapolis, IN: Hackett.

Arrow, K. 1962 'Economic Welfare and the Allocation of Resources for Invention' in *The Rate and Direction of Inventive Activity: Economic and Social Factors* Princeton, NJ: Princeton University Press.

Arrow, K. 1972 'Gifts and Exchanges' *Philosophy and Public Affairs* 1, pp. 343–362.

Augustine 1972 *City of God* Harmondsworth: Penguin.

Austin, J. 1954 *The Province of Jurisprudence Determined* London: Weidenfeld and Nicolson.

Baier, A. 1989 'Hume, the Women's Moral Theorist' in E. Kittay and D. Meyers eds. *Women and Moral Theory* Totowa, NJ: Rowman and Littlefield.

Barker, E. 1928 *Political Thought in England 1848–1914* 2nd edn. London: Oxford University Press.

Barone, E. 1935 'The Ministry of Production in the Collectivist State' reprinted in F. Hayek ed. *Collectivist Economic Planning* London: Routledge and Kegan Paul.

Barry, B. 1990 *Political Argument* 2nd edn. New York: Harvester Wheatsheaf.

Becker, G. 1978 *The Economic Approach to Human Behavior* Chicago: University of Chicago Press.

Becker, G. 1981 *A Treatise on the Family* Cambridge, MA: Harvard University Press.

Benson, J. 1983 'Who is the Autonomous Man?' *Philosophy* 58, pp. 5–17.

Berlin, I. 1969 *Four Essays on Liberty* Oxford: Oxford University Press.

Blackburn R. 1991 'Fin de Siècle: Socialism after the Crash' *New Left Review* 185, pp. 5–67.

Brandt R. 1979 *A Theory of the Good and the Right* Oxford: Clarendon.

Brennan, G. and J. Buchanan 1980 *The Power to Tax* Cambridge: Cambridge University Press.

Broome, J. 1991a *Weighing Goods* Oxford: Blackwell.

Broome, J. 1991b 'Utility' *Economics and Philosophy* 7.

Buchanan, A. 1985 *Ethics, Efficiency and the Market* Oxford: Clarendon.

Buchanan, J. 1969 'External Diseconomies, Corrective Taxes and Market Structure' *American Economic Review* 59, pp. 174–177.

Buchanan, J. 1972 'Towards Analysis of Closed Behavioural Systems' in J. Buchanan and R. Tollison eds. *Theory of Public Choice* Ann Arbor: University of Michigan Press.

Buchanan, J. 1975 *The Limits of Liberty* Chicago: University of Chicago Press.

Buchanan, J. 1978 'From Private Preferences to Public Philosophy: The Development of Public Choice' in J. Buchanan ed. *The Economics of Politics* London: Institute of Economic Affairs.

Buchanan, J. 1979a 'Natural and Artificial Man' in *What Should Economists Do?* Indianapolis, IN: Liberty Press.

Buchanan, J. 1979b 'Public Finance and Academic Freedom' in *What Should Economists Do?* Indianapolis, IN: Liberty Press.

Buchanan, J. 1986 'Rights, Efficiency and Exchange: The Irrelevance of Transaction Costs' in *Liberty, Market and the State* Brighton: Wheatsheaf.

Buchanan, J. and G. Tullock 1962 *The Calculus of Consent* Ann Arbor: University of Michigan Press.

Buchanan, J. and V. Vanberg 1991 'The Market as Creative Process' *Economics and Philosophy* 7, pp. 187–220.

Buchanan, J. and R. Wagner 1977 *Democracy in Deficit: The Political Legacy of Lord Keynes* New York: Academic Press.

Burke, E. 1826 *Works V* London: Rivington.

Cahn, S. 1964 'Fatalistic Arguments' *Journal of Philosophy* 61, pp. 295–305.

Cardan, P. 1974 *Modern Capitalism and Revolution* 2nd edn. London: Solidarity.

Cardano, G. 1968 *The Great Art* T. Witmer trans. Cambridge, MA: Massachusetts Institute of Technology Press.

Carter, C. 1968 *Wealth* Harmondsworth: Penguin.

Cicero 1941 *De Fato* XVI, 37–38 Cambridge, MA: Harvard University Press.

Coase, R. 1960 'The Problem of Social Cost' *Journal of Law and Economics* 3, pp. 1–22.

Cole, G. D. H. 1920 *Guild Socialism Restated* London: Leonard Parsons.

Collier, A. 1990 *Socialist Reasoning* London: Pluto Press.

Commons, J. 1934 *Institutional Economics: Its Place in Political Economy* New York: Macmillan.

Cooley, M. n.d. *Architect or Bee?* Slough: Langley Technical Services.

Cutler, A. 1988 'Social Theory and Social Policy' *Economy and Society* 17, pp. 251–271.

Cutler, A., B. Hindess, P. Hirst and A. Hussain 1977 *Marx's 'Capital' and Capitalism Today* London: Routledge and Kegan Paul.

Dales, J. H. 1968 *Pollution, Property and Prices* Toronto: University of Toronto Press.

Dasgupta, P. and P. David 1991 'Resource Allocation and the Institutions of Science' Stanford, CA: Stanford University.

David, P. 1992a 'Intellectual Property Institutions and the Panda's Thumb' *Centre for Economic Policy Research* no. 287, Stanford, CA: Stanford University.

David, P. 1992b 'Knowledge, Property and the System Dynamics of Technological Change' *World Bank Annual Conference on Development Economics* Washington, DC: World Bank.

Davies, M. 1983 'Boethius and Others on Divine Knowledge' *Pacific Philosophical Quarterly* 64, pp. 313–329.

Dearlove, J. 1989 'Neoclassical Politics: Public Choice and Political Understanding', *Review of Political Economy* 1, pp. 208–237.

Devlin, P. 1965 *The Enforcement of Morals* Oxford: Oxford University Press.

Dewey, J. 1935 'Liberty and Social Control' *Social Frontier* November.

Dewey, J. 1938 *Experience and Education* New York: Macmillan.

Dore, R. 1993 'What Makes the Japanese Different?' in C. Crouch and D. Marquand eds. *Ethics and Markets* Oxford: Blackwell.

Downs, A. 1957 *An Economic Theory of Democracy* New York: Harper and Row.

Downs, A. 1967 *Inside Bureaucracy* Boston, MA: Little, Brown.

Dummett, M. 1978 'Bringing About the Past' in *Truth and Other Enigmas* London: Duckworth.

Durkheim, E. 1964 *The Division of Labor in Society* G. Simpson trans. New York: Free Press.

Dworkin, G. 1988 *The Theory and Practice of Autonomy* Cambridge: Cambridge University Press.

Dworkin, R. 1977 *Taking Rights Seriously* London: Duckworth.

Dworkin, R. 1978 'Liberalism' in S. Hampshire ed. *Public and Private Morality* Cambridge: Cambridge University Press.

Eisenberg, R. 1987 'Proprietary Rights and the Norm of Science in Biotechnology Research' *Yale Law Journal* 97, pp. 177–231.

Elster, J. 1986 'The Market and the Forum: Three Varieties of Political Theory' in J.Elster and A. Hylland eds. *Foundations of Social Choice Theory* Cambridge: Cambridge University Press.

Elster, J. and J. Roemer eds. 1991 *Interpersonal Comparisons of Well-Being* Cambridge: Cambridge University Press.

Fairclough, N. 1993 'Critical Discourse Analysis and the Marketization of Public Discourse: the Universities' *Discourse and Society* 4, pp. 133–168.

Fauvel, J. and J. Gray eds. 1987 *The History of Mathematics: A Reader* London: Macmillan.

Feyerabend, P. 1978 *Against Method* London: Verso.

Fleetwood, S. 1995 *Hayek's Political Economy: The Socio-economics of Order* London: Routledge.

Fleetwood, S. 1996 'Order Without Equilibrium: A Critical Realist Interpretation of Hayek's Notion of Spontaneous Order' *Cambridge Journal of Economics* 20, pp. 729–747.

Foucault, M. 1980 *Power/Knowledge* New York: Pantheon.

Foucault, M. 1986 'What is Enlightenment?' in P. Rabinow ed. *The Foucault Reader* Harmondsworth: Penguin.

Fraser, N. 1995a 'From Redistribution to Recognition? Dilemmas of Justice in a "Post-Socialist" Age' *New Left Review* 212, pp. 68–91.

Fraser, N. 1995b 'Recognition or Redistribution: A Critical Reading of Iris Young's *Justice and the Politics of Difference*' *Journal of Political Philosophy* 3, pp. 166–180.

Friedman, M. 1979 'The Methodology of Positive Economics' in F. Hahn and M. Hollis eds. *Philosophy and Economic Theory* Oxford: Oxford University Press.

Fukuyama, F. 1992 *The End of History and the Last Man* London: Hamish Hamilton.

Funtowicz, S. and J. Ravetz 1993 'Science for the Post-Normal Age' *Futures* 25, pp. 739–755.

Gaskin, R. 1994 'Fatalism, Foreknowledge and the Reality of the Future' *Modern Schoolman* 71, pp. 83–113.

Gilligan, C. 1982 *In a Different Voice* Cambridge, MA: Harvard University Press.

Goldman, A. 1989 'Ethical Issues in Proprietary Restrictions on Research Results' in V. Weil and J. Snapper eds. *Owning Scientific and Technical Information: Value and Ethical Issues* New Brunswick, NJ: Rutgers University Press.

Goldsmith, M. 1980 'Hobbes's "Mortal God": Is There a Fallacy in Hobbes's Theory of Sovereignty?' *History of Political Thought* I, pp. 33–50.

Graves, R. 1885 *Life of Sir William Rowan Hamilton vol. 2* Dublin: Hodges, Figgis.

Gray, J. 1984 *Hayek on Liberty* Oxford: Blackwell.

Gray, J. 1989 'On Negative and Positive Liberty' in *Liberalism: Essays in Political Philosophy* London: Routledge.

Gray, J. 1992 *The Moral Foundations of Market Institutions* London: IEA Health and Welfare Unit reprinted in J. Gray 1993 *Beyond the New Right* London: Routledge.

Gray, J. 1993a *Post-Liberalism* London: Routledge.

Gray, J. 1993b 'An Agenda for a Green Conservatism' in *Beyond the New Right* London: Routledge.

Griffin, J. 1986 *Well-Being* Oxford: Clarendon.

Griffin, J. 1991 'Against the Taste Model' in J. Elster and J. Roemer eds. *Interpersonal Comparisons of Well-Being* Cambridge: Cambridge University Press.

Griffin J. 1996 *Value Judgement: Improving Our Ethical Beliefs* Oxford: Oxford University Press.

Haack, S. 1974 *Deviant Logic* Cambridge: Cambridge University Press.

Habermas, J. 1986 *Autonomy and Solidarity* London: Verso.

Hagstrom, W. 1965 *The Scientific Community* New York: Basic Books.

Hahn, F. 1984 'Reflections on the Invisible Hand' in *Equilibrium and Macroeconomics* Oxford: Blackwell.

Hahn, F. 1989 'On Market Economics' in R. Skidelsky ed. *Thatcherism* Oxford: Blackwell.

Hahn, F. and M. Hollis 1979 'Introduction' in F. Hahn and M. Hollis eds. *Philosophy and Economic Theory* Oxford: Oxford University Press.

Hare, R. 1963 *Freedom and Reason* Oxford: Oxford University Press.

Harrod, R. 1938 'The Scope and Method of Economics' *Economic Journal* 48, pp. 383–412.

Harsanyi, J. 1982 'Morality and the Theory of Rational Behaviour' in A. Sen and B. Williams eds. *Utilitarianism and Beyond* Cambridge: Cambridge University Press.

Hart, H. L. 1961 *The Concept of Law* Oxford: Clarendon.

Hayek, F. A. 1931 *Prices and Production* London: Routledge and Sons.

Hayek, F. A. 1933 *Monetary Theory and the Trade Cycle* London: Jonathan Cape.

Hayek, F. A. ed. 1935 *Collectivist Economic Planning* London: Routledge and Kegan Paul.

Hayek, F. A. 1944 *The Road to Serfdom* London: Routledge and Sons.

Hayek, F. A. 1949a 'Economics and Knowledge' in *Individualism and Economic Order* London: Routledge and Kegan Paul.

Hayek, F. A. 1949b 'The Uses of Knowledge in Society' in *Individualism and Economic Order* London: Routledge and Kegan Paul.

Hayek, F. A. 1949c 'The Socialist Calculation Debate: The Competitive "Solution" ' in *Individualism and Economic Order* London: Routledge and Kegan Paul.

Hayek, F. A. 1955a *The Counter-Revolution of Science* London: Free Press.

Hayek, F. A. 1955b *Scientism and the Study of Society* New York: Free Press.

Hayek, F. A. 1960 *The Constitution of Liberty* London: Routledge and Kegan Paul.

Hayek, F. A. 1973 *Law Legislation and Liberty: Volume 1* London: Routledge and Kegan Paul.

Hayek F. A. 1976 *Law, Legislation and Liberty: Volume 2* London: Routledge and Kegan Paul.

Hayek, F. A. 1978 'Competition as a Discovery Procedure' in *New Studies in Philosophy: Politics, Economics and the History of Ideas* Chicago: University of Chicago Press.

Hayek, F. A. 1979 *Law Legislation and Liberty: Volume 3* London: Routledge and Kegan Paul.

Hayek, F. A. 1984 'Two Pages of Fiction: The Impossibility of Socialist Calculation' in C. Nishiyama and K. Leube eds. *The Essence of Hayek* Stanford, CA: Hoover Institution Press.

Hayek, F. A. 1988 *The Fatal Conceit* London: Routledge.

Hegel, G. 1967 *Philosophy of Right* T. Knox trans. Oxford: Oxford University Press.

Hegel, G. 1977 *Phenemonology of Spirit* A. Miller trans. Oxford: Oxford University Press.

Heilbroner, R. 1975 *An Inquiry into the Human Prospect* London: Calder and Boyars.

Heilbroner, R. 1990 'The Triumph of Capitalism' *The New Yorker* 23 January.

Herodotus 1954 *Histories* Harmondsworth: Penguin.

Hettinger, E. 1989 'Justifying Intellectual Property' *Philosophy and Public Affairs* 18, pp. 31–52.

Hicks, J. 1946 *Value and Capital* 2nd edn. London: Oxford University Press.

Hicks, J. 1981a 'The Foundations of Welfare Economics' in *Wealth and Welfare* Oxford: Blackwell.

Hicks, J. 1981b 'The Rehabilitation of Consumers' Surplus' in *Wealth and Welfare* Oxford: Blackwell.

Hindess, B. 1987 *Freedom, Equality, and the Market* London: Tavistock.

Hirsch, F. 1977 *Social Limits to Growth* London: Routledge and Kegan Paul.

Hirschleifer, J. 1985 'The Expanding Domain of Economics' *American Economic Review* 75, pp. 53–68.

Hirschman, A. O. 1970 *Exit, Voice and Loyalty* Cambridge, MA: Harvard University Press.

Hirschman, A. O. 1977 *The Passions and the Interests* Princeton, NJ: Princeton University Press.

Hirschman, A. O. 1982 'Rival Interpretations of Market Society: Civilising, Destructive, or Feeble?' *Journal of Economic Literature* 20, pp. 1463–1484.

Hirschman, A. O. 1985 *Shifting Involvements: Private Interests and Public Affairs* Oxford: Blackwell.

Hirst, P. ed. 1989 *The Pluralist Theory of the State* London: Routledge.

Hobbes, T. 1968 *Leviathan* Harmondsworth: Penguin.

Hobbes, T. 1991 *De Cive* Indianapolis, IN: Hackett.

Hodgson, G. 1984 *The Democratic Economy* Harmondsworth: Penguin.

Hodgson, G. 1988 *Economics and Institutions* Cambridge: Polity.

Hodgson, G. 1993 'Institutional Economics: Surveying the "Old" and the "New" ' *Metroeconomica* 44, pp. 1–28.

Holland, A. and O'Neill, J. 1997 'The Ecological Integrity of Nature over Time: Some Problems' *Global Bioethics*

Hume, D. 1975 *Enquiries Concerning Human Understanding and Concerning the Principles of Morals* Oxford: Oxford University Press.

Hume, D. 1985a 'Of Civil Liberty' *Essays, Moral, Political, and Literary* Indianapolis, IN: Liberty Press.

Hume, D. 1985b 'Of the Rise and Progress of the Arts and Sciences' in *Essays Moral, Political, and Literary* Indianapolis, IN: Liberty Press.

Hume, D. 1985c 'Of the Independency of Parliament' in *Essays Moral, Political, and Literary* Indianapolis, IN: Liberty Press.

Hume, D. 1985d 'Of the Origin of Government' in *Essays Moral, Political and Literary* Indianapolis, IN: Liberty Press.

Hume, D. 1985e 'Of Interest' in *Essays Moral, Political and Literary* Indianapolis, IN: Liberty Press.

Hume, D. 1985f 'Of the Standard of Taste' in *Essays Moral, Political and Literary* Indianapolis, IN: Liberty Press.

Hume, D. 1985g 'The Sceptic' in *Essays Moral, Political and Literary* Indianapolis, IN: Liberty Press.

Hurka, T. 1993 *Perfectionism* Oxford: Oxford University Press.

Hurley, S. 1989 *Natural Reasons* Oxford: Oxford University Press.

Irwin, T. 1987 'Generosity and Property in Aristotle's *Politics'* Social Philosophy and Policy* 4, pp. 37–54.

Irwin, T. 1988 *Aristotle's First Principles* Oxford: Clarendon.

Jameson, F. 1991 *Postmodernism, or the Cultural Logic of Late Capitalism* London: Verso.

Jevons, W. S. 1970 *The Theory of Political Economy* Harmondsworth: Penguin.

Kant, I. 1991a 'An Answer to the Question: "What is Enlightenment?" ' in H. Reiss ed. *Kant Political Writings* Cambridge: Cambridge University Press.

Kant, I. 1991b 'Idea for a Universal History with a Cosmopolitan Purpose' in H. Reiss ed. *Kant Political Writings* Cambridge: Cambridge University Press.

Keat, R. 1993 'The Moral Boundaries of Markets' in C. Crouch and D. Marquand eds. *Ethics and Markets* Oxford: Blackwell.

Keat, R. 1994 'Scepticism, Authority and the Market' in R. Keat, N. Whitely and N. Abercrombie eds. *The Authority of the Consumer* London: Routledge.

Keat, R. 1997 'Colonisation by the Market: Walzer on Recognition' *Journal of Political Philosophy* 5, pp. 93–107.

Kellner, D. 1992 'Popular Culture and the Construction of Postmodern Identities' in S. Lash and J. Friedman eds. *Modernity and Identity* Oxford: Blackwell.

Kelly, P. ed. 1991 *Locke on Money* Oxford: Clarendon.

Kenny, A. 1992 *What is Faith?* Oxford: Oxford University Press.

Keynes, J. M. 1961 'Economic Possibilities for our Grandchildren' in *Essays in Persuasion* London: Macmillan.

Kirzner, I. 1972 *Competition and Entrepreneurship* Chicago: University of Chicago Press.

Kirzner, I. 1979 *Perception, Opportunity and Profit* Chicago: University of Chicago Press.

Kirzner, I. 1985 *Discovery and the Capitalist Process* Chicago: University of Chicago Press.

Kneale, W. 1955 'The Idea of Invention' *Proceedings of the British Academy* XLI, pp. 85–108.

Kuflik, A. 1989 'Moral Foundations of Intellectual Property Rights' in V. Weil and J. Snapper eds. *Owning Scientific and Technical Information: Value and Ethical Issues* New Brunswick, NJ: Rutgers University Press.

Kukathas, C. 1990 *Hayek and Modern Liberalism* Oxford: Clarendon.

Laclau, E. and C. Mouffe 1985 *Hegemony and Socialist Strategy: Towards a Radical Democratic Politics* London: Verso.

Lafargue, P. 1917 *The Right to Be Lazy* C. Kerr trans. Chicago: Kerr.

Lamberton, D. 1971 *Economics of Information and Knowledge* Harmondsworth: Penguin.

Lancaster, K. 1983 *Introduction to Modern Microeconomics* Tunbridge Wells: Costello.

Lane, R. 1978 'Markets and the Satisfaction of Human Wants' *Journal of Economic Issues* 12, pp. 799–827.

Lane, R. 1991 *The Market Experience* Cambridge: Cambridge University Press.

Lange, O. 1956 'On the Economic Theory of Socialism' in O. Lange and F. Taylor *On the Economic Theory of Socialism* B. Lippincott ed. New York: McGraw-Hill.

Lange, O. and F. Taylor 1956 *On the Economic Theory of Socialism* B. Lippincott ed. New York: McGraw-Hill.

Larmore, C. 1987 *Patterns of Moral Complexity* Cambridge: Cambridge University Press.

Latour, B. and Woolgar, S. 1979 *Laboratory Life: The Social Construction of Scientific Facts* London: Sage.

Lavoie, D. 1985 *Rivalry and Central Planning: The Socialist Calculation Debate Reconsidered* Cambridge: Cambridge University Press.

Lawson, T. 1994 'Realism and Hayek: A Case of Continuous Transformation' in M. Colona and H. Hageman eds. *The Economics of Hayek, vol. 1: Money and Business Cycles* Aldershot: Edward Elgar.

Le Grand, J. and S. Estrin eds. 1989 *Market Socialism* Oxford: Clarendon.

Lewis, D. 1989 'Dispositional Theories of Values' *Proceedings of the Aristotelian Society* supplementary series 63, pp. 113–137.

Lindley, R. 1986 *Autonomy* London: Macmillan.

Little, I. 1957 *Welfare Economics* 2nd edn. Oxford: Oxford University Press.

Loasby, R. 1986 'Organisation, Competition and the Growth of Knowledge' in R. Langlois ed. *Economics as Process: Essays in the New Institutional Analysis* Cambridge: Cambridge University Press.

Locke, J. 1975 *Essay Concerning Human Understanding* Oxford: Clarendon.

Locke, J. 1991 *Some Considerations of the Consequences of the Lowering of Interest, and Raising the Value of Money* in P. Kelly ed. *Locke on Money* Oxford: Clarendon.

Lukasiewicz, J. 1967 'On 3-valued Logic' in S. McCall ed. *Polish Logic* Oxford: Oxford University Press.

MacIntyre, A. 1985 *After Virtue* 2nd edn. London: Duckworth.

Mackenzie, M., P. Keating and A. Cambrosio 1990 'Patents and Free Scientific Information in Biotechnology: Making Monoclonal Antibodies Proprietary' *Science, Technology and Human Values* 15, pp. 65–83.

Macpherson, C. B. 1973 *Democratic Theory* Oxford: Clarendon.

Macpherson, C. B. 1978 *Property: Mainstream and Critical Positions* Oxford: Blackwell.

Mahoney, M. 1989 *The Mathematical Career of Pierre de Fermat* Princeton, NJ: Princeton University Press.

Mäki, U. 1990a 'Mengerian Economics in Realist Perspective' in B. Caldwell ed. *Carl Menger and his Legacy in Economics* Durham, NC: Duke University Press.

Mäki, U. 1990b 'Scientific Realism and Austrian Explanation' *Review of Political Economy* 2.3, pp. 310–344.

Mäki, U. 1992 'Social Conditioning in Economics' in N. de Marchi ed. *Post-Popperian Methodology of Economics: Recovering Practice* Boston, MA: Kluwer.

Mandeville, B. 1988 *The Fable of the Bees or Private Vice, Publick Benefits* Indianapolis, IN: Liberty Press.

Mao Tse Tung 1967 *Selected Works* II Peking: Foreign Languages Press.

Maritain, J. 1958 *Reflections on America* New York: Charles Scribner.

Marshall, A. 1962 *Principles of Economics* 8th edn. London: Macmillan.

Martell, L. 1992 'New Ideas of Socialism' *Economy and Society* 21, pp. 152–173.

Martinez-Alier, J. 1996 'The Merchandising of Biodiversity' *Capitalism, Nature and Socialism* 7 pp. 37–54.

Martinez-Alier, J., G. Munda and J. O'Neill 1997 'Incommensurability of Values in Ecological Economics' in C. Spash and M. O'Connor eds. *Valuation and Environment: Principles and Practices* Aldershot: Edward Elgar.

Marx, K. 1969 *Theories of Surplus Value: Part II* London: Lawrence and Wishart.

Marx, K. 1970 *Capital I* London: Lawrence and Wishart.

Marx, K. 1973 *Grundrisse* Harmondsworth: Penguin.

Marx, K. 1974a *German Ideology* C. Arthur ed. 2nd edn. London: Lawrence and Wishart.

Marx, K. 1974b *Critique of Hegel's Doctrine of the State* in L. Colletti ed. *Early Writings* Harmondsworth: Penguin.

Marx, K. 1974c 'On the Jewish Question' in L. Colletti ed. *Early Writings* Harmondsworth: Penguin.

Marx, K. 1974d *Economic and Philosophical Manuscripts* in L. Colletti ed. *Early Writings* Harmondsworth: Penguin.

Marx, K. and F. Engels 1968 *Manifesto of the Communist Party* in *Selected Works* London: Lawrence and Wishart.

Mason, A. 1990 'Autonomy, Liberalism and State Neutrality' *Philosophical Quarterly* 40, pp. 432–452.

Mauss, M. 1954 *The Gift* London: Cohen and West.

Meikle, S. 1979 'Aristotle and the Political Economy of the Polis' *Journal of Hellenic Studies* 79, pp. 57–73.

Meikle, S. 1985 *Essentialism in the Thought of Karl Marx* London: Duckworth.

Meikle, S. 1995 *Aristotle's Economic Thought* Oxford: Clarendon.

Menger, C. 1950 *Principles of Economics* Glencoe, IL: Free Press.

Menger, C. 1985 *Investigations into the Method of the Social Sciences with Special Reference to Economics* F. Nock trans. New York: New York University Press.

Merton, R. 1968 *Social Theory and Social Structure* New York: Free Press.

Mill, J. S. 1884 *A System of Logic* New York: Harper and Brothers.

Mill, J. S. 1929 *The Subjection of Women* London: Dent.

Mill, J. S. 1975 *Considerations on Representative Government* London: Oxford University Press.

Mill, J. S. 1991 *On Liberty* J. Gray and G. Smith eds. London: Routledge.

Mill, J. S. 1994 *Principles of Political Economy* Oxford: Oxford University Press.

Miller, D. 1989 *Market, State and Community: The Theoretical Foundations of Market Socialism* Oxford: Clarendon.

Mises, L. von 1920 'Die Wirtshaftrechung im Sozialistischen Gemeinwesen' *Archiv für Sozialwissenschaften* 47, trans. 1935 'Economic Calculation in the Socialist Commonwealth' in F. Hayek ed. *Collectivist Economic Planning* London: Routledge & Kegan Paul.

Mises, L. von 1922 *Die Gemeinwirtschaft: Untersuchungen über den Sozialismus* Jena: Gustav Fischer; trans. 1981 *Socialism: An Economic and Sociological Analysis* Indianapolis, IN: Liberty Press.

Mises, L. von 1949 *Human Action* London: Hodges.

Mises, L. von 1960 *Epistemological Problems of Economics* Princeton, NJ: Van Nostrand.

Mises, L. von 1981 *Socialism* Indianapolis, IN: Liberty Press.

Montesquieu, Baron de 1989 *The Spirit of the Laws* Cambridge: Cambridge University Press.

Mueller, D. 1979 *Public Choice* Cambridge: Cambridge University Press.

Mulgan, R. 1977 *Aristotle's Political Theory* Oxford: Clarendon.

Munda, G. 1995 *Multicriteria Evaluation in a Fuzzy Environment: Theory and Applications in Ecological Economics* Berlin: Physica-Verlag.

Munda, G., P. Nijkamp and P. Rietveld 1994 'Fuzzy multigroup conflict resolution for environmental management' in J. Weiss ed. *The Economics of Project Appraisal and the Environment* Aldershot: Edward Elgar.

Nelkin, D. 1984 *Science as Intellectual Property* New York: Macmillan.

Nelson, J. O. 1995 'That a Worker's Labour Cannot be a Commodity' *Philosophy* 70, pp. 157–166.

Neurath, O. 1912 'The Problem of the Pleasure Maximum' in 1983 *Philosophical Papers 1913–1946* R. S. Cohen and M. Neurath eds. Dordrecht: Reidel.

Neurath, O. 1913 'The Lost Wanderers of Descartes and the Auxiliary Motive' in 1983 *Philosophical Papers 1913–1946* R. S. Cohen and M. Neurath eds. Dordrecht: Reidel.

Neurath, O. 1919 'Through War Economy to Economy in Kind' in 1973 *Empiricism and Sociology* Dordrecht: Reidel.

Neurath, O. 1928 'Personal Life and Class Struggle' in 1973 *Empiricism and Sociology* Dordrecht: Reidel.

Neurath, O. 1935 'Pseudorationalism of Falsification' in 1983 *Philosophical Papers 1913–1946* R.S. Cohen and M. Neurath eds. Dordrecht: Reidel.

Neurath, O. 1942 'International Planning for Freedom' in 1973 *Empiricism and Sociology* Dordrecht: Reidel.

Neurath, O. 1944 *Foundations of the Social Sciences* Chicago: University of Chicago Press.

Neurath, O. 1946 'The Orchestration of the Sciences by the Encyclopedism of Logical Empiricism' in 1983 *Philosophical Papers 1913–1946* R. S. Cohen and M. Neurath eds. Dordrecht: Reidel.

Newman, J. 1884 *Oxford University Sermons* London: Rivingtons.

Nietzsche, F. 1967 *On the Genealogy of Morals* W. Kaufmann and R. Hollingdale trans. New York: Random House.

Nietzsche, F. 1968 *The Anti-Christ* R. J. Hollingdale trans. Harmondsworth: Penguin.

Nietzsche, F. 1974 *The Gay Science* W. Kaufmann trans. New York: Random House.

Niskanen, W. 1971 *Bureaucracy and Representative Government* Chicago: Aldine-Atherton.

Niskanen, W. 1973 *Bureaucracy: Servant or Master* London: Institute of Economic Affairs.

Novak, M. 1982 *The Spirit of Democratic Capitalism* New York: Simon and Schuster.

Nove, A. 1983 *The Economics of Feasible Socialism* London: Allen and Unwin.

Nozick, R. 1980 *Anarchy, State and Utopia* Oxford: Blackwell.

Nussbaum M. 1990 'Aristotelian Social Democracy' in R. Douglass, G. Mara and H. Richardson eds. *Liberalism and the Good* London: Routledge.

Oakeshott, M. 1962a 'On Being Conservative' in *Rationalism in Politics* London: Methuen.

Oakeshott, M. 1962b 'Rationalism in Politics' in *Rationalism in Politics* London: Methuen.

Olson, M. 1965 *The Logic of Collective Action* Cambridge, MA: Harvard University Press.

Olson, M. 1982 *The Rise and Decline of Nations* New Haven, CT: Yale University Press.

O'Neill, J. 1989 'Markets, Socialism and Information' *Social Philosophy and Policy* 6, pp. 200–210.

O'Neill, J. 1992a 'Journalism in the Market Place', in A. Belsey and R. Chadwick eds. *Ethical Issues in Journalism and the Media* London: Routledge.

O'Neill, J. 1992b 'Altruism, Egoism, and the Market' *Philosophical Forum* 23, pp. 278–288.

O'Neill, J. 1993a 'Science, Wonder and the Lust of Eyes' *Journal of Applied Philosophy* 10, pp. 139–146.

O'Neill, J. 1993b 'Ethics' in W. Outhwaite and T. Bottomore eds. *Twentieth Century Social Thought* Oxford: Blackwell.

O'Neill, J. 1993c 'Intertextual Reference in Nineteenth Century Mathematics' *Science in Context* 6, pp. 435–468.

O'Neill, J. 1993d *Ecology, Policy and Politics: Human Well-Being and the Natural World* London: Routledge.

O'Neill, J. 1994a 'Essentialism and the Market' *Philosophical Forum* 26, pp. 87–100.

O'Neill, J. 1994b 'Humanism and Nature' *Radical Philosophy* 66, pp. 21–29.

O'Neill, J. 1994c 'Should Communitarians Be Nationalists?' *Journal of Applied Philosophy* 11, pp. 135–143.

O'Neill, J. 1995a 'Polity, Economy, Neutrality' *Political Studies* 43, pp. 414–431.

O'Neill, J. 1995b 'Intrinsic Evil, Truth and Authority' *Religious Studies* 31, pp. 209–19.

O'Neill, J. 1995c 'In Partial Praise of a Positivist' *Radical Philosophy* 74, pp. 29–38.

O'Neill, J. 1996 'Contingent Valuation and Qualitative Democracy' *Environmental Politics* 5, pp. 752–759.

O'Neill, J. 1997a 'Cantona and Aquinas on Good and Evil' *Journal of Applied Philosophy* 14, pp. 95–105.

O'Neill, J. 1997b 'Time, Narrative and Environmental Politics' in R. Glottlieb ed. *New Perspectives in Environmental Politics* London: Routledge.

O'Neill, J. 1997c 'Value Pluralism, Incommensurability and Institutions' in J. Foster ed. *Valuing Nature?* London: Routledge.

O'Neill, J. 1997d 'King Darius and the Environmental Economist' in J. O'Neill and T. Hayward eds. *Justice, Property and the Environment: Social and Legal Perspectives* Aldershot: Avebury.

O'Neill, J. 1997e 'Ecology, Socialism and Austrian Economics' in E. Nemeth, R. Heinrich and A. Soulez eds. *Enzyklopedie und Politik* Vienna: Weiner Reihe.

O'Neill, J. 1998 'Practical Reasoning and Mathematical Analysis' *History and Philosophy of Science*.

O'Neill, J. and Y. Solomon 1996 'Education Elitism and the Market' in B. Brecher, O. Fleischmann and J. Halliday eds. *The Political Theory of Higher Education* Aldershot: Avebury.

Ophuls, W. 1977 'The Politics of a Sustainable Society' in D. Pirages ed. *The Sustainable Society* New York: Praeger.

Orwell, G. 1968 *Collected Essays, Journalism and Letters vol. 4* London: Secker.

Parfit, D. 1984 *Reasons and Persons* Oxford: Clarendon.

Pateman, C. 1988 *The Sexual Contract* Cambridge: Polity.

Peacock, M. 1993 'Hayek, Realism and Spontaneous Order' *Journal of the Theory of Social Behaviour* 23, pp. 249–264.

Pearce, D., A. Markaandya and E. Barbier 1989 *Blueprint for a Green Economy* London: Earthscan.

Perry, R. 1940 *Freedom: Its Meaning* New York: Harcourt, Brace.

Perry, T. 1976 *Moral Reasoning and Truth* Oxford: Oxford University Press.

Pierson, N. 1935 'The Problem of Value in the Socialist Society' in F. Hayek ed. *Collectivist Economic Planning* London: Routledge and Kegan Paul.

Pigou, A. 1920 *The Economics of Welfare* London: Macmillan.

Plato 1974 *The Republic* D. Lee trans. Harmondsworth: Penguin.

Pocock, J. G. A. 1985 'The Political Economy of Burke's Analysis of the French Revolution' in *Virtue, Commerce and History* Cambridge: Cambridge University Press.

Polanyi, K. 1957a 'Aristotle Discovers the Economy' in G. Dalton ed. *Primitive, Archaic and Modern Economies* Boston, MA: Beacon Press.

Polanyi, K. 1957b 'The Economy as Instituted Process' in G. Dalton ed. *Primitive, Archaic and Modern Economies* Boston, MA: Beacon Press.

Polanyi, K. 1957c *The Great Transformation* Boston, MA: Beacon Press.

Polanyi, K. 1963 *Biographical Notes* unpublished.

Porter, T. 1995 *Trust in Numbers: The Pursuit of Objectivity in Science and Public Life* Princeton, NJ: Princeton University Press.

Power, M. 1994 *The Audit Explosion* London: Demos.

Price, R. 1988 'Self-Love, "Egoism" and *Ambizione* in Machiavelli's Thought' *History of Political Thought* 9, pp. 237–261.

Putnam, H. 1975 'Time and Physical Geometry' in *Mathematics, Matter and Method* Cambridge: Cambridge University Press.

Quine, W. 1953 'On a So-called Paradox' *Mind* 62, pp. 65–67.

Quine, W. 1987 'Future' in *Quiddities* Harmondsworth: Penguin.

Radnitzky, G. 1987a 'The "Economic" Approach to the Philosophy of Science' *British Journal for the Philosophy of Science* 38, pp. 159–179.

Radnitzky, G. 1987b 'Cost-benefit Thinking in the Methodology of Research: the "Economic Approach" applied to Key Problems of the Philosophy of Science' in G. Radnitzky and P. Bernholz eds. *Economic Imperialism: The Economic Approach Applied Outside the Field of Economics* New York: Paragon House.

Radnitzky, G. and P. Bernholz eds. 1987 *Economic Imperialism: The Economic Approach Applied Outside the Field of Economics* New York: Paragon House.

Railton, P. 1986 'Moral Realism' *Philosophical Review* 95, pp. 163–207.

Ravetz, J. 1973 *Scientific Knowledge and its Social Problems* Harmondsworth: Penguin.

Rawls, J. 1972 *A Theory of Justice* Oxford: Oxford University Press.

Raz, J. 1986 *The Morality of Freedom* Oxford: Clarendon.

Reekie, W. 1984 *Markets, Entrepreneurs and Liberty* Brighton: Wheatsheaf.

Ricardo, D. 1973 *Principles of Political Economy* London: Dent.

Robbins, L. 1935 *An Essay on the Nature and Significance of Economic Science* London: Macmillan.

Robbins, L. 1938 'Interpersonal Comparisons of Utility' *Economic Journal* 48, pp. 635–641.

Roemer, J. 1994 *A Future for Socialism* London: Verso.

Rorty, R. 1989 *Contingency, Irony, and Solidarity* Cambridge: Cambridge University Press.

Rose-Ackerman, S. 1977 'Market Models for Pollution Control' *Public Policy* 25, pp. 383–406.

Rousseau, J. 1984 *A Discourse on Inequality* M. Cranston trans. Harmondsworth: Penguin.

Ryle, G. 1960 *Dilemmas* Cambridge: Cambridge University Press.

Ryle, G. 1963 *The Concept of Mind* Harmondsworth: Penguin.

Sale, K. 1985 *Dwellers in the Land: The Bioregional Vision* San Francisco, CA: Sierra Club.

Samuelson, P. 1937 'A Note on Measurement of Utility' *Review of Economic Studies* 4, pp. 155–161.

Samuelson, P. 1938 'The Empirical Implications of Utility Analysis' *Econometrica* 5, pp. 344–356.

Sandel, M. 1982 *Liberalism and the Limits of Justice* Cambridge: Cambridge University Press.

Sayer, A. 1995 *Radical Political Economy* Oxford: Blackwell.

Schapiro, D. 1989 'Reviving the Socialist Calculation Debate: A Defense of Hayek Against Lange' *Social Philosophy and Policy* 6, pp. 112–138.

Schecter, D. 1994 *Radical Theories* Manchester: Manchester University Press.

Schotter, A. 1981 *The Economic Theory of Institutions* Cambridge: Cambridge University Press.

Schumpeter, J. 1934 *The Theory of Economic Development* Cambridge, MA: Harvard University Press.

Schumpeter, J. 1987 *Capitalism, Socialism and Democracy* London: Unwin.

Selucky, R. 1979 *Marxism, Socialism, Freedom* London: Macmillan.

Sen, A. 1987a *The Standard of Living* Cambridge: Cambridge University Press.

Sen, A. 1987b *On Ethics and Economics* Oxford: Blackwell.

Sen, A. 1993 'Capability and Well Being' in M. Nussbaum and A. Sen eds. *The Quality of Life* Oxford: Clarendon.

Shackle, G. 1979 *Imagination and the Nature of Choice* Edinburgh: Edinburgh University Press.

Shackle, G. 1983 'The Bounds of Unknowledge' in J. Wiseman ed. *Beyond Positive Economics* London: Macmillan.

Shapin, S. 1994 *A Social History of Truth* Chicago: University of Chicago Press.

Simon, H. 1972 *Theories of Bounded Rationality, Decision and Organisation* Amsterdam: North Holland.

Simon, H. 1979 'From Substantive to Procedural Rationality' in F. Hahn and M. Hollis eds. *Philosophy and Economic Theory* Oxford: Oxford University Press.

Skillen, A. 1977 *Ruling Illusions* Hassocks: Harvester Press.

Smith, A. 1981 *An Inquiry into the Nature and Causes of the Wealth of Nations* Indianapolis, IN: Liberty Press.

Smith, A. 1982a *The Theory of Moral Sentiments* Indianapolis, IN: Liberty Press.

Smith, A. 1982b *Essays on Philosophical Subjects* Indianapolis, IN: Liberty Press.

Smith, A. 1982c *Lectures on Jurisprudence* Indianapolis, IN: Liberty Press.

Smith, A. 1987 *Correspondence of Adam Smith* E. Mossner and I. Ross eds. Indianapolis, IN: Liberty Press.

Smith, B. 1986 'Austrian Economics and Austrian Philosophy' in W. Grassl and B. Smith eds. *Austrian Economics* London: Croom Helm.

Smith, B. 1990 'Aristotle, Menger and Mises: An Essay in the Metaphysics of Economics' in B. Caldwell *Carl Menger and his Legacy in Economics* Durham, NC: Duke University Press.

Smith, G. 1990 'Markets and Moral: Self, Character and Markets' in G. Hunt ed. *Philosophy and Politics* Cambridge: Cambridge University Press.

Stanfield, I. 1978 *The Economic Thought of Karl Polanyi* London: Macmillan.

Steele, D. 1992 *From Marx to Mises: Post-Capitalist Society and the Challenge of Economic Calculation* La Salle, IL: Open Court.

Stobaeus 1939 *Extracts* ii, 31, 114 in I. Thomas ed. *History of Greek Mathematics* London: Heinemann.

Sugden, R. 1981 *The Political Economy of Public Choice* Oxford: Martin Robertson.

Tawney, R. 1964 *Equality* London: Unwin.

Taylor, C. 1971 'Interpretation and the Science of Man' *Review of Metaphysics* 25, pp. 1–45.

Taylor, C. 1985 'Atomism' *Philosophy and Human Science* Cambridge: Cambridge University Press.

Taylor, C. 1992 *Multiculturalism and 'The Politics of Recognition'* Princeton NJ: Princeton University Press.

Taylor, F. 1966 *On the Art of Cutting Metals* New York: American Society of Mechanical Engineers.

Taylor, M. 1976 *Anarchy and Cooperation* New York: Wiley.

Taylor, R. 1957 'The Problem of Future Contingencies' *Philosophical Review* 66, pp. 1–28.

Titmus, R. 1970 *The Gift Relationship* London: Allen and Unwin.

Tomlinson, J. 1982 *The Unequal Struggle? British Socialism and Capitalist Enterprise* London: Methuen.

Tomlinson, J. 1990 'Market Socialism' in B. Hindess ed. *Reactions to the Right* London: Routledge.

Tullock, G. 1970 *Private Wants, Public Means* New York: Basic Books.

Veblen, T. 1919 *The Place of Science in Modern Civilisation and Other Essays* New York: Huebsch.

Vlastos, G. 1962 'Justice and Equality' in R. Brandt ed. *Social Justice* Englewood Cliffs, NJ: Prentice-Hall

Wade Hands, D. 1994 'The Sociology of Scientific Knowledge' in R. Backhouse ed. *New Directions in Economic Methodology* London: Routledge.

Wainwright, H. 1994 *Arguments for a New Left: Answering the Free Market Right* Oxford: Blackwell.

Walzer, M. 1983 *Spheres of Justice* Oxford: Blackwell.

Walzer, M. 1984 'Liberalism and the Art of Separation' *Political Theory* 12, pp. 315–330.

Warnock, M. 1989 *Universities: Knowing Our Minds* London: Chatto and Windus.

Weber, M. 1978 *Economy and Society* Berkeley: University of California Press.

Weil, S. 1952 *Gravity and Grace* London: Routledge and Kegan Paul.

Weiner, C. 1989 'Patenting and Academic Research: Historical Case Studies' in V. Weil and J. Snapper eds. *Owning Scientific and Technical Information: Value and Ethical Issues* New Brunswick, NJ: Rutgers University Press.

Whitehead, A. N. 1911 *An Introduction to Mathematics* London: Oxford University Press.

Wiggins, D. 1980 'Weakness of Will, Commensurability, and the Objects of Deliberation and Desire' in A. Rorty ed. *Essays on Aristotle's Ethics* Berkeley: University of California Press.

Wightman, W. 1962 *Science and the Renaissance vol. I* London: Oliver and Boyd.

Williams, B. 1972 *Morality* Cambridge: Cambridge University Press.

Winch, P. 1967 'Authority' in A. Quinton ed. *Political Philosophy* Oxford: Oxford University Press.

Wiseman, J. 1989 *Cost, Choice and Political Economy* Aldershot: Edward Elgar.

Wittgenstein, L. 1958 *Philosophical Investigations* Oxford: Blackwell.

Wittgenstein, L. 1960 *Blue Book* Oxford: Blackwell.

Wolf, C. 1987 'Market and Non-market Failure: Comparison and Assessment' *Journal of Public Policy* 7, pp. 43–70.

Wolff, R. P. 1970 *In Defence of Anarchism* New York: Harper and Row.

Wood, A. 1981 *Karl Marx* London: Routledge and Kegan Paul.

Wood, A. 1990 *Hegel's Ethical Thought* Cambridge: Cambridge University Press.

Woolgar, S. and B. Latour 1979 *Laboratory Life: The Construction of Scientific Facts* London: Sage.

Wright, G. H. von 1984 'Determinism and Future Truth' in *Truth, Knowledge and Modality* Oxford: Blackwell.

Yeo, S. 1987 'Three Socialisms: Statism, Collectivism, Associationalism' in W. Outhwaite and M. Mulkay eds. *Social Theory and Social Criticism: Essays for Tom Bottomore* Oxford: Blackwell.

Ziman, J. 1978 *Reliable Knowledge* Cambridge: Cambridge University Press.

INDEX

Ackerman, B. 18
acquisition, economic and chrematistic 28–9, 199
altruism 6, 7, 158–159, 160–164, 167, 200, 201, 202–203: *see also* egoism, self interest
appearance 107–9; and commerce 179–183; and recognition 107–109
Aquinas, T. 39, 183
Aristotle 4, 5, 6, 8–10, 16, 17, 21–27, 28–29, 31–32, 37, 39, 40, 49, 51, 99, 106, 123, 125, 131, 149, 158, 168, 171, 180 189, 199–200; Aristotelianism 8–10, 16, 28, 49, 100, 106, 157, 165
Arrow, K. 149, 200
associations 2–3, 98–100, 106, 107, 110–111, 141, 142, 159, 163, 169–171, 173, 174–175, 176–178, 191–192, 203 *see also* socialism, associational
Augustine 182–183, 202–203
Austrian economics 1, 6, 8, 19–20, 37, 41, 44, 55–56, 58, 64, 78, 95, 112–113, 122, 119, 129–132, 138–141, 145, 159, 165, 196 *see also* Hayek, Kirzner, Menger, Mises
authoritarianism 16, 31–32, 88–89
authority 84–92, 95, 110; epistemological 85–88, 95, 97; social/epistemological distinction 88–9
autonomy 6, 30, 33–34, 49, 64–72, 175, 185, 188, 189; aesthetic account of 89–92; and authority 84–100; character and identity 73–77; conditions for 70; and equality 96–100; ethical 91; and feminism 73, 75–76 intellectual 90–91; and the market 77–83, 84, 94, 99; misconceptions concerning 71; and

morality 89–90, 92; perfectionist account of 69–72, 92–96; and reason 85–89, 94; strong interpretation of 85–92, 94, 96; and trust 96–100; virtues and vices of 69–70, 90–92
avarice 171–173, 202

Baier, A. 75
Barker, E. 174, 175
Barone, E. 112
Benson, J. 188
Berlin, I. 25, 67
Bohm-Bawerk 37
Buchanan, J. 94–95, 172, *see also* public choice theory
Burke, E. 172
business cycle 135–136, 197

calculation *see* socialist calculation debate
capitalism 5, 62, 141–142, 175, 198
Cardan, P. 142
Cardano, G. *see* Tartaglia/Cardano dispute
central planning 130, 132–134, 142, 174–175 196
character: and habit 201–202; and identity 73–77
choice 24, 77–78, 94, 114, 117, 120, 122, 124, 125, 127, 128, 131, 141, 175, 193; *see also* public choice theory, rationality
citizen/ship 2, 104
civil society 1, 30–33, 78, 106–107, 163, 175–176
classical economics 35, 36, 41–52, 44, 55, 56, 59–60, 62, 165, 167, 176 *see also*, Smith, Hume

219

self-interest, egoism and avarice 168–173; *see also* choice
public goods 20, 54, 150–151
public use of reason 84–85, 100–101

quality 94–95

rational economic agents 35–6, 168, 203
rationalism 123–124, 128, 141, 194; and autonomy 85–89; and socialist calculation debate 114–121; *see also* pseudorationalism
rationality: and commensurability 114–128, 141–142; expressive 126–127; limits of 127–128; narrative 127, procedural 126
Ravetz, J. 146, 147–148
Rawls, J. 75, 123
Raz, J. 70, 126
realism 195
recognition 2, 101, 102, 175; of appearance 107–109; desired for its own sake 105–108; desire for 103–106; and intellectual property 147; market model of 106–109; and science 108, 156–157, 158; of standing and virtue 103–104, 107, 109–110
respect 68
rights 123; *see also* property rights
Robbins, L. 44–46, 54, 113, 121, 183–184
Roemer, J. 119
Rousseau, J.-J. 79–80

Samuelson 182
Schumpeter, J. 141, 179
science 2–3, 95, 97, 108, 163, 195, 199; communism of 157, 200; coordination of 129–130; and democracy 152–153; and innovation 152; and market mechanisms 144–145, 152, 156, 167; practice/institution distinction 157; property in 148–149, 151–159; and recognition 108, 156–157, 158, 167; and public choice 163
self-interest 137, 157–158, 160, 162, 164, 165–167, 168–171, 200, 202–203; *see also* egoism, altruism
self-sacrifice 160, 200, 201
self-sufficiency 22–24, 96, 125
Sen, A. 182, 184
situationism 188
Smith, A. 1, 3, 7, 32, 33, 35, 36, 41–42,

55, 57, 59–62, 77, 79–81, 102, 106, 109, 110–111, 167, 175, 186, 191, 203
socialism 2, 3, 29–31, 32, 104, 109, 112, 137; associational 3, 110–111, 174–175, 176–178; market socialism, 2, 112 118–119, 137–138
socialist calculation debate 112–113, 140–141; plurality of debates 112–121; and commensurability 113–121, 129, 140–142; and epistemology 113, 119–121, 129–142, 143–145
Solon 29
sophism 1, 199
sovereign consumer 84, 89–90
standing 103–104, 107, 109, 191
Stoicism 60, 61, 80, 110–111
subjective determination of well-being 38, 40–41, 42, 44; and autonomy 49; confusion concerning 46; and diversity 49–51; sophisticated 47–49
subjectivism 38–46, 58, 59, 91–92, 131; explanatory and ontological 41–43; meta-ethical 43; and political neutrality 46; preference satisfaction and well-being 38–41; radical 130–131, 183, 196; and value freedom 43–46
suspicion 189
syndicalism 174

Tartaglia/Cardano dispute 144, 145–146, 148, 151, 153, 157, 198
Tawney, R.H. 97–98, 100, 105, 109–110
Taylor, C. 112
Taylorism 141–142
thumos 103, 105
Titmus, R. 200
totalitarianism 30, 32–33, 176–177
trade secrets 153–155
trumping principle 123, 124
trust 96–100, 153
truth 184, 195

unity of the sciences 195–196
umpiring principle 122–123
utilitarianism 36, 41, 49, 122, 182–183
utility 35–37, 41, 53–55, 161, 163, 165–166, 168, 182, 202; interpersonal comparisons of 45–46, 54, 184

value freedom 43–46
value-pluralism 25–26, 125–128; *see also* commensurability
value-subjectivism 95